Palgrave Macmillan Series in International Political Communication

Series editor: Philip Seib, University of Southern California (USA)

From democratization to terrorism, economic development to conflict resolution, global political dynamics are affected by the increasing pervasiveness and influence of communication media. This series examines participants and their tools, their strategies and their impact. It offers a mix of comparative and tightly focused analyses that bridge the various elements of communication and political science included in the field of international studies. Particular emphasis is placed on topics related to the rapidly changing communication environment that is being shaped by new technologies and new political realities. This is the evolving world of international political communication.

Editorial Board Members:

Hussein Amin, American University in Cairo (Egypt)
Robin Brown, University of Leeds (UK)
Eytan Gilboa, Bar-Ilan University (Israel)
Steven Livingston, George Washington University (USA)
Robin Mansell, London School of Economics and Political Science (UK)
Holli Semetko, Emory University (USA)
Ingrid Volkmer, University of Melbourne (Australia)

Books Appearing in this Series

Media and the Politics of Failure: Great Powers, Communication Strategies, and Military Defeats
By Laura Roselle

The CNN Effect in Action: How the News Media Pushed the West toward War in Kosovo
By Babak Bahador

Media Pressure on Foreign Policy: The Evolving Theoretical Framework
By Derek B. Miller

New Media and the New Middle East
Edited by Philip Seib

The African Press, Civic Cynicism, and Democracy
By Minabere Ibelema

Global Communication and Transnational Public Spheres
By Angela M. Crack

EXPLAINING NEWS

National Politics and Journalistic Cultures in Global Context

Cristina Archetti

EXPLAINING NEWS
Copyright © Cristina Archetti, 2010.

All rights reserved.

First published in 2010 by
PALGRAVE MACMILLAN®
in the United States—a division of St. Martin's Press LLC,
175 Fifth Avenue, New York, NY 10010.

Where this book is distributed in the UK, Europe and the rest of the world,
this is by Palgrave Macmillan, a division of Macmillan Publishers Limited,
registered in England, company number 785998, of Houndmills,
Basingstoke, Hampshire RG21 6XS.

Palgrave Macmillan is the global academic imprint of the above companies
and has companies and representatives throughout the world.

Palgrave® and Macmillan® are registered trademarks in the United States,
the United Kingdom, Europe and other countries.

ISBN: 978–0–230–62282–1

Library of Congress Cataloging-in-Publication Data

Archetti, Cristina.
    Explaining news : national politics and journalistic cultures in global
    context / Cristina Archetti.
        p. cm.—(Palgrave macmillan series in international political
            communication)
    Includes bibliographical references.
    ISBN 978–0–230–62282–1 (alk. paper)
    1. Press and politics—Case studies. 2. September 11 Terrorist
Attacks, 2001—Press coverage. 3. Afghan War, 2001—Press coverage.
I. Title.

PN4751.A85 2009
070.4′49973931—dc22   2009046438

A catalogue record of the book is available from the British Library.

Design by Newgen Imaging Systems (P) Ltd., Chennai, India.

First edition: July 2010

10 9 8 7 6 5 4 3 2 1

Printed in the United States of America.

*To Maria Concetta Militi and Renato Archetti,
my mum and dad, for teaching me the importance of
perseverance and hard work.*

Contents

ILLUSTRATIONS

FIGURES

TABLES

ACKNOWLEDGMENTS

This book would have not been written without the help and support of many people. It is based on my doctoral thesis, whose completion would have not been possible without my supervisors, Dr. Robin Brown and Professor Philip Taylor. I thank Professor Taylor for the amazing skill of saying that single sentence that would instantly allow me to place into perspective both academic and personal problems. To Dr. Robin Brown I owe my love for theory, methods, as well as almost all I know about research. He provided guidance, uncomfortable questions, and a great deal of freedom to follow my ideas, even when they were leading to unproductive dead ends. He never caught me when I fell. He provided the toughest criticism I could ever encounter. His patient (and less patient) comments allowed me both to improve my work and grow as an academic.

I thank the whole Institute of Communications Studies (ICS) at Leeds University (UK) for making me look forward to go to work, where I could meet such supportive and cheerful colleagues everyday.

In addition to my parents, to whom this book is dedicated, my sister, Sonia, and my brothers, Marco and Emanuele, were a major source of motivation and encouragement. The material for this book has been presented at a number of conferences, and many colleagues from all over the world have contributed with their questions and comments to the development of my thoughts on the subject. Professor Lance Bennett very kindly commented on an early draft and provided stimulating criticism. The anonymous reviewer of the manuscript also gave me insightful suggestions as to how the work could be further improved. I wish I had met Professor Jay Blumler earlier in the editing process. I am very grateful to him for finding the time not only to read the manuscript, but also to point out problem areas in my research and suggest new directions for future investigation in great detail. I have tried as much as possible to take both comments and critiques received onboard. To do justice to the good advice I was not able to follow this time I'll have to write another book.

My greatest gratitude is for Robin, my husband, who understands when I am in a bad mood for no other reason than that I haven't finished a draft or have spent my day in the sunless basement of a library—who is truly happy to see me succeed and who, I know, will always be the inspiration (and the toughest test) of my most creative ideas.

ABBREVIATIONS

9/11	September 11, 2001
APEC	Asia Pacific Economic Cooperation
CDA	Critical Discourse Analysis
CDS	*Il Corriere della Sera*
CNN	Cable News Network
DAWN	*Dawn*
EU	European Union
F	France
G8	Group of 8
GDP	Gross Domestic Product
I	Italy
IC	International Communications
IR	International Relations
IE	Idea Element
IMF	International Monetary Fund
LIB	*Libération*
LM	*Le Monde*
NAT	*Nation*
NATO	North Atlantic Treaty Organization
NGO	Nongovernmental Organization
NYT	*New York Times*
NWICO	New World Information and Communication Order
OECD	Organization for Economic Cooperation and Development
PK	Pakistan
PM	Prime Minister
REP	*La Repubblica*
SPSS	Statistical Package for the Social Sciences
UAE	United Arab Emirates
UN	United Nations

UNESCO	United Nations Educational, Scientific and Cultural Organization
UNGA	United Nations General Assembly
U.S.	United States
U.S.S.R.	Union of Soviet Socialist Republics
WOT	War on Terrorism
WSJ	*Wall Street Journal*

INTRODUCTION

This book addresses the question of what shaped the international elite press coverage in the aftermath of 9/11. In doing so it raises broader theoretical and methodological issues about the nature of news in contemporary society, as well as the state of communication research.

In 1978 Gaye Tuchman famously argued in *Making News* that news was a "window on the world."[1] Through its frame, individuals in society learned "of themselves and others, of their own institutions, leaders, and life styles, and those of other nations and their peoples."[2] At the beginning of the twenty-first century, if anything, news is even more pervasive. It surrounds us 24/7 on TV screens, in print, on the Internet, and it follows us through the day by being delivered to our mobile phones. The portion of reality that we directly witness as individuals, in an increasingly global world, merely varies between the infinitely small and the plain insignificant. Almost all we know about reality, indeed, comes from the news we consume. News affects our knowledge, our attitudes, and as a consequence, our behavior. News shapes our understanding of public issues, from domestic policy to conflicts, and to international crises.[3] Print news coverage can make a difference in the way voters interpret election campaigns and judge candidates.[4] Live TV news, under certain circumstances, increases the visibility of world leaders in the eyes of international audiences, thereby having an influence on the policy-making process.[5] Objective news, the ideal staple diet of informed citizens, is regarded as the very lifeblood of democracy.[6] News shapes our lives. But what shapes the news?

Finding an answer to this question has important implications for the way we understand the role of the media in society. There is a range of views about the effects that the information contained in the news can have. For example, the media can either constructively contribute to democratic debate, or through the search for profits and the "dumbing down" of the information they deliver to the public—also known as "infotainment"—be a cause of "civic decay."[7] It is the assessment of the extent to which media organizations are in control of the news they produce that can tell whether it is meaningful to blame the media for the social problems they are believed to encourage,[8] or whether, by bringing more attention to international conflicts, they can perhaps awake the world's conscience.[9]

Despite the relevance of the matter, a number of possibly conflicting claims are made in relation to the role of the news media in society and what they produce. For some, news is a powerful tool through which the dominant political ideology is reproduced in society.[10] For others, news is the means through which the media fulfill their role of democratic "watchdog."[11] In an increasingly interconnected world, news could be seen as the result of global processes that escape the control of any single government or media organization.[12] Alternatively, news could be interpreted as the creation of media organizations ruled by their own internal dynamics.[13] In several accounts news is the result of a combination of political, economic, cultural, and social factors.[14]

This book elaborates a multidisciplinary model to explain what shaped the elite press coverage in the September 11, 2001, aftermath in the United States, France, Italy, and Pakistan. It dissects the news about two global crises that have defined our time—9/11 and the 2001 war in Afghanistan—by systematically comparing the reactions to and portrayals of these crises by the presidents, prime ministers, foreign and defense ministers, and major newspapers in the four countries: the *New York Times* and the *Wall Street Journal* in the United States, *Le Monde* and *Libération* in France, *La Repubblica* and *Il Corriere della Sera* in Italy, the *Dawn* and the *Nation* in Pakistan. The study examines the extent to which news coverage was shaped by national governments' reaction to the events, whether the coverage presented global features against local interpretations, and the degree to which the journalists who covered the events individually contributed to shaping the stories they wrote. It challenges the idea that processes of globalization are leading to an increasing homogenization of news on a worldwide scale. Instead, it makes the point that the national political dimension and the norms of each news media organization are crucial in understanding the social construction of events, even those that appear global in scope. The analysis suggests that, although audiences around the world read about the same events, the two crises were framed in completely different terms in each newspaper. In fact, advances in communication technologies allowed journalists, political actors, and audiences to witness world events as if they were living in a "global village." However, the ways 9/11 and the war in Afghanistan were framed by journalists for the eyes of the readers of each newspaper, as will be illustrated, were still shaped by the structures of the old non-globalized world.

This book argues that elite press news cannot be understood by looking at the extent to which it reproduces political messages, nor can it be explained through international macro dynamics in isolation from each other. Elite press news is, indeed, shaped by media professionals, but the constraints affecting their decisions of "what is news" and which sources should be allowed to "speak" within the news come from far beyond the newsroom. The analysis of the international news coverage in the aftermath of 9/11 shows that elite press news is shaped by *national interest, national journalistic culture,* and the *editorial policy* of each individual media organization. These three variables affect the sense of *newsworthiness* of media professionals, therefore playing the role of multiple filters on the journalists' selection of sources within the news coverage.

The analysis, by spanning the global, national, and individual news organizational dimensions—which studies so far have tended to investigate separately—takes up ambitious theoretical and methodological challenges. They exceed the limits of the study. The model generated by the empirical investigation, in this perspective, is ultimately only a snapshot of the contemporary media landscape. It certainly does not claim to explain all news everywhere in the world. The study's findings cannot be extended, for example, to transnational newspapers, nonprint media, a context like the blogosphere, or the coverage of events of either a nonpolitical nature or with mainly domestic rather than international repercussions. It is nonetheless a first step toward developing a multidisciplinary explanation of the nature of news in the twenty-first century. It aims to be the beginning of a long-term international comparative research program to develop a better understanding of the connection between journalism, international politics, and society in a globalized world—a path that other researchers will perhaps be inspired to pursue.

The reason for writing this book, in fact, lies in the realization that the fragmentation of communication research has led to a sort of "scientific dead end." It is true that the existence of different theories can be an indicator of a healthy debate within an academic discipline. The potential contradictions among existing theories, however, appear to mutually undermine their explanatory power rather than contributing to further accumulation, refinement, or updating of our understanding of communication phenomena. This situation is largely because, within the discipline of Communications, different fields of study tend to focus on single and mutually exclusive perspectives of analysis. When it comes to explaining news, for example, Political Communications tends to approach it as the result of a struggle between political actors and journalists within a national context. One main focus of investigation within the field is the issue of media independence against the attempt by political actors at controlling media coverage. Examples of this research tradition are the studies covering the relationship between journalists and official sources,[15] political campaigning and media management,[16] the way power and economic interest affect journalistic practices.[17] International Communications tends to approach the study of news in a macro perspective. For some, globalization processes lead news to become increasingly homogenous on a worldwide scale. According to others, globalization is "resisted" through cultural differentiation at the national or regional level (localization). In yet another perspective, news is affected by power and economic imbalances between developed and developing countries (media flows). To this strand of research belong the studies investigating, respectively, the homogenizing role of news agencies;[18] the way in which cultural variables differentiate the production,[19] reception, and interpretation of media messages;[20] the analysis of media products' imports and exports across the globe.[21] News Sociology studies, instead, tend to focus on micro interactions within news organizations and the way news is mainly shaped by negotiations among media professionals. Ethnographic studies and investigations of production processes in specific news organizations are examples of this last approach.[22]

Within this context, this book is a reaction to yet largely unmet calls for multidisciplinarity and paradigm regeneration coming from several directions. It particularly aims to address theoretical and methodological issues related to the study of news across Political Communications, International Communications, and News Sociology in three ways. First, the study shows the limitations of current theoretical approaches in explaining news. In Political Communications this issue is linked to the fact that the field is largely based on studies with a national scope. Jay Blumler and Michael Gurevitch, in this respect, have called for more international comparative research: they point out that although more comparative studies appeared in the 1990s, there is still need for comparative *conceptualizations and designs*.[23] They criticize the current theoretical vacuum of the field. It is not that there are no theories, they write, but they can be termed at most "middle-range theories."[24] International Communications, instead, could benefit from integrating micro approaches into the mostly macro perspective of the field. Stig Hjarvard, in fact, has criticized the narrowness of news flows studies, arguing that "both the realm of foreign news and the outside social world have been considered to be much simpler and homogeneous than is really the case."[25] What is needed, instead, is a middle-range analysis in the perspective of interaction that stresses the interrelatedness between social actors and between different factors in the news process. On the front of the globalization versus localization debate, Kalyani Chadha and Anandan Kavoori highlight the inadequacy of current approaches by calling for a model of media globalization that recognizes "the continuing role of the national...rather than the somewhat Manichean homogenization versus heterogenization debate that does little to illuminate the complexities of contemporary media developments as they are manifest across national contexts around the globe."[26] The multidisciplinary model presented in this book attempts to bridge the perspectives of these different fields. It explains the dynamic way in which social actors—not only media professionals, but also politicians and members of the wider public—interact with each other and are constrained in the way they act and construct the world by structures they themselves help to create over time at the international, national, and media-organizational levels.

Second, the study reveals the theoretical inconsistencies of the three fields and the fact that some of the claims within their current respective debates are supported by little rigorous empirical evidence. International Communications is particularly haunted by contradictory views. Oliver Boyd-Barrett, for example, argues that international communications "has moved through theories of international communications as propaganda, through to modernization and free flow, to dependency and cultural or media imperialism, supplanted in turn by theories of the 'autonomous reader' and culminating in discourses of globalization that play upon an infinite variety of combinations of 'global' and 'local.'"[27] This "narrative of linearity," as he puts it, is "suspect": "intellectual development of the field...appears not to proceed on the basis of exhaustive testing but lurches from one theory, preoccupation, dimension to another with inadequate attention to accumulative construction."[28] The study, in this context, by relying on an international comparative research design, measures both quantitatively and qualitatively the extent to which the coverage of 9/11 and the war in Afghanistan was "global" rather than "local."

Third, the study confirms the need for renewing old paradigms and finding new ones. Blumler and Gurevitch make the point that social sciences are more exposed to the risk of becoming obsolete than are physical sciences. The advances of communication technologies in the last few decades, in particular, have had such a profound impact on the way political actors communicate with the public, on media formats' proliferation, and on the dynamics of information distribution across the globe, that our theoretical horizons might require a paradigm shift.[29] The problem of theories' slow adaptation to world changes is also emphasized by Brigitte Nacos, Robert Shapiro, and Pierangelo Isernia. They argue that "indeed, much of what we know about the predominant patterns in news reporting about foreign affairs, the nature and formation of public opinion, and the intricate relationships involving mass media, public attitudes, and foreign policymaking is based on research conducted during the Cold War era."[30] What this book fundamentally argues is that some of the current paradigms are not only old—when applied to an international comparative perspective they are also wrong. To truly explain news in the twenty-first century we need to bring together the analytical tools of Political Communications, International Communications, and News Sociology.

This book is essentially about assessing the validity of some of the current main explanatory approaches to news within the case study of the post-9/11 coverage. It could be compared to a forensic analysis of international news. In the same way in which detectives in the TV series *CSI: Crime Scene Investigation* carry out chemical tests, collect evidence, and then carefully piece the data together to establish a cause of death, this book takes the reader through the tests, the gathering of data, and the progressive as well as systematic assembling of evidence to solve the mystery of what shaped the news that followed 9/11.

The purpose of the first part of the book is addressing the "dilemma" of news by showing that there is very little consensus when it comes to explaining what news is, where it comes from, how it is constructed and by whom, what explains its changes across different media outlets and countries. Chapter 1 introduces a multidisciplinary model of the construction of elite news in the aftermath of 9/11. It outlines the constructionist ontology of the world on which the model is based, as well as the three key interrelated variables that were found to explain news variation across the countries and newspapers under study: national interest, national journalistic culture, and the editorial policy of each media organization. Chapter 2 reviews some of the mainstream existing (and conflicting) perspectives about news. It provides a critical overview of the three fields of study whose internal debates are addressed by the empirical investigation: Political Communications, International Communications, and News Sociology. The discussion comparatively addresses both their theoretical and methodological problems. The chapter also contains an explanation of the methodologies that were chosen to meet these challenges in the empirical investigation.

The second part of the book covers the empirical investigation of the international press coverage and the political discourses in the aftermath of 9/11. It presents the results of a study that combined process tracing with quantitative and qualitative content analysis of both governmental discourses and news coverage of eight elite newspapers across the United States, Italy, France, and Pakistan. The study tested the validity of the explanatory approaches to news illustrated in Chapter 2 by systematically assessing the role of different variables. The purpose of this part of the book is not only showing the findings of the investigation, but also taking the reader through the actual contents of the political discourses and media coverage in the aftermath of 9/11. The analysis therefore includes plenty of translated excerpts of both political statements and actual news stories. More specifically, Chapter 3 contains the process-tracing analysis of political statements. It illustrates the extremely diverse way in which governmental actors—presidents, prime ministers, defense and foreign ministers—constructed (framed) the issues of 9/11 and the war in Afghanistan in the four countries under study. Chapter 4 contains the process-tracing analysis of the news coverage. It presents the analysis of both first pages and editorials of the eight newspapers mentioned earlier. Chapter 5 combines the previous process-tracing observations with qualitative and quantitative content analysis. It shows that the coverage patterns identified in the case study over the 64 days between September 11, 2001, and November 14, 2001 (the fall of Kabul during the war in Afghanistan), challenge mainstream explanatory frameworks about news within Political Communications, International Communications, and News Sociology. Chapter 6 covers the theoretical and methodological lessons that can be drawn from the study, as well as the benefits deriving from multidisciplinary and international comparative analysis.

CHAPTER 1

The Construction of News:
A Multidisciplinary Explanation

The study presented in this book is based on a constructionist understanding of society.[1] The actors it describes are politicians, journalists, editors, as well as sources journalists approach in the newsgathering process. All these social actors interact within more or less material structures—governmental institutions, international alliances, national institutional practices, existing political agendas, media systems, editorial policies, media organizations' routines and budgets—that constrain their behavior at different levels. At the same time as acting within these structures, social actors contribute over time to changing and reshaping them. Political actors, for example, might exploit an international crisis situation for rearranging the priorities on an existing policy agenda. Editors, while respecting the mission statement of a news organization, might want to readjust the focus of the coverage it produces so that it better suits audience interests in an increasingly competitive market.[2]

News is part of the very process through which the world is constructed and social meanings created. Gaye Tuchman, for example, writes that it is the meanings within the news that contribute to "perpetually defining and redefining, constituting and reconstituting social phenomena."[3] In a world that is constructed, however, news is constructed, too.[4] For Philip Schlesinger, news is "the product of judgments concerning the social relevance of given events and situations based on assumptions concerning their interest and importance."[5] Making news, in his words, is "putting 'reality' together."

The comparative analysis of the elite press framing of 9/11 and the war in Afghanistan suggests that news is *doubly* constructed. It is constructed by media professionals, who physically assemble it by gathering information. It is also constructed, in meaning, by sources, which might well include editors or journalists themselves, "speaking" within the news text and competing among each other to communicate to the public their interpretation of events. The framing of 9/11 and the war in Afghanistan in the news can effectively be explained by the selection of newsworthy sources within the coverage by journalists. It is the range of sources, their variety of origin (foreign rather than national) and identity (politicians, intellectuals, social actors, religious leaders, etc.) that determine the scope and variety of the news coverage. The choice by journalists and editors of which sources are newsworthy is guided by national interest, national journalistic culture, and editorial policy. These variables act as multiple and progressive filters on the media professionals' judgments of newsworthiness: they shape their *news values*.

Before explaining the way in which the concepts of national interest, national journalistic culture, and editorial policy are defined for the purposes of the empirical investigation and how they shape journalists and editors' news values, I am going to discuss newsworthiness.

Newsworthiness

The literature refers to *news values* in relation to the news-making process, particularly in relation to how journalists, among the countless events happening in the world, are able to select what is most "interesting" or "important" to potential readers in order to fill the daily newshole. David White, in a famous study about the selection of news, examined the way an editor, whom he called "Mr Gates," decided what was "in" and "out."[6] He found that the reasons for the selection of stories (such as "no space," "not too important," "don't care for suicide stories") were "highly-subjective value judgments."[7]

One of the most quoted studies of news values is an article published in 1965 by Johan Galtung and Mari Ruge.[8] On the basis of the coverage of four international crises by Norwegian newspapers they identified 12 criteria according to which "events become news":[9] frequency, intensity ("threshold"), unambiguity, cultural proximity ("meaningfulness"), predictability ("consonance"), unexpectedness, continuity, "composition" (meaning the event suits the needs of the news agenda of a media organization), reference to elite nations, reference to elite persons, human interest ("personalization"), and negativity.[10]

News values in the view of both White and Galtung and Ruge constitute, in practice, an understanding by media professionals about "what is news." It appears to be a "gut feeling" that almost naturally leads journalists and editors to agreeing about the selection of certain events rather than others. While this approach helps in explaining how news comes to exist, it does not tackle the question of where the news values come from and how they got into the mind of the media professionals in the first place. Indeed, a variety of studies confirm that news values, far from being universal, differ depending on the countries and media organizations considered. Noha Mellor, for example, writing about the making of Arab news, defines the already mentioned article by Galtung and Ruge as the "most influential study on *Western* news values."[11] As she observes, while in the West human interest is an increasingly important criteria for selecting stories, news in the Arab world is more closely associated with "social responsibility."[12] The majority of Saudi journalists, for example, think that the main function of the press—which is arguably going to affect their selection of what is newsworthy—is enhancing Islamic values.[13]

Vincent Campbell also argues that different countries "exhibit very different, culturally-specific attitudes towards events' news value."[14] In his analysis, for journalists in authoritarian regimes "a pro-social function is usually part of the job, promoting activities of the state rather than focusing more on a critical watchdog role."[15] Munir Nasser confirms that, in developing countries, journalists see themselves as "educators and nation builders" rather than conveyors of information.[16] Restrictions on Western-style investigative reporting are justified on the ground that developing countries' societies are "too fragile to stand too much probing into the failures of government."[17] Alcino Da Costa, in his analysis of African news, also shows how media in African countries provide the public with "reassuring news" in the attempt to avoid "troublesome reactions."[18] News in developing countries therefore focuses more on positive events rather than disasters, corruption, and wars.[19] As Paul Lendvai put the principle to select what was news in the old Soviet Union: "[G]ood news is news—bad news is not really news at all."[20]

This book is based on the realization that news values vary, and with them the formulation by media professionals of judgments about what is newsworthy.[21] More specifically, the perception of sources' newsworthiness in the minds of media professionals— that is, who should be allowed to "speak" in the news and who shouldn't—I argue, is shaped by three variables: national interest, national journalistic culture, and editorial policy. I am now going to define these concepts and explain how each of them shapes media professionals' news values in the context of the post-9/11 elite press coverage.

NATIONAL INTEREST

Within the constructionist ontology of the book national interest is socially constructed rather than fixed and determined by material resources. Several studies have explained the way shared meanings are constructed by way of communicative interactions among international actors. Thomas Risse calls this process "arguing."[22] Frank Schimmelfenig refers to "bargaining" and "rhetorical action."[23] Both Marc Lynch and Risse talk about "communicative action,"[24] while Kenneth Schultz writes about "signalling."[25] All these analyses agree on the idea that national priorities are not a given, but are subject to redefinition, negotiation, and change over time.

This view fits the theory of "securitization" elaborated by the Copenhagen School, mainly represented by Barry Buzan, Ole Waever, and Jaap de Wilde.[26] They regard the very issue of security as constructed through speech-acts. Which issues belong to the "security" box cannot be determined *a priori*, but they are the result of rhetorical choices. In other words, how issues are constructed and perceived is the result of a process involving a selection of language, which is not just seen as describing reality but as creating it.

National interest is defined in this book using Joseph Nye's words as

> the set of national priorities regarding relations with the rest of the world. It is broader than strategic interests, though they are part of it. It can include values such as human rights and democracy, if the public feels that those values are so important to its identity that it's willing to pay a price to promote them.[27]

This notion suits not only the idea that national interest might evolve over time, but also that what national interest is in the first place is open to redefinition.

While the book is based on the belief that it is social actors who decide what should be labeled "national interest," I am more specifically arguing that national interest is constructed on the basis of a country's *political culture*.

As Richard Wilson points out, there are different approaches to political culture:

> Assumptions emphasize different factors, such as how individuals and/ or groups are socialized, how different individuals organize their thinking about rules and norms, how discourse affects the legitimacy of political institutions, how and why individuals orient their thinking

and communication in terms of salient myths, rituals, and symbols, and how moral criteria are apprehended and with what consequences for political behaviour.[28]

William Reisinger has, indeed, pointed to the "profusion of definitions" concerning political culture.[29] For Gabriel Almond and Sidney Verba "the term 'political culture'. . . refers to the specifically political orientation—attitudes toward the political system and its various parts, and attitudes toward the role of the self in the system."[30] Elsewhere, Verba defines political culture as the embedding of political systems in sets of meanings, specifically in symbols, beliefs, and values.[31] Lucien Pye enlarges the definition to include "both the political ideals and the operating norms of a polity."[32]

The concept of political culture therefore shifts between approaches locating it at the level of individual psychological factors and perspectives including norms of behavior at a broader societal level, which more closely resemble the idea of "structures."

What is common among political culture studies is the focus on "preference formation," particularly on explaining the way culture constrains preferences and preferences affect culture. The utility of political culture studies, according to Wilson is, in fact, in their capacity to explain "why people choose particular courses of action over others and the likelihood that these choices will be widely shared."[33] This means, in alternative terms, explaining how and why people make decisions that affect the political life in a country.[34]

In this book I choose to define political culture as a form of structure rather than a set of individual beliefs. This, however, within the study's structurationist view of the world, does not exclude individuals' contributions in creating a country's political culture over time, and in turn, their being affected by it. In fact even Almond, who privileges the individual approach, says that "the causal arrows between culture [individual subjective orientations] and structure [governmental structure and performance]. . . go both ways."[35]

On the basis of the process-tracing analysis of the political statements made by authorities in the United States, France, Italy, and Pakistan in the aftermath of 9/11, which will be illustrated in Chapter 4, I take the political culture of a country to be the combination of four main aspects: *national identity, existing policy agendas, relations with foreign countries (international relations), and a country's positioning within the international system.*

John Hutcheson et al. write that "national identity. . . is a constructed and public national self-image based on membership in a political community as well as history, myths, symbols, language, and cultural norms commonly held by members of a nation."[36] Schlesinger defines national identity as a form of collective identity, "one of inclusion that provides a boundary around 'us' and one of exclusion that distinguishes 'us' from 'them.'"[37] "Policy agendas" refer to sets of domestic and foreign policy activities. They are pursued and prioritized consistently with the country's identity and in accordance with existing national institutional and legal frameworks. "International relations" refers to a country's relations with foreign countries, which includes belonging to international organizations as the UN or NATO, membership of supranational institutions such as the EU, belonging to international alliances such as the international coalition against terrorism. Sharing the membership of an international organization or alliance means sharing its purposes and values. The EU, for example, brings together member states that share commitment to free market, respect for human rights and democratic institutions.[38] "Positioning within the international system" is the place within the international system a country constructs on the basis of its sense of identity and its international relations. This is very different from geographic position, although being close to a theater of war, for example, or sharing a border with another country could have an effect on it. Nonetheless, positioning within the international system is the result of a construction process rather than reducible to geography only. India and Pakistan, for example, might be very close geographically. Politically their perceived position could not be further. Even countries that appear very distant geographically might be joined in an international alliance. For example, countries as diverse as the United States, Turkey, and Norway belong to NATO.

These four aspects are tightly interlinked. Vivien Schmidt and Claudio Radaelli say, in fact, that "collective identity determines not only what 'we' are and where 'we' come from but also what can and cannot be achieved."[39] What the book argues, in addition to this, according to what the analysis of the political statements in the empirical investigation will show, is that who we are (national identity) affects what we do (policy agendas), but also who we do it with (international relations) and where we stand (positioning within the international system).

National identity, policy agendas, international relations, and positioning in the international system all evolve over time, dynamically affecting each other: policy agendas might affect a country's positioning in the international system, its relations with foreign countries, and will eventually have an impact on its national identity. An example is offered by Pakistan in the aftermath of 9/11. The decision by President Musharraf to join the international coalition against terrorism led the country to dramatically distance itself from the Taliban regime, which it had previously supported, and to reposition itself much more closely to the United States, both politically and ideologically.

Not only was Pakistan's identity suddenly reshaped to emphasize the country's new role as a "frontline state"[40] in the war on terrorism (WOT), but this led also to the development of more cooperative relations with the United States. In addition to the American government's decision to remove the sanctions that were placed on Pakistan and India after their nuclear tests in 1998, State Secretary Colin Powell, when he visited the country on October 15, 2001, promised an aid package of $650 million to support Pakistan's increased military expenditure and to compensate for the loss of exports due to the military operations in the region.[41] This led to a chain reaction in the international community, which soon followed the American steps in establishing new—or reviving old—ties with Pakistan. Here are a few examples of the headlines in the Pakistani newspaper the *Dawn* in the immediate aftermath of Pakistan's decision to join the antiterrorism coalition and that well document the effects of Pakistan's repositioning in the international system: "Japan to provide $40m aid soon" (September 22), "Australia revives military ties" (September 22), "IMF likely to okay plan for Pakistan" (September 23), "Mubarak [Egyptian president] extends support to Pakistan" (September 24), "Access to European markets soon: officials" (September 26). As Samina Yasmeen confirms in her analysis of the Pakistani policy response to 9/11, Pakistan moved, within weeks, from being identified as a "failed or failing state," "imploding under the pressure of mounting lawlessness, sectarian strife and near economic bankruptcy," to "a major participant in the war against terrorism."[42]

The four aspects of a country's political culture—national identity, policy agendas, international relations, and positioning within the international system—are defined through negotiations with actors at the international level as who we are, what we do, and where we stand in the international arena are defined in relation to foreign "others," too.

Political culture affects what political actors can say and do. Within the constructionist ontology of the book, political culture performs the role of a flexible structure that restricts the range of choices available to political actors. As Henning Boekle, Jörg Nadoll, and Bernhard Stahl write (although in relation to national identity only), existing discourses (or structures) cannot cause specific behaviors in the sense that they *determine* them.[43] Political culture provides "reasons" (and justifications) for different behaviors. The way in which national identity concretely affects a state's foreign policy conduct depends on the situation-specific factors and on the development of the political discourse.[44] The discourse structure also provides a range of "acceptable" behaviors.

* * *

National interest, in this book, is based on national political culture, but evolves more rapidly than the latter. To illustrate this point, while Pakistan's political culture could not change altogether from one day to the next, in the immediate aftermath of 9/11 some of the country's national priorities were redirected following a phone call from State Secretary Powell to President Musharraf: "You are either with us or against us."[45] While Pakistan kept on regarding itself as a "fortress of Islam" and a member of the community of Muslim states (national political culture), the national priority became joining the international coalition against terrorism. This short-term decision feeds back into the political culture by changing the positioning of Pakistan within the international system. The shaping of a country's national interest, similarly to what happens with the political culture, occurs in relation to the national interests of other countries.

National interest guides the selection of newsworthy sources by journalists and editors. It guides the selection of the identity of the sources, which could be, for example, allied countries' leaders, international organization officials, or religious leaders from other Muslim countries. Whether the sources are mainly national or international, as the comparative analysis of the coverage of 9/11 reveals, depends on the relations of a country with the rest of the world.

Sunanda Datta-Ray illustrates how the change in American national priorities following 9/11 suddenly made Afghanistan a newsworthy topic:

> "Afghanistanism" was the term for news that was remote or irrelevant for…colleagues on *The New York Times*. "Who can check up on or take offence at news from Afghanistan?" Operation Enduring Freedom and the war on terrorism changed all that, making Afghanistan front-page news only because of the involvement of Americans and American interests.[46]

National interest contributes to selecting a first "pool" of potentially newsworthy sources, as it can be seen on the first layer of figure 1.1. National interest determines the ratio between international and national sources within the coverage at the national level. The chart illustrates, as an example, the impact different national priorities have on both American and French coverage. As will be illustrated later in the analysis, the French government's interest in developing countries and the Arab world leads to a greater selection of foreign sources in the coverage than in the United States. The administration's focus on domestic politics, instead, translates into mainly national sources within the news. These "pools" of sources are further both cut down and integrated by a second variable: national journalistic culture.

NATIONAL JOURNALISTIC CULTURE

National journalistic culture is the set of moral ideals, as well as reporting and editing practices, that characterize journalists in a country and lead to different perceptions of their own role within that country's society, affect the way they gather news, handle sources, and write their stories. Within the book the main distinction between journalistic cultures is between objective journalism and interpretative journalism.

Michael Schudson defines "objectivity" in American journalism as "at once a moral ideal, a set of reporting and editing practices, and an observable pattern of news writing."[47] This definition can be applied, in principle, to interpretative journalism, too. In both kinds of journalistic cultures journalists express allegiance to the moral ideal by reproducing the norm in formal codes of professional ethics, by incorporating it in textbooks and in educational curricula, by developing the idea in professional journals.[48] The application of the norm can be identified by means of content analysis that "measure the degree of impersonality and non-partisanship in news stories."[49] The difference is that objective journalism guides journalists "to separate facts from values and to report only the facts."[50] Reporters should report "news" without commenting on it. In interpretative journalism, instead, reporters present opinions rather than (or besides) facts to the readers. Schudson calls interpretative journalism, which he identifies with continental European journalism, "partisan"[51] as in his view newspapers outside the United States "are the declared allies or agents of political parties and their reporting of news is an element of partisan struggle."[52] I prefer for this book the more general label of "interpretative journalism" as the analysis will reveal that opinions expressed within news stories, even in media organizations that do take political sides, do not necessarily conform to the latter's ideologically partisan leanings.

National journalistic culture is the result of the creation of ethical norms over time through the practices of news media professionals. Their establishment can be understood within the broader political, economic, and social context in which they develop. National journalistic culture, in other words, is shaped by society, although this "shaping" should be understood in constructionist terms. Journalistic culture evolves through the continuous interaction between agents belonging to media organizations and external agents belonging to other organizations and institutions. The effects of such interactions continuously feed back into the agents' respective organizations affecting their norms of behavior and practices over time. Jean Chalaby is therefore right, in this perspective, when he claims that (objective) journalism is "an Anglo-American invention."[53] One of the reasons why American journalism developed the normative ideal of objectivity, as Schudson writes, was the need felt by journalists to protect their integrity from public relations practitioners who started multiplying in the early twentieth century and who aggressively worked to place official stories—sometimes plain misinformation—in the press.[54] The move toward adopting rules of conduct, and specifically toward objectivity, was supported by the political Progressive movement against party corruption, which made objectivity look like "a natural and progressive ideology for an aspiring occupational group at a moment when science was god, efficiency was cherished, and increasingly prominent elites judged partisanship a vestige of tribal 19th century."[55] This did not happen in continental Europe, where journalists had developed a self-perception of "high literary creators and cosmopolitan thinkers," had an established tradition of professionalism, and did not see much virtue in separating journalism from political ideology.[56]

I am going to present further evidence of the way different national political, economic, and social contexts contribute to shape journalistic practices in different countries, the perception of journalists' own role within the societies in which they operate, and the very content of the news they produce. Paolo Mancini, for example, explains why the attempt by both the U.S. government as well as business at importing the objectivity model into Italian journalism in the post-WWII period did not yield to its actual implementation.[57] In his view, the form and function of journalism are shaped by the political and economic system of the country. A first reason why Italian journalism, particularly the press, cannot possibly be "objective" is, in his analysis, its historical lack of autonomy. While in the United States and the United Kingdom, in the first part of the twentieth century, the press detached itself from the political movement from which it was born by self-funding through advertising revenues, state intervention and support from corporations with political interests in Italy did not allow journalism in the country to divorce from ideological and economic interests.[58] The tendency of the Italian press to be partisan finds its roots in the advocacy journalism going back to the Risorgimento.[59] As Carlo Sorrentino points out, the literary tendencies of Italian journalism are supported by the "liberal paternalism" of the first part of the twentieth century, which pursued "general and high values in the attempt of hiding social conflict."[60] Newspapers, in this perspective, played a "pedagogic role" that consisted in educating the reader.[61] The result was, and still is, that the press does not talk *about* citizens, as objective journalism tends to do in providing information about what happens in the world, but talks *to* them.[62]

In France, as Clyde Thogmartin writes, a similar tradition of literary journalism, or "sitting journalism," is partly due to the French press lack of resources:

> Most of the small turn-of-the-century opinion papers did not have a journalist to spare to chase down a story in the streets, or the space to print one if he found it. The old mass circulation papers also got by with surprisingly small editorial staffs, preferring to rely on dispatches from Havas [French news agency] that each editorialist could rewrite with his own spin. After World War II, the extreme poverty of the reborn press discouraged any aggressive chasing about for news.[63]

In Arab countries, instead, journalism revolves around politics, and in relation to issues that enjoy a "pan-Arab consensus," such as the Palestinian-Israeli conflict, "objectivity in the sense of balanced reporting of conflicting views seems to be virtually non-existent."[64] Such features can be explained by considering that journalism has evolved as a government institution. Muhammed Ayish, specifically referring to television journalism, says that for last three decades of the twentieth century objectivity was almost completely absent as "television services had functioned more as government propaganda machines than as independent sources of information."[65] This has its historical roots in the fact that before the 1990s Arab television was dominated by a government monopoly of broadcasting. In turn, government control was based on the idea that broadcasting was a tool of national development that should be under political control.[66] The traditional official focus of news has affected the sense of newsworthiness of journalists and the interest of the public, which, also due to the political and economic developments of the past 50 years, is highly politically engaged.[67]

In the United States, where journalism is traditionally expected to aspire to objectivity, reporters are gatherers of facts. This means that they tend to approach news sources to ask for their interpretation of events and present them to the readers without—at least is the aim—evaluating them. In France or Italy, where the expected function of journalism is providing commentary, journalists tend to see themselves as intellectuals. They approach sources to gather some raw information and opinions. They, however, elaborate on them and present the readers with their own comments. As an example presented by Thogmartin very well illustrates, this translates into very different practices:

> You are a journalist, you have just finished a long piece of reporting, you transmit it to your editor in chief, who does not like it. In the Anglo-Saxon countries, the journalist goes back into the field; in France, he shuts himself up in his office and thinks.[68]

The social embedding of journalistic practices, or national journalistic culture, affects the journalists' very sense of what is news and what is newsworthy. This, again, also applies to sources. More precisely, in this book, national journalistic culture influences the selection of newsworthy sources in the coverage by affecting the ratio between official and nonofficial sources. Going back to the previous examples, while in France "journalists tend to think that there are more interesting things to do in life than pester some politician or official who has never said anything interesting in the first place for one more quote,"[69] in the Arab world "news is politics."[70]

I am talking about official sources because they are the main suppliers of raw information about the issue of terrorism and security, the focus of the empirical investigation of this book. The observation, however, could be applied to other issues by changing the category of who the "authorities" are. Nonofficial sources are, in the case of 9/11, commentators, intellectuals, academics, researchers from think-tanks asked to give an evaluation of the situation in the West. These sources extend to religious leaders and *ulema* in Pakistan.[71] Interpretative journalism tends to give more space to nonofficial sources, particularly commentators, than objective journalism does, as can be observed in layer 2 of figure 1.1. The chart shows the way national journalistic culture leads to selecting more official sources in the American rather than the French coverage.

The judgment about sources' newsworthiness is, however, affected by one more variable: the editorial policy of each news organization.

EDITORIAL POLICY

The editor (or editorial board) of each media organization sets the news agenda. This means establishing the relative size of the "newshole" for the different issues that are going to be covered in the news. This choice is made in accordance with the mission statement of the media organization, its focus of interest—for example, business or domestic affairs rather than foreign policy—and is made with economic considerations in mind: both budgets as well as anticipation of readers' interests. As Einar Ostgaard writes:

> Each single news medium...runs on a budget and has to consider costs, whether or not it is intended to make profits for the publisher. The space or time given to foreign news may thus be restricted by financial considerations, and whether these considerations in the last resort are based on competition for space by other news material or by advertisements, or lack of money to pay for reports from other countries, or from other causes, the effect is the same: economic factors are at work also at this stage of the news flow, restricting the amount of foreign news which is presented to the public.[72]

In this view editorial policy translates into both a limit to the kind of stories that can be reported and the extent to which news should be devoted to a certain topic.[73] Editorial policy affects the way individual journalists write their stories as it shapes their sense of what is news in the first place: what is "newsworthy."

Within a constructionist view of the world, editorial policy is defined within a country's national journalistic culture. However, while all editors in France might attribute to opinion greater newsworthiness than in the United States, where just fact should become news, there are further differences at the level of each newspaper. Some newspapers might not deal with certain issues but very marginally because they are not newsworthy to the organization's specific agenda. The study finds, for example, that *Libération* does not cover the issue of 9/11 in as much detail as *Le Monde*. This difference in priorities concerning the coverage reflects the fact that *Libération*

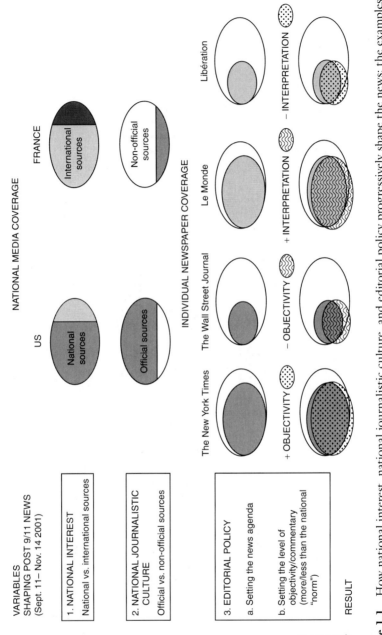

Figure 1.1 How national interest, national journalistic culture, and editorial policy progressively shape the news: the examples of the United States and France

was established in 1973 as the voice of "all the leftist political ferment" of French society and was therefore concerned with domestic issues.[74] The very title *Le Monde*—"the world"—reveals instead a strong international vocation. Its first page in 1944 famously had just one story on domestic politics.[75]

Even within the same journalistic culture different newspapers might present different levels of commentary/objectivity than the national "norm." Within the same American objective journalism the *Wall Street Journal* shows a higher presence of evaluative statements (interpretation) in the news than the *New York Times*.[76] This reflects the editorial philosophy of the business news organization, which openly states: "We often take sides on the major issues of politics and society, with a goal of moving policies or events in what we think is the best direction for the country and the world."[77] The editorial policy therefore also shapes the way national journalistic culture is implemented at the level of the single media organization.

Editorial policy acts as a further selector of the pools of newsworthy sources previously identified in figure 1.1. The third layer in the chart shows the double effect of editorial policy on the coverage: setting the size of the newshole (layer 3.a) and defining whether there is going to be more (or less) objectivity/commentary than the national journalistic norm would lead to expect (3.b). The chart, more specifically, visually illustrates the way a different selection of sources leads to different contents in the coverage. The news in each newspaper appears like a canvas with different shades. It is, in fact, the sources who "color" the coverage by expressing ideas—each idea being represented by a pixel in the image. Newspaper coverage in the United States presents darker shades of gray, representing the prevalence of national and official sources rather than international and nonofficial sources (lighter shades) as in France. Coverage in each newspaper ("individual newspaper coverage") further differentiates itself from the national coverage ("national media coverage") through the size of its agenda in relation to a specific issue and either the "objectivity" or "interpretation" lens through which journalists/editors produce the news (respectively, the dotted or wavy "screens" superimposed on the "results" layer in the chart).

CHAPTER 2

News Theories:
Conflicting Perspectives

If a researcher was respectively to approach the literature of different fields of study with the same question, "What shapes the news?" he or she would find completely different explanations. Studies in Political Communications, for example, tend to argue that political actors have a major role in shaping a country's news stories. Scholars of International Communications point at least at three possibilities: for some news is shaped by unbalanced and unidirectional flows between richer and poorer countries, the advocates of globalization support the idea that news is becoming homogeneous on a worldwide scale, supporters of the Localization hypothesis reject the idea of global news in favor of its diversification along cultural, linguistic, or ethnic lines. Research in News Sociology, instead, emphasizes how the news product of each media organization is the unique output of patterns of micro interactions among media professionals and between them and the rest of society.

This chapter provides a critical overview of the current state of analytical approaches to news within Political Communications, International Communications, and News Sociology. These, of course, are not the only approaches to the study of news, but represent three established, fairly distinct, and mainstream areas of research. They are chosen for review for two purposes. The first is showing the extreme diversity of existing explanatory frameworks. The discussion particularly highlights the fact that, when it comes to analytically dissecting the claims made within these debates, it is difficult to understand what they empirically mean, what are the factors (variables) or indeed the causal mechanisms that are supposed to shape the news. For example, within International Communications, the Globalization and Localization perspectives make two diametrically opposite claims about the way news should vary at the international level: either a tendency toward worldwide homogenization or a diversification of coverage along national, if not regional, lines. Despite these fairly clear-cut predictions, the two theoretical stances are vague when it comes to name what it is, exactly, that is being "globalized" or "localized." The approaches neither unambiguously identify which *variables* drive the processes of either globalization or localization, nor explain *how* these variables produce the said globalization or localization of news. The discussion comparatively addresses both theoretical and methodological problems with existing approaches.

The second aim of the review is selecting five alternative perspectives to be tested in the empirical case study of 9/11 and its aftermath. They are Indexing from Political Communications; Media Flows, Globalization, and Localization from International Communications; Hierarchy-of-Influences from News Sociology. Each of the five approaches is disassembled into three components: a *hypothesis*, or prediction about the way news (the dependent variable) should vary at either the international, national, or subnational level; *independent variables*, which are expected to produce those changes; and *causal mechanisms*, through which the independent variables should lead to the predicted news outcomes.[1]

Details about the combination of methodologies that were used in the empirical study to test both the hypotheses and the role of the independent variables are provided at the end of the chapter. It is in order, however, to stress here a couple of important caveats. First, the hypotheses that are outlined in this chapter are, to some extent, both obvious and extreme. In fact, on the one hand, even before conducting any empirical investigation, there is little doubt that each of the predictions is going to materialize *to some extent*. News coverage will certainly match at least some of the views within the political debate of a country: the link between 9/11, terrorism, and security makes political authorities an extremely newsworthy source of information for journalists. It is reasonable to expect, since the world's attention focused on the United States and its reaction to the events, that there will be unbalances in the level of reporting across countries. Thinking back about newspapers' first pages in the aftermath of the events and the presence of the very same pictures and titles, reproduced over and over again, in so many countries around the world suggests that there is most likely going to be some evidence of a "globalization" of coverage.[2] At the same time, while most of the world condemned the attacks, some voices framed the events in a radically different way. Iraqi news, for example, described 9/11 as "the American cowboy gathers the results of its crimes against humanity."[3] Media coverage could therefore also be expected to be shaped by "local" ways of interpreting the same global issues. Common sense suggests that news is going to present different characteristics in different newspapers. Left-wing newspaper *Libération* did not write an editorial entitled "We are all Americans" in the aftermath of the events like *Le Monde* did,[4] but published, instead, the slightly less sympathetic "The new global disorder: The day when America became vulnerable."[5]

On the other hand, none of the hypotheses are going to be confirmed in full. For example, it is extremely unlikely that news, anywhere, is going to reproduce the contents of the political discourse only, or that news is literally going to be the same on a global scale across national borders and media organizations. The strength of the study lies in its capacity to test the different hypotheses *simultaneously* to assess their *relative validity* by actually measuring the extent of news coverage similarity and difference across the international, national, and media-organizational levels. In other words, the study assesses the extent to which, for example, news is "globalized" rather than "indexed" to political discourse, or "nationalized" rather than being the product of each single media organization. The opportunity of analyzing the variation of news across the international, national, and media-organizational levels on the same data ultimately enables outlining a hierarchy of relative influences shaping the news. This further leads the way toward refining existing theories, completing them, and understanding their limits, eventually building new theory.

A second warning applies to the variables identified for each of the hypotheses. A concept such as "political culture"—a variable that is expected to affect the correlation between media coverage and political discourse—is highly complex. As the discussion in Chapter 1 has pointed out, political culture can be defined in many different ways. In this book, however, as already explained, it refers to the combination of national identity, policy agendas, international relations, and the positioning of a country within the international system. The choice of adopting this and other definitions that might be regarded as restrictive in a context in which many interpretations exist is the outcome of a pragmatic balancing of complexity with the measurement of intangible concepts in the empirical investigation.

POLITICAL COMMUNICATIONS

Political Communications addresses different aspects of the role of communications within the political process.[6] The question of what affects the content of media coverage, mainly approached as "news," has attracted considerable attention among researchers. The idea that political actors are an essential source for the media and contribute to shaping news coverage is widespread.[7] The extent to which political actors affect media coverage and the shape taken by their influence have been conceptualized in different ways over time. The hegemonic approach tends to see the media spontaneously reproducing the ideology of the political system.[8] As Daniel Hallin puts it, "[I]f ideology is a symphony, it is a symphony without a conductor."[9] In this view even what looks like an oppositional relationship to political authority is actually, as in the case of the reporting of the Vietnam War, "a response to the degree of consensus or dissensus among political elites."[10]

The agenda-setting approach, instead, focuses on the "theoretical metaphor" of the "agenda."[11] Studies within this strand of literature concentrate on identifying specific issues or topics being communicated by political actors to the media.[12] Agenda setting acknowledges an effort by political actors to shape the news for their own interest. Dan Berkowitz says, for example, that

> when policymakers attempt to influence public opinion, they often see the mass media as a convenient channel for transmitting their messages. Sometimes, they intentionally attempt to place stories, while other times, they position themselves as useful news sources whom journalists can come to depend on. They also develop a sense of how to avoid the media agenda.[13]

While the view that media and politicians have an ambivalent relationship and can influence each other is not new, more recent developments in the field have explored the circumstances or the conditions under which a party has more influence on the other.[14] Hallin himself has raised doubts about the validity of hegemonic interpretations.

> I don't find myself using the term hegemony much in my more recent work. I have grown tired of the enterprise of demonstrating that the media are neither neutral nor are they most of the time "watchdogs" acting to check the power of the state or other dominant interests.... The strongest critique of the concept of hegemony, it seems to

me, would be to say not that it is false—is it really plausible, after all, that major cultural institutions would not be closely tied to the structure of power?—but that it is too obvious to be interesting.[15]

Lance Bennett and Steven Livingston also express the idea that news content is the result of a "negotiated process":[16]

> Rather than advocate one extreme or the other regarding press-government autonomy or dependence, it makes sense to think of journalists as semi-independent players in the news game. There is no inherent contradiction in the idea that press-government relations are characterized by potentially extreme variations from independence to dependence. Rather than continuing to debate the extremes of autonomy or dependence, it makes more sense to explore the uneasy and often disjointed combinations of the two.[17]

Several studies have, indeed, pointed out that, far from being a passive recipient of political actors' influence, the press enjoys margins of independence.[18] Karen Callaghan and Frauke Schnell, in a study about the way framing of the issue of gun control in the United States was influenced by both politicians (interest groups) and the media, conclude, for example: "[W]e conceptualize the media's role as a dual one: as institutional players who construct and promote unique frames of their own, as well as a conduit for the dissemination of other players' frames."[19]

The "bottom line," however, as Scott Althaus puts it, is that "we simply don't know how independent news discourse might be from the parameters of official debate."[20] Out of the many possibilities the "indexing hypothesis" was selected because it establishes a correlation between the debate of the political elite and the news.[21] Testing this approach by measuring the extent to which the media reproduce political messages also allows assessing the validity of alternative positions within the field.

The Indexing Hypothesis

The indexing hypothesis, originally developed by Bennett in 1990 in a study about the *New York Times* coverage of U.S. funding for the Nicaraguan contras, suggests that "mass media news professionals, from the boardroom to the beat, tend to 'index' the range of voices and viewpoints in both news and editorials according to the range of views expressed in mainstream government debate about a given topic."[22]

Other studies have confirmed Bennett's findings and refined the hypothesis by detailing the extent of the indexing of media coverage to domestic political debate in different circumstances. Bennett and Jarol Manheim analyze the *New York Times* coverage of the Gulf War and find a correlation between the range of coverage at each stage of the crisis and the range of debate among officials.[23] Andre Billeaudeaux and others examine the *New York Times* and the *Washington Post* coverage between September 11 and the beginning of the war in Afghanistan and conclude that the language of the U.S. administration produced effects ("discernible patterns") in the editorial contents of the two newspapers.[24] Jonathan Mermin finds evidence that American media coverage of foreign policy crises since the Vietnam War, although not shaped by one specific political actor, has been confined within the debate boundaries set by the U.S. government.[25] Livingston and Todd Eachus suggest that, while the indexing hypothesis is confirmed, in the post–Cold War era there is more scope for dissident voices, which would have been previously "marginalized," to be included in the mainstream press.[26] This occurs through "news icons": "dramatic, symbolically rich stories" used by journalists "as indicators of emerging social and political problems."[27] Althaus and others revise the indexing hypothesis, which they still believe is valuable in describing media approach to foreign policy, by extending the concept of official debate to foreign elites.[28] Content analysis of the *New York Times* coverage of the U.S.-Libya crisis of 1985–1986 reveals that journalists, to apply the objectivity rule of reporting, can turn to foreign sources if no opposition exists within the national political elite.[29] They can also marginalize some sources or give more space to others. John Zaller and Dennis Chiu, in a study of 42 foreign policy crises from the Soviet takeover of Poland in 1945 to the war in Kosovo in 1999, observe that media coverage follows the cues of officials, even if after the end of the Cold War media tend to become more independent of the U.S. Congress and the president. They distinguish between "source indexing" and "power indexing": the former essentially consists in journalists' direct dependence on sources for "everything they report"; the latter is the tendency to judge sources' newsworthiness on the basis of their capacity to affect future events.[30]

What Does "Indexing" Mean?

Despite being apparently straightforward, indexing reveals a much greater complexity when empirically unpacked. Althaus and others directly address a clarification of what "indexing to political elites' debate" should mean in practice. As the authors put it, "[I]ndexing seems to predict that the media hold a mirror to elite discourse and reflect that discourse to the public."[31] The empirical objective of the indexing concept is explaining "the closeness of fit between media discourse and debate among political elites."[32] This could lead, in their opinion, to three predictions: "[T]he breadth of media policy debate is less than or equal to, but never greater than, the official debate"; "the news closely reflects the distribution of expressed views among officials"; or "some combination of the first two."[33]

Even this clarification, however, raises some questions. What does it mean that the media "breadth" of debate is smaller or equal to the official one? What does "reflecting" the "distribution" of "views" exactly consist in? The difficulty in understanding what media content being "indexed" to the political debate actually means relates to several aspects. The first is defining what the nature of "indexing" is: it could be either a correlation, a compatibility, or a reproduction of contents. Depending on the definition of what indexing is, the data analysis could lead to different assessments of the levels of indexing within media coverage: "reproduction" of political messages—that is, contents detected within the coverage should be exactly the same as those in the political debate—could be a stricter criterion to meet than "compatibility." In the latter case contents would not have to be the same. They could be just "similar," although, in turn, a new definition would be needed about how similar contents should be in order to be coded as "compatible." And even when such clarification is made, what would the nature of such "contents" be?

Also on this last point the literature does not provide clear answers. Livingston and Eachus talk about "thematic shifts in news frames."[34] Billeaudeaux and others use a wide range of terms: "messages," "language," "themes," "positions," "voices."[35] Althaus and others, together with Robert Entman and Andrew Rojecki, refer to "views."[36] Bennett refers to "views," "voices and viewpoints" within the coverage.[37] The same terms are used by Livingston and Eachus.[38] David White refers to the presence of "frames" in the news.[39] Indexing is operationalized as the expression of support versus opposition to the government agenda in Bennett and Mermin.[40] It is the ratio of positive versus negative coverage in Zaller and Chiu.[41]

The two challenging issues here are, first, how to establish the relationship between political debate and media coverage in empirical terms, and second, how to draw conclusions from the data. In fact, political actors are a newsworthy source of information for journalists.[42] To an extent a certain level of "indexing" is always to be expected. The indexing hypothesis claims to expose a lack of independence by the press. While some would regard reporting official views as part of the democratic duty of the press (of voicing the views of elected officials), others would object that the press, by always remaining within the boundaries of official debate, is not fulfilling its role of democratic "watchdog."[43] What is indexing supposed to reveal to the researcher? At which point does indexing start telling the investigator something at all?—and something interesting rather than obvious? In fact, how close should the contents of the political debate and the media coverage be to allow the researcher to conclude that the media is not being critical enough, rather simply doing its job?

The key to understanding, let alone measuring, any relationship between media coverage and political debate is in the definition of the nature of the contents in question, in their detection in both political statements and news, in the assessment of their comparison as well as quantification. These tasks present challenges and will need to be operationalized carefully in the methodology section through an approach that records small contents differences and allows the quantification of the extent to which political messages are reproduced within the news. For the time being the prediction of a correlation between media coverage and political debate is defined as the reproduction, within the news, of the contents of the statements made by political actors (Hypothesis 1).

What Leads to the Correlation between News and Political Debate?

The same news outcome, a correlation of news contents to the contents of the political debate, could be achieved through alternative independent variables and causal mechanisms. Although Bennett's indexing hypothesis covers some possible explanations, they have been subject to critique. Not only will such critiques be highlighted here, but also alternative explanations drawn from additional literature within the field will be added to the range of variables and causal mechanisms to be tested during the study. The integrations, bringing the number of variables and causal mechanisms to six, come from International Relations, news management literature, and studies about the media coverage of political campaigns. The variables are a democratic form of government, objective journalistic culture, national political culture, media influence on political debate, news management by political actors, ideological orientation of a news organization. They will now be illustrated in turn.

Bennett explains the indexing of media coverage to political debate through two main variables. The first is the "symbiotic" relationship between political actors and the media within the news production process.[44] Political actors have, in fact, a "news-making edge," and they "enable journalists to fill the daily 'newshole' with a steady supply of economical, well-produced material."[45] Officials are also representatives of the people in a democratic country. By voicing the views of officials the press acts in a democratically responsible manner. This is enhanced by the journalists' newsgathering routines: the fact that journalists always have to rely on a source for reporting. The reliance on sources, in turn, is made stronger by a second variable, the objectivity norm of journalism. Professional reporters always try to present "both sides" of a story.[46] The role of the news production process (understood as newsgathering routines within each media organization) and the objectivity norm are also supported by Althaus and others.[47]

While there is no doubt that journalists all over the world need to fill a daily newshole, what Bennett as well as Althaus and others claim is that the tendency to give space in the news to official views is specifically affected by a country's *form of government*—in their case democracy—and *journalistic culture*—objectivity. The problem is that none of the authors can have controlled for those variables since their respective studies focused on the U.S. case only. Indeed, all indexing studies mentioned in this review have always focused on the contents of American elite newspapers, particularly (although not exclusively) the *New York Times*. Within the same national context, existing studies cannot have explored the possible effect of a different national journalistic culture, perhaps an interpretative kind of journalism rather than the American ideal of objective reporting.[48] Previous studies cannot have taken into consideration the impact of different journalistic routines than those existing in the United States, perhaps deriving from the fact that political authorities are not as approachable to journalists—let alone being available precisely to get their message into the news—as could happen in nondemocratic countries.

Indexing is regarded as a measure of political actors' "influence" on the media. However, it is questionable whether a correlation between the contents of the political debate and the media coverage alone can really be a measure of politicians' impact. The correlations of contents that have been used to test this hypothesis are indeed a highly questionable proof of the existence of a causal link between political influence (independent variable) and media coverage (dependent variable). To begin with, studies about indexing draw their conclusions about the influence of political actors on media coverage on the basis of media content alone.[49] Bennett originally looks at frequency, direction (support or opposition), and source of "opinions" voiced in the *New York Times* indexes only. As White, Althaus and others, and Zaller and Chiu notice, the author does not provide an independent measure of political content.[50] This is a serious shortcoming. As Zaller and Chiu put it:

> One concern is that it [Bennett's study] failed to develop a measure of congressional opinion that was independent of what the *New York Times* claimed it was. Thus if the newspaper gave a distorted impression of congressional opinion so as to make it seem consistent with its own editorial slant, it would create the impression that the paper was following the views of Congress even though it was not.[51]

Althaus and others say that the fact that the media simplify congressional debate or the fact that they emphasize some "themes and sources" more than others cannot really explain whether "the media are exercising some degree of independent choice within the parameters of official discourse—or that they are passively reflecting power relationships among elites."[52] Zaller and Chiu, on this point, also write that "thus far we have assumed that if any two actors take the same slant on a crisis, it must be because one has influenced the other. But there is another possibility: because members of Congress, presidents, and reporters are all members of the same political culture, they tend to have the same culturally conditioned response to events."[53] What their suggestion points to is that it could be entirely possible that there is a higher variable that shapes both political debate *and* media coverage. The source of the common "culturally conditioned response" by both political actors and reporters is a shared understanding of the issue. I take this to be a variable that exists at the national level, which I call *national political culture*, a combination, as explained in detail in Chapter 1, of a country's national identity, policy agendas, international relations, and positioning within the international system.

There is a fourth variable explaining news being indexed to political debate. Zaller and Chiu remark that the correlation between congressional and media opinion is interpreted as an influence by political actors on the media simply because prior studies have pointed at a reliance of journalists on official sources, but they admit that their own data is not sufficient to draw the inference of a causality link.[54] Indeed Zaller and Chiu argue that it is not possible to understand from Bennett's study whether it is the reporters following official cues or the other way around. In fact, it could be entirely possible that it is the political actors who use media coverage as a proxy for public opinion.[55] The study will therefore also take into consideration the possibility that it is the *media coverage that shapes the political debate.* The study additionally examines suggestions coming from elsewhere in the field on the relationship between political actors and the news. Literature about the use of spin and media management by political actors would explain the correlation between media coverage and political debate through *news management* techniques by political actors.[56] Drawing on an interview with Congressman Dick Cheney in 1989, John Maltese explains that the need by political actors to "control" the news comes from the news media interest in conflict: "[N]ews is drama, and drama thrives on conflict."[57] The news media search for drama can lead to a negative portrayal of officials:

> As a result of the media's preoccupation with conflict, good-faith debate within the administration is sometimes depicted as serious dissension among the ranks. Furthermore, stories about real conflicts increase the tension between those at odds and make the president look like a poor manager. To maintain control of the public agenda, then, the White House must not only minimize exposure of internal conflict but also aggressively promote the messages that it wants conveyed to the American people. Bluntly put, the White House must attempt to manipulate media coverage of the administration.[58]

The promotion of official messages can be accomplished through a variety of techniques, including publicizing speeches, providing interviews and articles to the media, planting stories, releasing negative news at times when journalists are distracted by other stories ("throwing out the bodies").[59] The main objective of all these activities is making sure that officials within the administration speak with one voice. Such coordination can take the form of the repetition of a "line of the day."[60] The consistency of views by political actors within government does not necessarily have to be expressed with the very same words. The key is rather consistency and "staying on message."[61]

The repetition of the same message is particularly effective in getting the government's story in the news. As Mary Matalin writes:

> The absolute rule of message dissemination and message penetration is consistency and repetition. The principle is the same for political campaigns or companies: Everyone says the same thing, *over* and *over.* What the press used to know about us—in the White House, at the RNC [Republican National Committee], in primaries, and in general election—was that we were impenetrable. You would never get anybody

inside who would say something different than the party line. It got to the point where reporters were disgusted. They'd roll their eyes and say, "We're not going to talk to you anymore because you all say the same thing." I'd start a sentence and they'd say, "Okay, we already heard that." And they knew that if they went to three people or four of fifteen, they'd get the same drill. And they'd have to print it because they couldn't get anything else.[62]

Entman also underlines the cognitive impact the repetition of the same messages has on journalists: "The more often journalists hear similar thoughts expressed by their sources and by other news outlets, the more likely their own thoughts will run along those lines, with the result that the news they produce will feature words and visuals that confirm the same framing."[63] The organized delivery of the official messages through distinct roles with specific tasks is referred to by Barbara Pfetsch as a "division of labour."[64]

The sixth and last variable producing indexing of news coverage to political debate is the *ideological orientation of a media organization.* Studies in the United States reluctantly acknowledge that newspapers' coverage might have an ideological bias on the ground that journalism has to be objective. If bias exists at all, it is the reflection of the social background of reporters, who tend to be more "liberal" overall than the general public.[65] Alternatively, news bias leans toward conservatism on the ground that the media tend to reproduce the ideology of the system.[66] This view is contested by Benjamin Page, who, by analyzing the coverage of three case studies between 1991 and 1992 in a range of elite newspapers in the United States, finds evidence that coverage of the same issues varied significantly among different media and conformed to newspapers' long-term editorial positions, either liberal and prodemocratic (as in the case of the *New York Times*) or conservative and pro-Republican (as for the *Wall Street Journal*).[67] The finding is confirmed by Kim Kahn and Patrick Kenney, who, by examining newspaper coverage of 60 senatorial campaigns over three election years in the United States, similarly conclude that news coverage is slanted in favor of the candidate endorsed on newspapers' editorials.[68]

The view that newspapers are ideologically biased is almost taken for granted outside the United States. In continental Europe, newspapers are commonly identified by their political orientation.[69] Also studies from outside Europe confirm the relevance of ideological biases in shaping coverage. Deo Ngonyani, for example, by studying media coverage of student protests by national newspapers in Tanzania concludes that news organizations "construct reality in a manner consistent with their underlying ideologies."[70]

International Communications

The review of International Communications introduces three approaches to the study of news based on the Media Flows, Globalization, and Localization theories. These approaches respectively identify three possible variations of news at the international level: unidirectional flows of news from rich to poor countries, news homogenization at a worldwide level, cross-national differentiation of coverage. The Media Flows approach will be presented first, followed by Globalization and Localization.

There are two main challenges in relation to disassembling the International Communications theoretical approaches and understanding what they involve for the empirical study. The first consists in identifying hypotheses, independent variables, and causal mechanisms for each of the approaches within what cannot but be called a confused theoretical landscape. Globalization and localization perspectives, in fact, point to two diametrically opposite predictions about the way news should vary at the international level: either worldwide homogenization or diversification of coverage along national lines. Neither approach, however, unambiguously identifies which variables drive the processes of either globalization or localization, nor explains how these trends materialize in the news text. Further complications are added by the perspective of "domestication," in which globalization and localization of news coverage could well coexist. The second challenge is extracting independent variables and causal mechanisms that are workable in terms of the study's constructionist social ontology. For example, the Media Flows theoretical approach explains news flows among countries through structural macroeconomic imbalances. These processes will have to be translated, by relying on additional literature from the field, into structural constraints on groups of individuals rather than being taken as mostly agent-less processes.

The Media Flows Hypothesis

Although a considerable number of studies within the last 30 years have been drawing the same conclusions over and over again—that media flows exist—there is no agreement as to what the nature of the flows is and as to what actually drives them.

The concept of "media flow" appears to be the progressive empirical refinement of the earlier and more abstract notion of "cultural imperialism." Herbert Schiller, drawing on the neo-Marxist critical tradition, defined cultural imperialism as "the sum of the processes by which a society is brought into the modern world system and how its dominating stratum is attracted, pressured, forced, and sometimes bribed into shaping social institutions to correspond to, or even to promote, the values and structures of the dominant centre of the system."[71] Jeremy Tunstall described cultural imperialism as a situation in which "authentic, traditional local culture…is being battered out of existence by the indiscriminate dumping of large quantities of slick commercial and media products, mainly from the United States."[72]

Such statements were challenged for their lack of empirical basis: dependency literature, according to Robert Stevenson, was "notable for an absence of clear definitions of fundamental terms like imperialism and an almost total lack of empirical evidence to support the arguments."[73] This critique drove the development of the concept of "media imperialism," which Oliver Boyd-Barrett introduced as a "distinct analytical tool" from cultural imperialism.[74] The author defined it as "the process whereby the ownership, structure, distribution or content of the media in any one country are singly or together subject to substantial external pressures from the media interests of any other country or countries, without proportionate reciprocation of influence by the country so affected."[75] According to the author, the concept could lend itself to a more rigorous study as it referred to a "more precise range of phenomena" than the general cultural imperialism.[76] Boyd-Barrett tied media imperialism to the idea of "unidirectional" and unbalanced "flows." In his words: "While there is a heavy flow of exported media products from the US to, say, Asian countries, there is only a very slight trickle of Asian media products to the US."[77] According to him the most visible form of media imperialism was the export of media contents, particularly TV programs and news.[78]

This view was supported by a series of empirical studies confirming the existence of unbalanced, unidirectional flows of TV program materials and foreign news.[79] As Kaarle Nordenstreng and Tapio Varis put it:

> There is no need—in fact, no justification—for a question mark after the title of this publication ["Television Traffic—A One-Way Street?"]. Globally speaking, television traffic does flow between nations according to the "one-way street" principle: the streams of heavy traffic flow one way only.[80]

The concept of "Media Flows" has survived to this day virtually unquestioned. A study conducted by Varis at the beginning of the 1980s confirmed the results of a report published a decade earlier: "[T]he 1983 study confirms that no major changes in the international flow of television programmes and news have taken place since 1973."[81] A number of studies within the last decade not only support the idea of media flows, but often tend to take as a given their very existence.[82] Daya Thussu, for example, claims that the West dominates the world's media: "The general pattern of media ownership indicates that the West, led by the USA, dominates the international flow of information and entertainment in all major media sectors."[83] The author investigates the way global media are exploited by the United States to sell "neo-imperial conflicts" in the post–Cold War period. He finds that there is a "growing tendency among US-dominated global news networks [Sky News in Europe, Star News Asia from Hong Kong, Brazil's Globo News, CCTV in China, and Doordashan in India] generally to follow Washington's foreign policy agenda, couching imperial military actions in terms of 'humanitarian interventions' undertaken to promote freedom and democracy."[84]

Boyd-Barrett has argued more recently that the concept of media imperialism is still useful for understanding a wider "colonization of communications spaces," which transcends the unequal relations among nations to explore also intranational media relations, inequality among genders or ethnicities.[85] The very idea that there are "alternative" news agencies, such as the Chinese Xinhua, or alternative "voices," such as Al-Jazeera, to those of Western outlets implies an assumption: that the views aired in the Western media constitute the mainstream perspective on world events.[86]

Despite the existence of a vast body of empirical evidence supporting the idea of unbalanced flows of information, the nature of the flows is not clear. Nordenstreng and Varis take the flows to be constituted by the quantity of TV programs sold and bought, not necessarily just news.[87] Even by looking at studies specifically focusing on *news*, however, it is uncertain what should be taken as a proof of the flows' existence. Annabelle Sreberny-Mohammadi and others in their 1985 UNESCO study refer to "topics" and "themes" within TV news (part of the "news presentation").[88]

Considering the emphasis within the literature on the unidirectional nature of information exchanges, for the purpose of the study, news media flows will be defined as an unreciprocated exchange of news contents from one country to the other (Hypothesis 2).

What Drives News Flows?
The well-established idea that unbalanced information flows exist and that they are observable in empirical terms is not backed by as

much precision when it comes to defining which variables exactly drive them. An in-depth reading of the literature reveals that a number of variables play different roles depending on the very way flows are defined, examined, and on the nature of the issue in relation to which the flows are analyzed. These aspects will now be looked at in more detail.

Even if all studies talk about "flows," in reality each project adopts a slightly different definition, which leads to drawing different conclusions about what drives them. Douglas Van Belle, for example, analyzes U.S. news media coverage (TV and press) of foreign disasters and concludes that geographical proximity is the most significant factor shaping the news.[89] Kyungmo Kim and George Barnett, instead, operationalizing the news flow as the number of newspapers and periodicals traded among countries, find a range of significant variables: while economic development is the most important factor in shaping the flows, the authors argue that the languages spoken in a country, physical location, political freedom, and population also play a role.[90]

Different authors suggest an array of causes involving different types of imperialism, power, colonial domination. What seems to connect all of them is the reference to *economic imbalances*: news flows unidirectionally from rich to poor countries, so that, using Ostgaard's terms, the former are news "givers" and the latter news "takers."[91] The importance of economic imbalances—differences in economic resources among countries—emerges from several key studies within the field. Johan Galtung, for example, explains news flows through the concept of "structural imperialism," a structural imbalance that materializes as a dominance relationship between Center and Periphery. For Galtung the world consists of Center and Periphery nations, each of which, in turn, has center and periphery.[92] What the author focuses on is "the mechanism underlying this discrepancy, particularly between the centre in the Centre, and the periphery in the Periphery."[93] Imperialism, according to him, is a "dominance relation between collectivities, particularly between nations. It is a sophisticated type of dominance relation which cuts across nations, basing itself on a bridgehead which the centre in the Centre nation establishes in the centre of the Periphery nation, for the joint benefit of both."[94] Galtung distinguishes five types of imperialism: economic, political, military, communication, and cultural. A combination of the last two, communication and cultural imperialism, constitutes "news communication" imperialism.[95] This last kind, as the author points out, translates into an imbalance of news contents.

Nordenstreng and Varis, instead, explain the one-way street news flow through economic imbalances. They write, "[T]he overall picture is very clear: it is the major Western industrialized countries (U.S.A., U.K., France, FRG [Federal Republic of Germany]) that account for most of the programme flow between nations": "It may be concluded that the supply of foreign material is mostly provided to the world TV market by the rich and dominant countries, and that, accordingly, economic resources are the major explanation."[96] These considerations lead the authors to conclude that "the term 'communication imperialism'... should not be understood as a separate phenomenon but rather as a particular aspect of a single mechanism of imperialism basically determined by economical relations within and between nations."[97]

Although Boyd-Barrett writes that more research into the causes of media imperialism is necessary, he similarly suggests that the relationships of domination are rooted into the international political and economic developments of the late nineteenth and twentieth centuries.[98] In his opinion they are "the inevitable or highly probable outcomes of an imbalance of power resources."[99]

Sreberny-Mohammadi and others, in a seminal study comparing foreign news in 29 countries, concluded that "geographical proximity and former colonial orientations have thus been established as the two leading criteria" in shaping news.[100] Geographical proximity and former colonial orientation confirm, according to the authors, that Galtung's structural imperialism thesis is still valid:

> News geography is primarily a matter of news history, and ... the news capitals which are best covered in terms of the production and distribution of news stories thus systematically occupy central positions in the world news geography. This also reflects the continuing orientations of the peripheral nations toward the metropolitan centres in the post-colonial world, a prime determinant of news focus suggested by Galtung many years ago.[101]

The explanation of how economic imbalances translate into flows, formulated in terms of the study's social ontology, is the reliance by poor countries' journalists on Western news agencies because of a lack of equipment and resources.[102] The reliance on news agencies by developing countries is, in the literature, one of the common explanations for these countries' news "dependency" on the West.[103] This state of affairs, so the argument goes, leads to news that reflects the perspective of the richer countries. This was the reasoning behind the New World Information and Communications Order (NWICO) debate in the 1970s and 1980s: "Concern about news agencies within academe was always associated with the dominance-dependency model and the NWICO debates which it fed.... Unable to control their external image, developing nations had even less control over other people's representations of them."[104] Van Belle calls this the "logistic perspective" of explaining how technical and structural impediments might affect news coverage: "[C]ountries and locals with well-developed communications infrastructure are expected to gain more coverage than those that do not because it is easier to gather and transmit the news from them."[105]

While economic imbalances shape the direction of the news flows from richer countries toward poorer countries, their scope is affected by *cultural proximity* and *geographical proximity*. Galtung and Mari Ruge describe cultural proximity as the very factor that allows journalists to notice events in the first place. They compare the multitude of events happening in the world to the noise of a broadcasting station. In the same way in which an imaginary radio listener, in order to make sense of the continuous "cacophony" emitted by a radio set, needs to "scan" the noise to perceive meaningful sounds, a journalist selects events. The way such selection occurs is not random. As they write: "The more consonant the signal is with the mental image of what one expects to find, the more probable that it will be recorded as worth listening to."[106] In other words, they say that "what we choose to consider an 'event' is culturally determined."[107] Herbert Kariel and Lynn Rosenvall, in analyzing news flows on Canadian newspapers, also find that cultural affinity is a "striking factor in determining the source of news printed in a newspaper."[108] Canadian newspapers show "remarkable cultural affinities toward [the cultural homelands of] their readers": "The French language newspapers towards France and the English language ones towards the United Kingdom."[109]

Geographic proximity also affects the flows because journalists, as again Van Belle points out, acting as gatekeepers in the news selection process "might dismiss a story because it occurs in a location or affects people they believe the consumers of the news will not be interested in."[110]

The two variables are distinct because even countries that are geographically close, such as India and Pakistan, could be culturally very different.

The Globalization Hypothesis

Globalization and news appear to be tightly related. Anthony Giddens, for example, writes that the "sense of living in 'one world'" is the result of the "transformation of technologies of communication."[111] They contribute to "a fundamental aspect of globalization,...which might be referred to as cultural globalization."[112] He continues, "[T]he global extension of the institutions of modernity [capitalist economy, nation-state system, world military order, industrial development] would be impossible were it not for the pooling of knowledge which is represented by the 'news.'"[113]

Although the term "globalization" is widespread in the literature, its meaning is often left to a tacit understanding between writers and readers rather than explicitly defined. In fact, by looking more in detail at definitions, it is difficult to distinguish "globalization" from a general notion of "Americanization" and from "media flows."

The development of a global media network is often uncritically assumed to be a synonym with worldwide homogenization of media contents.[114] As Lisbeth Clausen writes, "[M]odernization and cultural globalization theories almost ritually refer to the 'globalization of media' as an evident factor in the globalization process."[115] The general "conflation" of the communications *infrastructure* with the idea of a homogenization of the contents within the communication *process* is precisely the target of a critique by John Tomlinson, who points out that "though communications technologies are absolutely central to the globalization process, their development is clearly not identical with cultural globalization."[116] The author refers, in his analysis, to the idea of a *cultural* globalization. In the literature, however, it is not always possible to understand what the object of the globalization process is. As Boyd-Barrett puts it, globalization is "a process simultaneously economic, political and cultural: it has to do with the belief system, which has been commodified within a political-economic dynamic."[117] Even when talking about the globalization of news—and in the example just made the author is actually referring to that—the focus of the globalization process is often sidetracked by value judgments about the process. Tomlinson spells out two main shortcomings of the literature about globalization: the first is the tendency to regard the distribution of cultural goods around the world, mainly by the United States, as self-evident; the second is the making of "unwarranted leaps of inference from the simple presence of cultural goods to the attribution of deeper cultural or ideological effects."[118] The result is that rigorous empirical investigations of the evidence supporting the very idea of globalization are largely absent from the literature. The most empirically based studies almost invariably involve news agencies on English language news, which raises doubts about their ability to capture the complexity of news exchanges beyond the mainstream media.[119]

The fact that the empirical meaning of globalization has not been subject to careful investigation is remarked by Marjorie Ferguson. The author, by highlighting the problems related to the very meaning of globalization, the evidence of its existence, and its evaluation, concludes that the notion is largely a "myth."[120] Terhi Rantanen also spots a theoretical gap in the lack of explanations about the way in which media should produce globalization. Despite the ubiquity of the terms "media" and "globalization," the author says, it is not yet clear what their relationship is:

> Two words, "media" and "globalization," seem to be repeated over and over again. The two go together like a horse and carriage to use a pre-globalization metaphor although their mutual connection has not always been visible. The early globalization theorist Marshall McLuhan made this connection by combining "the medium is the message" with his "global village"...and since then the link between globalization and media has been acknowledged by many, but studied by few. When globalization and media are connected, we also need to know *how* they are connected.[121]

In the literature, globalization is often assumed to be the outcome of cultural imperialism. Boyd-Barrett, for example, writes that "globalization is Westernization."[122] Globalization is also equated with Americanization by Thussu.[123] For the purpose of selecting a third hypothesis to be tested in the study, however, international homogenization of news is not taken to coincide necessarily with an Americanization of news. News coverage is rather expected to present homogeneous features on an international scale (Hypothesis 3).

What Explains the Globalization of News?

Indeed, it is not clear what leads to the supposed globalization of news. The globalization phenomenon is related to technological advances of modernity by Giddens, to the development of communications by Marshall McLuhan and Quentin Fiore, and to the growth of "information 'superhighways'" by Boyd-Barrett.[124]

Robert McChesney argues that what causes globalization is media convergence. The author writes that digital and satellite technologies make global markets both cost effective and profitable, thus encouraging the rise of a global media market.[125] These explanations are not acceptable by the social ontology of this study since they do not acknowledge the role of individual agents: technological advances and a global media market seem to materialize outside the realm of human responsibility.

A perspective that is more suitable to the study's structurationist ontology is offered by research that identifies journalists' *reliance on the same news sources*, particularly news agencies, and reporters' adoption of the same *global journalistic standards* as the major factors explaining the worldwide homogenization of news. In this perspective advances of communication technology and media convergence are still present, but are explained through human agency. Chris Paterson, Boyd-Barrett and Rantanen, and Clausen argue, in fact, that it is more specifically news agencies that are responsible for the globalization of news.[126] Paterson particularly draws attention to the way increasingly concentrated ownership of news services as well as broadcasters' dependency on news providers leads to the use of the same sources to shape "our global reality."[127] News agencies, as he explains, in the attempt to satisfy the needs of their customers, "create the appearance of objectivity and neutrality. In so doing they manufacture an ideologically distinctive and homogeneous view of the world."[128] This is reflected by the use of "standard frames or themes of news coverage."[129] In the author's view the technological variable responsible for globalization is accompanied by the development of professional standards at the international level, media ownership, as well as political ideology. Michael Gurevitch, Mark Levy, and Itzhak Roeh also identify a "shared professional culture" to explain the commonality of contents among the TV programs they analyze.[130] Professional culture contributes to creating homogeneity by providing common news values. This implicitly translates into a globalization of the same model of journalism. This point is also made by Stephen Reese, who writes that the "synchronization and spatial reach of world communication" enables the rise of a deterritorialized "discursive space."[131] He compares the coordination that increasingly takes place across national boundaries among broadcast organizations to a "global newsroom."[132] It is the interaction among professionals within it that leads to developing "consensual professional values and outlook as to what the news should look like."[133]

The Localization Hypothesis

If globalization is not a well-defined concept, localization is even less so. The "local" dimension to which the localization perspective refers, in fact, can exist at different levels: from the individual level, in which, for example, each person interprets a media message, to the national or the regional. Cultural and ethnographic studies approach the globalization phenomenon from the point of view of the reception and reading of global texts, emphasizing their differentiation at the local level.[134] Marwan Kraidy calls this "multidisciplinary concern over the fragmentation and fusion of cultural forms" "hybridity."[135] As the author puts it, hybridity "emerged in the post-cultural imperialism malaise of the 1990s" precisely to counter the dominance and homogenization perspectives.[136] Since globalization is often tacitly assumed to be a kind of political or cultural imperialism, localization is seen as a form of "resistance."[137]

When localization is not seen as an alternative to globalization, it exists in parallel to it. This view is embodied by the perspective of "domestication." Clausen's comparative study of news contents and news production processes in Denmark and Japan, for example, concludes that homogenization and particularization of news are not mutually excluding phenomena. Communication technology and news agency access contribute to the worldwide diffusion of information about events. The result is that news in different parts of the world covers the same issues. The same information, however, is framed differently at the national level by news producers who try to make it understandable to local audiences. In other words, international news is "domesticated" by news producers, leading, in terms of contents, to distinctive national perspectives.[138]

Clausen's study largely confirms previous findings by Gurevitch, Levy, and Roeh. Grounding their observations on a content analysis of TV news stories aired by 18 different news services over a two-week period in 1987, they conclude that

> the convergence of different news services on the "same" set of stories should not necessarily be viewed as leading to a "homogenization" of news around the world. Indeed, if the "same" events are told in divergent ways, geared to the social and political frameworks and sensibilities of diverse domestic audiences, the "threat" of homogenization might have little basis.[139]

For the purpose of the study, the localization perspective is turned into the prediction that news will present a diversification of contents along national lines (Hypothesis 4). In other words, not only will news in the United States be different from, for example, news in France—as it is not at all surprising to expect—but news from different organizations within the same country will present a common national perspective. News by media organizations within the same country will, as a result, present greater similarities compared with news produced by organizations from foreign countries.

What Leads to News Localization?

The independent variables leading to a national differentiation of news within the literature are the role of *producers who domesticate news* to the taste and interest of national audiences and the role of the *national journalistic culture.* In relation to the former, Clausen explains that, in the "domestication" process, the meaning of international news is constructed by news producers, who act as mediators between the global and the local at the national level:

> News producers at the national broadcast stations, who work in the space between the global and the national, have included a reflexive hunch in their strategy for the selection and production of international stories. The Janus-faced ability of both knowing international affairs and knowing the receiving audience was found to be essential in the framing of international news information and an important element in the process of presenting events to a national audience.[140]

Kalyani Chadha and Anandan Kavoori also make the point that, despite globalization, a diversification of contents tends to occur at a national level:

> While it is true that the media play a self-evident technological role as one of the drivers of globalization (and indeed one might argue that there could be no globalization without them), they simultaneously engage with and are transformed by its dynamics. In other words, there exists a dialectical interplay between these two elements that is negotiated and articulated at the level of the nation-state, resulting in far-reaching structural and institutional changes within national media landscapes. These changes include a pattern of commercialization of broadcasting frequently at the initiative of the state, the emergence of nationally based multi-media conglomerates as well as the national domestication of formats.[141]

The domestication of formats, in the authors' view, consists in both the linguistic and presentation style adaptation of media products in order to meet national cultural tastes and preferences.[142]

As far as the second variable is concerned, localization of news is associated by Gurevitch, Levy, and Roeh to national diversities. The authors explain that, while the shared professional culture of journalism leads to commonality of media reporting across countries, contents are not entirely the same: "[N]ational social and political differences, as well as differences in journalistic norms between nations" also play a part in shaping patterns of news coverage.[143]

These considerations suggest a role for national journalistic culture. Objective journalistic culture is posited by the indexing hypothesis as one of the variables leading to a reproduction of political messages in the news. Here, the national journalistic culture expected to lead to a diversification of news along national lines could be either objective or interpretative.

News Sociology

News Sociology engages directly with the questions of what is news and what are the factors shaping it. The general answer provided by the field is that news is a social product shaped by the interactions between media professionals, media organizations, and society.[144] As Walter Gieber put it over 40 years ago: "[N]ews is what newspapermen make it."[145] This, however, in research terms, is translated into multiple focuses within the field, depending on which level of analysis is being addressed. In Berkowitz's words: "The study of news is much like viewing a hologram. A person can get closer or farther away. A person can stand in different places. Each new perspective will reveal a different aspect of the same holographic picture."[146] The main levels of analysis are the individual, the organizational, and the societal.

The way individual preferences and attitudes affect media contents is mainly covered by studies interpreting the role of the media professional as a "gatekeeper."[147] According to Pamela Shoemaker, "[S]imply put, gatekeeping is the process by which the billions of messages that are available in the world get cut down and transformed into the hundreds of messages that reach a given person every day."[148]

Moving up to a broader perspective from the individual level is the study of the social environment in which journalists operate. This level of analysis downplays individual judgment, while focusing on the way individuals are constrained by the policies and imperatives of the news organization. The analysis concentrates, as Berkowitz writes, "not on journalists' decisions but rather on the social forces that shape and constrain those decisions."[149] The organizational level highlights the bureaucratic character of news production, the conventions by which work is accomplished and the management of organizational conflict.[150] It is within the media organization that professionalism and journalistic ethics develop. Gaye Tuchman points out that the very definition of journalistic "objectivity" is shaped within interorganizational relationships.[151] Besides the individual norm of objectivity and news values, it is routines within the media organization that help journalists manage the unexpected and meet organizational expectations and deadlines.[152] It is again at this level that the relationship between journalists' ethical norms and organizational policies are investigated. In this perspective, several studies focus on the way journalists are socialized into news organizations.[153] Charles Bantz, placing emphasis on the way "patterns of meanings" and relative "expectations that define appropriate action" are created, goes as far as claiming that media organizations are "cultures" in their own right.[154] The formalization of such shared meanings is embodied by organizations' policies.

At a societal level, there are yet more influences at work: political/ideological, economic, and cultural. Society's political and economic influences are approached, for example, by Hallin and Paolo Mancini.[155] The authors, comparing presidential TV coverage in Italy and the United States, explain how differences in media coverage stem from the political culture of the countries rather than from the characteristics of the television medium.[156] This influence is mediated by economic structures. Edward Herman and Noam Chomsky, in their propaganda model, also focus on the way the media reflect the interests and ideologies that dominate private and state activities.[157] Herbert Altschull more specifically explores the way financial arrangements and ownership affect news organizations. The author argues that "the news media inevitably reflects the interests of those who pay the bills."[158] In other words, "key to understanding the economic influence on news is the idea that an organization must keep its content within the bounds of acceptability to its financiers."[159]

Within this level of analysis are also what Michael Schudson calls "culturological" approaches to the study of news.[160] They are useful in understanding the differences between journalistic practices in different countries.[161] Renate Köcher, for example, explains how political, legal, and historical contexts affect the perception by journalists of their role in different countries. Journalists in the United Kingdom are defined as "bloodhounds" hunting for news, while their German counterparts are labeled "missionaries" supporting the editorial line through their commentary.[162]

The Hierarchy-of-Influences Approach

The Hierarchy-of-Influences approach integrates the different levels of influence on news in one single perspective, whose essential claim is that even factors outside the newsroom affect the individual decisions by media professionals, and consequently, the coverage they produce.[163] News, because of the unique combinations of these influences, is therefore expected to be different in each media organization (Hypothesis 5).

More specifically, according to Reese, news is the product of five successive levels of influence with each level subsuming the one(s) prior: (1) individual preferences, training, and background of media professionals affect their news values, how they write and select stories. Individual preferences are constrained, however, by (2) routines: individuals "do not have complete freedom to act on their beliefs and attitudes, but must operate within a multitude of limits imposed by technology, time, space, and norms." But even routines are shaped by (3) organizational aspects such as policies of the news organization and the way power is exercised within it. The news organization is, then, part of society at large and is subject to (4) extra-media influences: institutions such as the government or advertisers, other media organizations. All these factors contribute to supporting the status quo, serving to making the media an instrument of social control. The last level of influence is therefore the (5) ideological.[164]

The Hierarchy-of-Influences model suggests, in practice, that anything in the society outside the media organization can affect the way news is produced. The objective of the study is testing the validity of variables affecting news at the international, national, and media-organizational levels. Variables identified within Indexing, Media Flows, Globalization, and Localization approaches already deal with levels above the media organization: they range, for instance, from the media management efforts by political actors, to national political culture, and national journalistic culture. Here, I will therefore concentrate on the way individual media professionals—not only journalists, but also editors—shape the news. This completes the spectrum of variables shaping the news at different levels the study aims to investigate.

What Shapes News in each News Organization?

The variables that differentiate news outputs from within media organizations are individual bias and editorial policy. *Individual bias* in the news is explained by Shoemaker as the product of multiple influences on each media professional. In her "new gatekeeping model" she links the individual level at which the gatekeeping activity occurs to the broader social context.[165] More precisely, she argues, gatekeeping occurs at three progressive levels. First, gatekeeping between organizations is embedded in the ideology and culture of the social system: influences at this level come from sources, advertisers, markets, interest groups, the government, and other social institutions. Second, gatekeeping within an organization is embedded in the communication and organizational routines, particularly group dynamics, referred to by the author as "groupthink phenomenon."[166] What particularly matters here is, however, a third aspect: intraindividual gatekeeping processes. They involve life experiences such as decision-making strategies, type of job, cognitive heuristics, role conceptions, values, attitudes, and ethics.[167] This last layer explains individual bias by both reporters (in news stories) and editors (in editorials).

Editorial policy can take different forms, from loosely setting the media agenda to tightly controlling the content of news. Philip Schlesinger defines editorial policy as the range of norms that make possible for the organization to construct news "in identifiable ways, in terms not only of the selection of stories, but also their angling and modes of representation."[168] This, in turn, can be more or less direct and explicit. As the author puts it in analyzing the way news is produced by the BBC:

> The command structure does not usually perform its work of editorial control through obvious routine intervention at the production level. Rather, in general, it works according to a system of retrospective review, as a result of which guidance is referred downwards and becomes part of the taken for granted assumptions of those working in the newsrooms. The general unobtrusiveness of this system, through which orientations first defined at the top of the hierarchy become quite unquestioningly adopted by those at the bottom, permits an orthodox ideology of editorial control to flourish.[169]

As Donohue, Olien, and Tichenor observe, however, "editors are often seen as having a 'buckstopping' role in the gatekeeping process. In the midst of a flow of information from a variety of sources and directions and in multiple forms, the editor must make the final decision about where, when, and how messages will be published."[170] John Soloski, describing his participant-observation of a medium-sized daily, confirms the point by describing the way the editors personally manipulate first-page coverage:

> The final control over the content of the newspaper lies in overseeing the production of the paper. The editor makes it a point to check all pages before they are removed from the production area, but he pays particularly close attention to the front page and the late page [the last news page to be produced, including late-breaking stories]. In fact, neither the front page nor the late page can be taken from the production area without the editor's permission, and even though it is difficult to change stories or headlines once copy is set and pasted on the pages, it was not uncommon for the editor to order some last-minute changes.[171]

The reasons for such control are related to both power dynamics within the news media organization, between the media organization and its owner, as well as to considerations related to the expected interest of the readers. Although the notion that news might be affected by editors, as Page writes, "[it] seems to strike a very sensitive nerve among journalists and communication scholars," the correspondence between news slant and editorial slant is not implausible.[172] As Page explains, "[O]wner and publisher influence is not at all inconsistent with journalists' subjective feelings of autonomy, because the values and beliefs of journalists (and editors who hire and supervise them) may already be largely in harmony with the values and beliefs of the owners—precisely because owners have the ultimate power to hire and fire."[173]

Editors' role of mediators of economic influences from the broader societal context is confirmed by Donohue, Olien, and Tichenor. They argue that "because of their [editors'] multiple roles as entrepreneurs and information gatekeepers, their concern with advertising income and profits is to be expected as part of their role definition."[174] It is true that the authors' study is based on the observation of editors working for daily and weekly Minnesota community newspapers. They are small circulation newspapers (about 60,000 daily copies). The authors do state that business aspects are dealt in bigger dailies by specialists outside the news-editorial department. Advertising and profit value, however, exist, as they put it, as a "corporate reality."[175] In other terms, editors, even if not directly involved with commercial issues, are aware of them, do have an audience in mind, and shape the newspaper content with the expectation that the product will meet the audience's approval.

MEETING THE METHODOLOGICAL CHALLENGES

This section explains the methodological choices for testing the validity of the competing explanations of news that have been outlined in the context of the empirical investigation.

The events of 9/11 and the war in Afghanistan were chosen as a case study for having been the focus of massive media coverage worldwide. They allow exploring both the global dynamics of news reporting as well as local coverage features.

The hypotheses were tested on the content of national elite newspapers. As Rodney Benson and Hallin argue, elite newspapers are not representative of the entire media discourse of a country, but they "occupy similar positions in prestige and influence in each society, making them suitable for a controlled comparative analysis."[176] The international comparative research design involved a range of international embedded cases:[177] the United States, Italy, France, and Pakistan. The time span for the study is September 11, 2001, to November 14, 2001. The period covers the 9/11 events, the first reactions to the terrorist attacks, the events leading to the intervention in Afghanistan (starting October 7), as well as the military operation Enduring Freedom until the conclusion of its first phase culminating in the fall of Kabul (November 13). The scope, 64 days, allows capturing both the immediate, spontaneous reactions to the events, as well as more reasoned interpretations of the situation, within political and news discourses alike.

The elite newspaper news sample included daily first-page and editorial articles from two elite newspapers per country, respectively, of a liberal and more conservative orientation: the *New York Times* and the *Wall Street Journal* in the United States, *Libération* and *Le Monde* in France, *La Repubblica* and *Il Corriere della Sera* in Italy, the *Dawn* and the *Nation* in Pakistan.

The choice of the embedded cases and the newspapers' selection meets the need to test, within the hypotheses, the relevance of different possible variables. In relation to Hypothesis 1 (correlation between political debate and news coverage or "indexing"), the embedded cases span from a country directly affected by the events, the United States, to European countries with no direct involvement (France and Italy), to a case very close to the theater of the military operations in Afghanistan (Pakistan). France and Italy at the time of the events had governments of a different political orientation: France had a center-left PM, while Italy was led by a center-right government. This could lead to different levels of closeness between media organizations and governmental actors, possibly affecting the extent to which news in different newspapers is "indexed" to authorities' debate. Overall, the four countries provide different political cultures in terms of institutional practices: the United States and France are presidential systems, Italy is a parliamentary republic, Pakistan, run by General Musharraf who came to power in October 1999 following a military takeover, does not fit the Western definition of a democracy.[178] The inclusion of a nondemocratic country allows controlling for possible differences in the relationship between political actors and journalists.

Hypothesis 2 (media flows), particularly the role of economic imbalances in news flows, can be tested across countries with different GDPs. According to data from the International Monetary Fund World Outlook, the United States is the richest country in the world, followed among the countries studied by France, then Italy, and finally Pakistan.[179] The expectation in cross-comparing the news among these countries is that news will be flowing out of the United States toward all other countries; that France, while at the receiving end of the flow from the United States, will export news toward Italy and Pakistan; that Italy will receive news flows from both the United States and France and export to Pakistan. Pakistan should be at the receiving end of all flows. News from poorer countries will present more similarity to the news from richer countries than the other way around. The choice of the embedded cases also allows controlling for variations in other factors that are expected to shape news flows: cultural and geographical proximity. The United States, Italy, and France could all be regarded as belonging to the same Western culture, while Pakistan—Asian and Muslim—represents a clearly distinguishable alternative. Within the same Western bloc, however, Italy and France are closer together in both geographical and cultural terms, which should further enhance the similarity of their news in comparison with both Pakistan and the United States.[180]

The four countries, distributed across America, the EU, and the non-Western world, enable testing Hypothesis 3, the possibility that news is becoming homogeneous on a worldwide scale (Globalization). This should appear in the form of news similarities across all eight newspapers within the four embedded cases.

The choice of two newspapers per country allows testing the Localization hypothesis (Hypothesis 4): the fact that newspapers from the same country present more similarities than with newspapers from a foreign country would constitute evidence that localization is truly occurring.

Hypothesis 5, according to which news is mainly shaped at the level of the single media organization, would be supported by little similarity of news contents among newspapers, even within the same country. The further distinction between first-page news and editorials allows assessing the impact of editorial policy. More specifically, a close correspondence between first-page news and the editorial line on the issue of 9/11 could suggest a control on first-page content by the newspaper's editor. This is not necessarily exercised personally by the editor, but could also be implemented through organizational routines and hierarchical arrangements within the news organization.

To assess the closeness of fit between political debate and the views expressed in the news coverage the study also content analyzed political statements (interviews, speeches, press conferences) by governmental actors (presidents, heads of state, prime ministers, foreign and defense ministers) in all countries under analysis for the same time span as for the news analysis.

* * *

The study faced the methodological challenge of approaching news stories in a way that made their contents comparable across the embedded cases. The way the study tackled the problem was by approaching contents in terms of a *framing* process.[181] The study used as a reference Entman's basic definition of frames. A frame, according to Entman, fundamentally involves selection and salience:

> To frame is to *select some aspects of a perceived reality and make them more salient in a communicating text, in such a way as to promote a particular problem definition, causal interpretation, moral evaluation, and/or treatment recommendation* for the item described.[182]

As an example of frame, the author mentions the Cold War: "The cold war frame highlighted certain foreign events—say civil wars—as problems, identified their source (communist rebels), offered moral judgments (atheistic aggression), and commended particular solutions (U.S. support for the other side)."[183]

Taking Entman's problem definition, causal interpretation, moral evaluation, and treatment recommendation as a basic structure for approaching the way an issue is framed, the 9/11 events could be seen as terrorist act (problem definition) by evil people (moral evaluation) motivated by hate for freedom and for America's way of life (causal interpretation). To bring to justice the perpetrators, the world should declare a war on terrorism (treatment recommendation). This, however, is the framing by a specific actor, in this case President Bush, at a specific time, the evening of September 11, 2001.[184] At a later stage, on September 19, at a meeting with the Indonesian president Megawati, the same 9/11 events are framed slightly differently. The events are a "crime" (problem definition) committed by "evildoers" (moral evaluation), motivated again by hate for freedom (causal interpretation), against whom a coalition of freedom-loving countries should fight a global war on terrorism that involves not only eradicating terrorist organizations and punishing those who support them, but also freezing terrorists' funds (treatment recommendation).[185] On September 11, 2001, Secretary of State Powell framed the events as a "tragedy" that has befallen "all nations of the world" (problem definition). The events were the result of terrorists' attempt to achieve "political purposes" (causal interpretation). People who "believe in democracy" should bring them to justice (treatment recommendation).[186] As seen, the contents of a frame, depending on the level of detail at which they are analyzed and on the time span under study, can change.

To capture small content changes over time within the framing process, the analysis focused on smaller units of analysis than a whole frame: *idea elements* (*IEs*).[187] They belong, depending on their relationship to the issue being framed, to different sections of the frame (Problem Definition, Causal Interpretation, Moral Evaluation, and Treatment Recommendation). IEs are simple ideas within the news text. For example, in relation to defining the 9/11 events, "war," "attacks," "tragedy," "event." In relation to the causal interpretation, terrorists are motivated by "hatred for human life," "hatred for America," "religious fanaticism," "ideology." The idea of "war," depending on the context in which it is used, can be coded also as a treatment recommendation. President Bush says, for example, that we should wage a "war against terrorism."[188]

IEs are used for both quantitative and qualitative analysis within the study. They are processed quantitatively to establish to what extent coverage in two different newspapers, for example, present similarities, but they are also looked at as the means through which social actors, in this case sources "speaking" within the news text, construct meaning (i.e., frame the 9/11 issue). In the following chapters I will refer to the framing of 9/11 and the war in Afghanistan within the news stories by providing examples of IEs. In this way the content analysis within this study differentiates itself from more traditional empirical quantitative analyses of news texts.[189]

The recording of IEs, rather than the frame as a complex whole, is useful considering the possibility that different aspects of the frame are addressed at different points in time. It may be that new IEs appear in the news coverage besides already existing ones leading to their gradual replacement: with reference to the case study, the specific idea about an intervention in Afghanistan replaces the general notion of pursuing and punishing those responsible for the attacks. New IEs can be introduced to complement already existing ones: for example, besides the idea that the war on terrorism consists in intervening against Osama bin Laden, the view that it is also about acting against all forms of terrorism. It can also be that new IEs are going to replace old ones from a specific point in time: the sudden change in U.S. governmental discourse from "we are not into nation building" to "we are supporting the achievement of a political solution in Afghanistan" toward the end of October 2001. IEs essentially constitute the "building blocks" through which social actors construct (frame) issues over time.

The decision to record IEs reflects the inductive approach to framing analysis described by Holli Semetko and Patti Valkenburg: the study records the IEs directly from the news stories, without assuming the existence of any specific frame *a priori*.[190]

The content analysis also recorded *sources*: they are all actors (politicians, commentators, international organizations' spokespersons, media organizations, such as news agencies...) who, within news stories, contribute to framing the issues under analysis—9/11 and the war in Afghanistan—with at least one IE. They do so through either a statement ("President Bush said: '[quote]'") or an attribution ("BBC reported that..."). It is important to note that sources are here understood as newsworthy actors making a statement *in the news text*, not as sources of information approached by journalists in the newsgathering process.

Testing the hypotheses consisted in making multiple comparisons of the IEs within the news coverage of either 9/11 or the war in Afghanistan across or within the embedded cases to verify to what extent the similarity or difference of news contents met the predictions made by the initial hypotheses. Testing the Indexing hypothesis, for example, involved a comparison of the IEs detected within news coverage in each country with the IEs recorded within the governmental statements of the same country. Testing the Globalization hypothesis meant comparing news coverage among all newspapers to assess the extent to which they presented common IEs.[191]

The research design of this study, however, exceeds content analysis. Content analysis of the way issues are framed is instrumental to testing processes that cannot be directly observed, such as political influence or international power relationships. As Klaus Krippendorf puts it: "What content analysts compare—the hypotheses they test—...do not concern differences among textual properties, but differences among the inferences drawn from texts, which are a function of the assumed context, not directly observed."[192] It therefore becomes important, for the validity of the study's results, to check through other means that the causal relationships contained in the approaches to news to be tested actually exist: "The point of requiring that content analysis be 'validatable in principle' is to prevent analysts from pursuing research questions that allow no empirical validation or that yield results with no backing except by the authority of the researcher."[193] In other words, just to make an example, the fact that media coverage reflects political statements cannot be considered evidence that political actors have an influence on the news. Media coverage and political statements could be correlated because of a third factor having an influence on both.

Alexander George and Andrew Bennett recommend researchers to "guard against the unjustified, questionable imputation of a causal relationship on the basis of mere consistency, just as safeguards have been developed in statistical analysis to deal with the possibility of spurious correlation."[194] They suggest addressing this problem through process tracing. Process tracing attempts uncovering causal links between the independent variables and the dependent variables, as well as evidence of the causal mechanisms posited by a theory.[195] It can be conducted in different ways: "[T]he simplest variety of process-tracing takes the form of a detailed narrative or story presented in the form of a chronicle that purports to throw light on how an event came about."[196] Process tracing, however, is not a merely chronological account of events. As Jeffrey Checkel points out, its aim is to trace the process in a "theoretically informed way": "between the beginning (independent variable[s]) and end (outcome of dependent variable), the researcher looks for a series of *theoretically predicted* intermediate steps."[197] For the "theoretical guesses," to use the same term as Bennett and George, the analysis will refer to the hypotheses identified in this chapter, their independent variables, and causal mechanisms.[198] It will, however, also have an exploratory role in trying to identify the way variables are connected to each other and how they lead to the news patterns identified in the empirical analysis.

CHAPTER 3

Political Discourse after 9/11

This chapter presents the results of the process-tracing analysis of political statements in the aftermath of 9/11. It compares the different ways in which governmental actors, presidents, prime ministers, defense and foreign ministers framed both the events of September 11 and the war in Afghanistan in the United States, Italy, France, and Pakistan between September 11 and November 14 (the fall of Kabul) 2001.

The framing of 9/11 and the military intervention in Afghanistan by governmental actors was very consistent and coherent in the United States and, to a less sophisticated extent, in Pakistan. Political actors in both countries carefully planned the delivery of messages related to the two issues in order to communicate their specific framing of the events to the media and the public. The analysis finds evidence, especially in the United States, of media management techniques: repetition of "messages of the day" and coordination across governmental departments. As the analysis will reveal, however, even if political actors have the power and resources to "manage" the issues, they are not entirely free in choosing how to frame them. Sense of identity of each country and existing policy agendas did shape—and heavily—the way political actors constructed their statements in all cases under study. Political statements were also shaped by broader international constraints, such as interactions with foreign politicians (international relations) and their position taking within the international system. In this respect the analysis contributes to illustrating the way national identity, policy agendas, international relations, and positioning within the international system—here all together referred to as "political culture"—provide the ground for the articulation of a country's foreign policy in the short term, particularly in response to changing events. The conclusions at the end of the chapter will recap all variables that were found to affect the political discourses in the four case studies. Among them the media were found to exercise some form of pressure on politicians, particularly in the Pakistani case, but not to the point of causing a shift in political priorities.

THE UNITED STATES: 9/11 AND THE WAR ON TERRORISM

The analysis of the American political discourse involved all public statements made by President Bush, Secretary of State Powell, and Secretary of Defense Rumsfeld in the aftermath of the 9/11 events.[1] It suggests a strong effort by the administration at managing the information provided to the public by means of cross-departmental coordination of messages. The sophistication of the authorities' messages in relation to 9/11 and its aftermath particularly emerges in the officials' extreme and consistent organization around a central notion: the idea of a war on terrorism (WOT).

After having briefly explored the contents of the WOT, I will turn to the more specific description of the forms taken by the U.S. authorities' "division of labor" and use of "lines of the day." The analysis, despite the administration's effort in delivering a highly complex interpretation of the events, also finds that the political messages are not created by individual governmental actors. Their statements contain references to already existing notions of national identity, which suggests a role for the political culture variable in shaping political discourse. The analysis also identifies another aspect of this variable shaping the political statements: interaction with foreign political actors (international relations).

The War on Terrorism: Delivering a Sophisticated Message

A key document in framing the 9/11 events as a WOT is a three-minute speech delivered by President Bush on September 12, 2001.[2] The statement clearly spells out all the central aspects of the WOT, which appear unchanged throughout the time span under analysis.

The events—a "tragedy"—are the result of "deliberate" attacks against "freedom and democracy." The events are more than "acts of terror"; they are "acts of war." With such actions the enemy has attacked "not just our [American] people, but all freedom-loving people everywhere in the world." In following speeches and interviews it will be said that the attacks were indeed an act of "war on civilization."[3]

The attacks have been carried out by a "different enemy" who wants to change "our way of life," "restricting our freedoms," who has "no regard for human life." No alternative interpretations are given on the reasons of the attacks. The mention of a "political purpose" behind the attacks by Powell on September 11 is an isolated remark.[4] The rational explanatory dimension of the conflict (causal interpretation) appears to be replaced by moral judgments (moral evaluation).

The moral dimension has a special significance in the WOT, which is defined as a "monumental struggle of good versus evil." Even if no explicit statement is made at this stage, there is a strong assumption that the United States and the "freedom-loving" nations of the world are on the good side and that—this is described with the tones of certainty—good will prevail: "We will win."

Formulating a recommendation on how to deal with the 9/11 crisis involves a prescription of what the United States is required to do at both the international and domestic levels. In the international context the United States is expected to face the enemy and "conquer it" by fighting a "battle," a "war" that will take "time and resolve." On September 12 this is not yet called a "war on terrorism." The expression will be used later (September 16), together with more details about a "different kind of enemy."[5] On September 12 the State Department adds that the effort against terrorism is going to take the form of a multifaceted attack along many dimensions— diplomatic, military, intelligence, law enforcement—[6]and that it will be a concerted, long-term commitment.[7] Although no perpetrator of the attacks has been identified at this stage, Secretary of State Powell says that the war will be waged not just against an organization, but a network of organizations.[8] This will be later identified as Al-Qaida.

These core ideas effectively set the directions along which the framing of the 9/11 issue will be further constructed through the addition of new idea elements (IEs). The core ideas provide the central thread for the development of what could be regarded as a proper narrative, which includes a whole vision of the world. Within this view, not only the world has radically changed, but also both "terrorism" and "war" have very specific meanings. I am going to describe these aspects in more detail.

A recurrent claim is that September 11 has "changed everything." This is explained as a change in the way governments look at international relations: there is a "new benchmark," a "new way of measuring the relationship [among states] and what we can do together in the future."[9] But 9/11 is also described as having a profound effect on society: "[T]he events of the 11ᵗʰ of September have fundamentally changed the way in which people look at terrorism and acts of terrorism."[10] As Powell puts it:

> Our lives have changed. For one thing, we're a little more conscious of security; we're concerned about how to go about protecting all of our facilities and our citizens. I think our lives changed in the sense that we got a better understanding of what's important, and we came together as a nation, we came together as a people, and some of the trivial issues that sometimes divided us were swept away with the magnitude of this tragedy.[11]

Terrorism, within this view, is a global threat, a "scourge," a "crime against all civilization and humanity." It knows "no ethnic, religious, national or geographic borders."[12] It is not motivated by ideology or rational thought; it is the expression of "flat evil."[13] Such an interpretation is peculiar to the U.S. political discourse, and as it will be seen later in the chapter, is not shared by its European and Asian counterparts.

The WOT is a "different kind of war" for three main reasons. First, it is waged against a different entity than a state: as presidential spokesperson Fleischer puts it, it is of a different type than "when you knew the capital of the country that attacked you."[14] Second, it involves a range of aspects going beyond the military and reaching into diplomacy, intelligence, financial regulation, law. Third, its visibility can vary: of the different measures used against terrorism, some will be "seen," such as the military strikes, whereas others will not. The shadowy areas are represented by intelligence and by measures, such as the fight against the financing of terrorism, that are not either obviously visible or suitable to be captured on camera. The campaign will last in the long term. As Powell states, "[I]t is a campaign that will go on for as long as it takes to be successful," "for as long as I can imagine,"[15] and it will be marked by "a number of battles."[16]

The intervention in Afghanistan, Operation Enduring Freedom, is part of the treatment recommendation offered by the administration on how to deal with the 9/11 events, and it is an aspect of the broader WOT. As President Bush remarks: "The first battle is being waged; but it's only one of a long series of battles."[17] The purpose of the military intervention is neutralizing terrorists' bases in Afghanistan. The fact that the fight against the Talibans, who are described as being very close to the terrorists, will free the country from a regime that has oppressed and brutalized its people, is seen as a microcosm of the function the WOT should have on a global scale: "We defend not only our precious freedom, but also the freedom of people everywhere to live and raise their children free from fear"; "[p]eace and freedom will prevail."[18] As Powell confirms: "In the first instance, we are interested in the Al-Qaida organization and Usama [*sic*] bin Laden, currently headquartered in Afghanistan.... But the struggle is really against terrorism wherever it is throughout the world, and wherever it threatens civilized societies."[19] The argument will be reiterated two years later as part of the rationale for the 2003 Iraq War.

Division of Labor

Almost all of the statements made by the U.S. government's representatives in the time span under analysis refer to the issue of 9/11. These statements, even when they introduce new ideas to frame the September 11 events, contribute to reinforcing notions that are already in place.

The U.S. government's framing of 9/11 is shaped almost exclusively by President Bush. The presidency and the State Department are particularly coordinated in their delivery, while the Department of Defense shows more independence. This difference, however, is just apparent and is explained by the use of a more technical vocabulary by the secretary of defense. The rhetoric of the Department of Defense, in fact, mainly concerns the new definition of warfare in the twenty-first century. As Rumsfeld says:

> This will be a war like none other our nation has faced.... Even the vocabulary of this war will be different. When we "invade the enemy's territory," we may well be invading his [*sic*] cyberspace. There may not be as many beachheads stormed as opportunities denied. Forget about "exit strategies;" we're looking at a sustained engagement that carries no deadlines. We have no fixed rules about how to deploy our troops; we'll instead establish guidelines to determine whether military force is the best way to achieve a given objective.[20]

The use of a slightly different rhetoric does neither challenge nor modify the portrayal of the events by the rest of the administration. On the contrary, the defense secretary's considerations very well fit within the world vision described by the other officials, therefore playing a role in consolidating the presidential framing.

Themes and Lines of the Day

A number of ideas take the form of themes and "lines of the day." Themes develop as a response to specific needs. An example is the theme of the WOT being waged against terrorists, not Muslims. As Powell states, "It's not a war against those who believe in Islam. It's a war against terrorism."[21] The analysis suggests that this theme is developed by the U.S. government in order to respond to international public doubts and uncertainties on the aims of the WOT. It is raised by the secretary of state first during an interview with Al-Jazeera on September 17, but is then reiterated by all members of the administration almost until the end of the war. During the first ten days following Powell's interview, the theme reappears on September 19 (Bush),[22] September 21 (Powell),[23] September 27 (Powell),[24] September 28 (Bush).[25]

Themes can, in turn, be conveyed by "lines of the day": they are specific key points to be conveyed in a coordinated manner by all the departments of the administration. Their aim is increasing the effectiveness of the messages by focusing on their repetition in almost identical form by all political actors. Repetition, in fact, is expected to increase the likelihood that journalists will pick up certain messages and reproduce them in their news stories.[26] The purpose here is increasing the visibility—and with it the newsworthiness in the eyes of the journalists—of governmental information. Some examples of recurring lines of the day over the first week following the attacks show the gradual evolution of the governmental messages and the repetition of the points the administration regards most important.

13 September. Terrorists are at war with civilized people: "we," the civilized nations, should unite against terrorism and respond with war.

15 September. An act of war has been declared by barbarians on America: we need to respond accordingly and do whatever it takes to win the war.

16 September. We are at war. We will do whatever necessary to deal with the (terrorist) threat. The prime suspects are Osama bin Laden and Al-Qaida. We need to go back to our work/normality.

17 September. This is a war to defend freedom. Freedom has a cost. We want justice. Justice comes in different forms.

18 September. The Administration does what needs to be done to fight terrorism.

Robert Singh remarks in analyzing the U.S. policy response to 9/11 that crafting the messages was a meticulously planned activity. The fact that the façade of consistency was carefully constructed is even clearer when considering that there actually were disagreements among members of the administration on the course of action following the attacks:

> Rational decision-making was especially important given the profound stakes. Central to internal deliberations were several issues of immense importance, not least the nature of the military response, the public framing of "war" and reforms to improve mainland security. On each, and despite internal disagreements, the administration reached rapid, clear and decisive conclusions: that it would not distinguish between terrorists and states harboring them (a message directed at Pakistan as much as the Taliban); that, for practical and diplomatic reasons— against the preference of Deputy Defense Secretary Paul Wolfowitz and Defense Policy chairman, Richard Perle—Iraq would be relegated to phase two or three of the war.[27]

Recycling Old Ideas: Shared Meanings Within the American Political Culture

The analysis of the WOT within the American political discourse suggests that the way political actors frame an issue, even an unprecedented event such as 9/11, is not isolated from preexisting statements. In the same way in which the intervention in Afghanistan has a sense within the broader WOT, also the WOT draws its logic from already existing and even broader systems of meaning. The framing of the 9/11 events by political actors in terms of a WOT does not therefore occur in a vacuum. The WOT contains a number of ideas that had already been used during the Cold War. According to John Hutcheson and others, the rhetorical campaign pursued by politicians in the aftermath of 9/11 was characterized by a demonization of the enemy.[28] This followed a "familiar" good versus evil imagery that had been used in the U.S./U.S.S.R confrontation and the 1991 Gulf War. The authors also find evidence of "affirmation of American values and ideals that drew upon the US "mythology" of individualism, liberty and equality" and an "affirmation of US international power and dominance, thereby tapping into the nation's long-established self-image as a world super-power."[29] An appeal to national unity against external threats to the American "democratic way of life" and a call to take action to defend liberties are also present in an even earlier presidential address—in the Four Freedoms speech of January 6, 1941, by President Roosevelt.[30]

What these examples suggest is that, to an extent, there cannot be entirely new ways in which political actors frame issues. Political discourse cannot simply be made up by individual officials. Authorities' statements appear to be shaped by the existing political culture.

Political Statements as Constructed: Interactions with Foreign Political Actors

There is just one noticeable change within the construction of the events by the administration in the immediate aftermath of 9/11, and this involves the framing of the war in Afghanistan. Before the start of the conflict, the American government denies being involved in any kind of nation-building activity: "[W]e're not into nation-building, we're focused on justice."[31] In the last week of October 2001, however, the administration suddenly changes its stance toward supporting an international effort to establish a new government for the Afghani people, a broad-based administration representing all elements of the Afghani society under UN aegis. A possible explanation for the change is the growing international pressure toward providing humanitarian assistance to the population affected by the conflict and ensuring stability in the region. This emerges in a press briefing by Powell en route to the Shanghai APEC summit on October 17:

> I will be spending time on the humanitarian issue because winter is approaching. Ramadan is approaching. Also, thinking not just about humanitarian relief but beyond that, the rebuilding of Afghanistan. Helping these people to reconstruct a life for themselves. This isn't the United States going in and nation-building with troops. This is helping the international community helping the people of Afghanistan to create hopeful conditions within the country so that they are not vulnerable to this kind of threat again in the future.[32]

The role of international pressure on the United States to get involved in Afghanistan beyond the military operation is also supported by the fact that the new policy direction is communicated in a joint statement following a meeting between President Bush and President Putin (October 21):

> The United States and Russia are ready to cooperate closely with the United Nations to promote a post-conflict settlement in Afghanistan that would provide for the formation of a representative, broad-based

government capable of ensuring the restoration of a peaceful Afghanistan that maintains good relations with countries of the region and beyond it.[33]

Among several other instances, Powell's words on November 11 eventually confirm that the position of the United States, within two months, has undergone a dramatic change:

> Our strategy for Afghanistan—let's not call it an exit strategy because this time we can't just exit, get up and walk away. We will be committed to humanitarian relief through the winter. And, after the demise of the Taliban regime, there will be a need for humanitarian relief. And we are committed to help with the reconstruction effort so that we can give the people of Afghanistan a sense of hope that the international community is not going to abandon them.... The United States will remain engaged as part of the international community, building hope and a sense of a positive future, a new future to the people of Afghanistan.[34]

FRANCE: INCORPORATING 9/11 INTO THE EXISTING POLITICAL AGENDA

The analysis of the French political discourse in the aftermath of 9/11 involves speeches, press briefings, and interviews by President Chirac, Prime Minister Jospin, Foreign Minister Védrine, and Defense Minister Richard.[35]

The French political statements following 9/11 present two essential characteristics. The first is the general consistency of their contents within the apparent absence of a tight information management strategy. The framing of the 9/11 events and their aftermath by the French authorities does not appear to be coordinated. In the United States, an information management effort is clearly identifiable in the form of the consistent repetition of the same "messages of the day" and an organized "division of labor." The U.S. president was the main deliverer of the framing of the events to the public; the rest of the administration played a supporting role. The political actors in France, instead, appear to be freer from such constraints. Besides the fact that their speeches are not entirely focused on the issue of terrorism, they do not use the same lines of the day.

This aspect will be illustrated by the analysis of early reactions to 9/11 by French authorities, who use contradictory terms to define the events. As evidence that, despite the contrasts in rhetoric, all French political actors share the same understanding of the terrorism issue, I am going to turn to the illustration of the causes of terrorism. They appear to be consistent across governmental departments. Further to this, the role of political culture, particularly already existing political agendas, will be illustrated through the consistent claims made by French politicians that 9/11 has "changed nothing."

The sharing of meanings rooted in the country's political culture among the French authorities does not rule out a constant process of transformation of the French framing of 9/11 and the war in Afghanistan, which, within the boundaries of the political agenda, keeps on evolving as a result of the interaction with international political actors. The second distinctive feature of the French political statements consists in an incorporation and integration of foreign political actors' viewpoints. The French political statements therefore get richer in ideas and more elaborated over time. It is possible to identify, especially in relation to the issue of the intervention in Afghanistan, the addition of new ideas to the official discourse every single time the French foreign minister meets the diplomat of another country. This confirms the importance of the interaction with foreign actors in the shaping of a country's political discourse, which has been detected in the analysis of American political statements, and will be illustrated as a last point.

Not being on Message: Is This a War?

While in the United States the 9/11 events are regarded as an "act of war" to which the U.S. administration should react by means of a "war on terrorism," there are dissonant interpretations within the French government. President Chirac, for example, at a meeting with President Bush says:

> I don't know whether we should use the word "war," but what I can say is that now we are faced with a conflict of a completely new nature. It is a conflict which is attempting to destroy human rights, freedom, the dignity of man. And I believe that everything must be done to protect and safeguard these values of civilization.[36]

The French foreign minister, however, defines the situation as a "war" on several occasions. An example is the following statement on September 16:

> Yes, these [9/11 events] are acts of war. It is a war like no other, which is not declared by anybody, there isn't a precise State [sic] behind it, it

is not clear how we should respond to it; but I can't see which other term we could possibly use [to define the situation].[37]

The term "war," he explains, should be understood in a political rather than juridical sense. Its meaning is further refined in another intervention:

> We can't say that we are at war as we were during the last two world wars. On the other hand, I don't know how else we could define what's happened in New York. It is, obviously, a will to [trigger a] war, it is a sort of war. But it is not the same as those of which we have memories. It is a war against terrorists.[38]

Defense Minister Richard has a very different assessment: "I realize that it is a peculiar terrorist aggression, that the American society, the American democracy is clearly under threat from such an action. A war, in my opinion, is of a different nature."[39]

Also the PM clarifies that French authorities are not dealing with a war:

> As far as the consultation with the Parliament is concerned, I have provided you with the essential information: you know that we cannot apply article 35 [of the French Constitution] which involves the "war declaration," because [what we are dealing with] is not a war.[40]

While the expression "fight against terrorism" (*lutte contre le terrorisme*) tends to become increasingly popular among all governmental actors in October, these examples stress the point of the lack of a strict message coordination among the governmental actors. This is confirmed by revelations about a tension in the relationship between Chirac and Jospin in October 2001 by Olivier Schrameck, the PM's chief of staff. He talks about a "bicephalous executive."[41]

Terrorism and Its Causes: Shared Meanings within the French Political Culture

Disagreement on the nature of the conflict with the terrorists does not prevent political authorities from sharing similar ideas in relation to the causes of terrorism. The reasons of political extremism are consistently addressed by all governmental actors and are described in a more sophisticated way than in Italy—terrorism, mainly in the Middle East, is motivated by poverty, as will be illustrated later—let alone in the United States, where the main motivations behind the terrorists' actions are evil and a hatred for "what the US stands for."

A first widespread notion in the French political statements is that the terrorists are "barbarians" and "criminals," "impostors who set a trap" (*imposteurs qui tendent un piège*). The trap consists in making "us" fall into the equation between Islam and terrorism, which would precipitate society into a clash of civilizations. President Chirac, on this point, declares:

> It is necessary not to confuse these fundamentalists, terrorist and fanatic groups [perpetrators of the hijackings] with the Arab or the Muslim world. This would be a fatal error [*erreur capitale*], it would be profoundly unjust and above all it would [mean] falling into the trap which, precisely, the terrorists have set for us. Their wish is triggering what somebody has called a clash of civilizations and which is absolutely absurd [*est le monde de l'absurde*].[42]

The point was raised so many times across all departments that McAllister, in describing the French authorities' response to 9/11, refers to it as "the 'no clash of civilization/crusade' mantra."[43]

A second idea is that the roots of terrorism, which need to be destroyed in order to remove the threat, are injustices and ideology. Conflicts and inequalities in the world are not the real causes of terrorism, but an alibi. This is the point made, for example, by Foreign Minister Védrine in an interview with the French daily *L'Humanité*:

> In the last twenty years, France has been targeted several times by terrorist groups. We have our own idea [*notre conception*] on the way of eradicating terrorism: a military action, even if sometimes necessary [*indispensable*] it is not enough, it is also necessary to fight against everything that causes [*alimente*] terrorism. There aren't just financial support and deranged ideologies, there are also situations of profound injustice [*des situations d'injustices criantes*][44] ... we should not make terrorism the favor of believing that it [terrorism] is nothing but the result of the world's injustices. There is terrorism which has developed from deranged interpretations of Islam or other religions or ideologies well before the conflict in the Middle East! Having said that, we haven't waited for the tragedy of 11 September to discover the terrible problems of this world.[45]

Elsewhere Védrine declares: "We have constantly been aware of intolerable situations in the world, which haven't created extremism, a folly in its own right, but which nourish it."[46] Jospin largely confirms the foreign minister's view when he says: "Terrorism is not explained, let alone justified, by the inequalities that divide the world and its conflicts. But it is necessary to realize that hatred is nourished by poverty, frustration and injustice."[47]

Such shared meanings among the French governmental authorities show, again, the role of political culture in shaping a country's political discourse.

The Already Existing Political Agenda

The whole crisis is seen through the lens of the already existing political agenda. As the PM puts it, the objective of France following the 9/11 events is

> to continue the full development on the international scene of the great themes of the French diplomacy [les *grands thèmes de la diplomatie française*], which are the reduction of the inequalities between North and South, the establishment [of the idea] that the problems can be resolved through multilateralism and not unilateralism, the necessity to understand that the complexity of the world calls for multipolarity, the will to bring regulation and therefore organization in the ongoing [process of] globalization and, of course, with the full backing [*le plein contact*] of our European partners, the idea that France keeps on having something to say [*continue à avoir un message à tenir*] at times of international crises.[48]

This is, in the words of the foreign minister, "the same old French policy" (*c'est la politique française de toujours*).[49]

For this reason the idea that "everything has changed," a central theme in the U.S. WOT framing, is rejected in favor of the diametrically opposite view that "nothing has changed." As Védrine says during an interview with Radio "Europe 1" on September 14, the problems that existed before 9/11 "are still there":

> I think that the problems that were in the world before 11 September are still there afterwards: the peace issue in the Middle East has not been tackled; the peace issue in the African region of the Great Lakes has not been tackled; the issue among India, Pakistan, and the Kashmir has not been tackled, I could make a long list. And the contradictions within the world, which have emerged with violence, and in a shocking but unfortunately real way at the Durban Conference [World Conference against Racism held from August 31 to September 7, 2001,

in South Africa], are still there. If the international community has anything of a community, it is just the name. The international community still has to be constructed. All of this has not changed, perhaps it presents itself under a more tragic and urgent light after this terrible day [September 11]. But we should keep on working on all these matters.[50]

The point is stressed, among the rest, on October 8: "There is a permanent action [by France against terrorism] and France has not waited for 11 September to start addressing it [terrorism], to be hugely involved on this front against all the wounds of the world, against all situations [of crisis] such as the Middle East."[51]

France has been, according to Védrine's statements, the origin of legal measures against terrorism: France was the first country to suggest the application of Article V of the NATO treaty;[52] the UN Resolution 1368 authorizing the use of military force in Afghanistan as a legitimate defense according to Article 51 of the UN Charter was also passed because of a French initiative.[53]

The analysis of the contents of the French political discourse suggests that 9/11 has simply made more relevant the efforts in which France was already engaged. They include achieving peace in the Middle East, what is defined by the defense minister as "an old French proposal" (*proposition ancienne de la France*);[54] pushing forward the project of EU enlargement and defense; and harmonizing policies in the matters of justice and police. This is the point in Jospin's words:

> The coherent responses to the terrorist threat are in the direction of public protection and intelligence [gathering]; the Government has already been working on it [tackling terrorism] in the long term and keeps on doing it under every respect. [The establishment of a] Europe of Defence—I have tried to give some evidence of it—is more than ever justified.[55]

Reference to the already existing agenda also underlines the importance of a *dialogue de cultures*. A dialogue of cultures is regarded as an essential tool against terrorism. As President Chirac remarks in his speech at the 31st General Conference of UNESCO on October 15, the dialogue among cultures that France has always supported can strengthen societies' cohesion. Tolerance and respect for each other improve coexistence and the understanding of diversity. A dialogue of cultures also directly undermines fanaticism—which has its roots in a lack of education and in obscurantism—the real ground of terrorism.[56]

Constructing the Political Statements: Negotiating with Foreign Officials over Afghanistan

The framing of the intervention in Afghanistan by French authorities particularly reflects a negotiated nature and is shaped by both French political actors' reactions to and their agreements with foreign politicians.

The military nature of the intervention is beyond question as the operation in Afghanistan is supported by the international community through UN Resolution 1368 authorizing the United States to legitimate defense. As Védrine explains:

> The Resolution of the [UN] Security Council recognizes that the Unites States are in a state of legitimate defense, it [resolution] does not address a particular country. It [addressing a country] would have been reckless at that point in time [12 September]. This does not mean: "you have the right to retaliate against *a* country," it is not a matter of retaliating against *a* country. The retaliation is against a system. If there is a target in this operation, it is not Afghanistan, it is Al-Qaida. The legitimate defence consists in a reaction to the networks [*réseaux*], which have organized the attacks. Up to now the information gathered by different services around the world is converging. These networks, their bases, their infrastructures, and all which supports them, must be destroyed [*doivent être cassés*].[57]

The action in Afghanistan is regarded as necessary (even "logical"):[58] it is against Al-Qaida and its sponsor, the Taliban regime. There is, however, a marked change of rhetoric shortly after the beginning of the operations. On October 9, the French government appears to realize that the United States may use the right to self-defense granted by Article 51 of the UN Charter against other states in the future. While the foreign minister says it is not possible to say how France would react in such circumstances, it could be anticipated that invoking the article would be seen as unjust.[59] Explicit statements about the fact that military operations should not extend beyond Afghanistan add to the range of ideas expressed about the issue. As Chirac later puts it, the military action remains "indispensable," but there is no reason to extend the military theater beyond Afghanistan.[60]

France is particularly active in framing the issue of Afghanistan. This involves, contrary to what happens in the United States, the elaboration of a political solution for the postwar period. Political provisions are contained in a "Plan for Afghanistan" presented by France to the UN on October 1. The plan covers the humanitarian political and economic aspects of the postwar scenario.[61] The details of the steps to be followed to achieve a political settlement, in particular, become the object of intense negotiations between French politicians and foreign diplomats. The diplomatic activity is especially lively at the end of October and beginning of November and the main points around which it revolves are the length and scope of the military operations, as well as the composition of the postwar Afghani government. Here are just a few examples of specific moments in which new ideas appeared and were incorporated into the French official framing of the issue as a result of meetings with foreign officials. At the Mediterranean forum, on October 25 in Agadir (Morocco): the military action is not going to extend beyond Afghanistan; the military objectives should be achieved as soon as possible.[62] On October 27 in Riyad (Saudi Arabia): after the military action a coalition government representing all Afghan people should be established.[63] On November 2 in Islamabad (Pakistan): the objective is the creation of a peaceful and stable Afghanistan.[64] On November 4 in Paris, Védrine, drawing on Brahimi (special representative to the UN for Afghanistan), says that there are several political processes. France should try to make them converge.[65] President Chirac, after having met Prime Minister Blair in London, expresses the idea of the establishment of a Palestinian state as a way of eliminating one of the alibis used by extremists.[66] On November 6, after a meeting between President Chirac and President Musharraf, the new ideas of a role for NGOs in Afghanistan and the creation of an interim government are incorporated into the French official views on the issue.[67] On November 12, in New York, all permanent members of the Security Council agree that the Northern Alliance should not advance into Kabul.[68]

9/11 SEEN FROM ITALY

The analysis of the Italian political discourse in the aftermath of 9/11 focuses on the speeches and press briefings by Prime Minister Berlusconi, President Ciampi, Foreign Minister Ruggiero, and Defense Minister Martino.[69] The Italian official public communication of the 9/11 events and their aftermath is characterized by being the least organized among those under analysis. Philip Daniels, in describing the Italian government's response to 9/11, writes that after the very immediate condemnation of the attacks and pledge of the country's solidarity with the United States, policy was characterized by "inertia, confusion over Italy's role in the 'war on terrorism.' "[70] The disagreements among senior ministers in the governing coalition, according to him, "conveyed the image of an inexperienced administration."[71] Even if Italian officials did not have a clear common message for the media and the public, the analysis finds nonetheless that their statements were shaped by the country's political culture. More specifically, the way officials framed the events was affected by a range of international institutional structures. The analysis shows that they were not just legal constraints, but contributed to shaping the very contents of the political statements. In fact, Italian authorities appeared to interpret the role of Italy within the fight against terrorism in the broader context of international alliances as communities of values. This point specifically shows the connection between national identity and institutional practices, particularly the belonging to international organizations. These aspects will now be illustrated, starting from the mixed messages the media and the public were exposed to in the aftermath of the 9/11 events, then moving on to the institutional, geopolitical, and cultural references that shaped the reaction of the Italian government.

Mixed Messages

The lack of coordination among official actors is supported by the fact that each of the politicians whose statements were analyzed expressed a different interpretation of the events. PM Berlusconi, for example, focused on the economic aspects of the struggle against terrorism. Berlusconi not only called for the convening of an extraordinary G8 meeting to discuss about an international response to terrorism, but also advocated a "Marshall plan for the Middle East."[72] Its purpose should have been tackling the poverty and the lack of hope that, in his view, feed terrorism in the area. President Ciampi, unlike the other Italian political authorities, sees the fight against terrorism as a struggle for democracy. He also talks at length about the special role of the Mediterranean area as a cultural meeting point of different civilizations. For example, he refers to the Mediterranean as a centre of "civilization and development" (*civiltà e benessere*)[73] and the natural context of action for Italy, given the country's geographical location and cultural tradition.[74]

It is not possible to observe any particular coordination effort among the different governmental departments, let alone an efficient communication strategy as in the case of the U.S. administration. Defense Minister Martino, for example, provoked a strong reaction from the opposition when he made the "casual sugges-tion," on September 20, that a NATO operation could be launched without the approval of parliament.[75] His statement had to be cor-rected the following day by Berlusconi through the assurance that the parliament would be involved in decisions about any Italian military involvement. Perhaps the most telling example of the lack of communication planning is Berlusconi's statement about Western civilizations' "superiority" to Islam at a press conference in Berlin on September 26.[76] The PM's declarations caused interna-tional outcry and condemnation,[77] which forced him to later clarify his views.[78]

The Institutional References

The institutional affiliations are important not only because they provide a legal framework, but also because they embody a set of values. As far as the legal framework is concerned, Foreign Minister Ruggiero, in his report to parliament about his visit to the United States,[79] clearly states that Italy's position is defined by the UN Security Council Resolution passed on September 12, the UN General Assembly Resolution passed on the same day, the Conclusions of the EU General Affairs Council (also dated September 12), the Joint Declaration by the EU Heads of State and Prime Ministers (September 14), the Declaration by the G8 Heads of State and Prime Ministers (September 19), the Conclusions and Action Plan of the EU Council Extraordinary Meeting (September 21).

The UN, EU, and G8 therefore have a direct influence in shap-ing the Italian political discourse. After the decision by the Atlantic Council that the terrorist attacks are covered by Article V of the Washington Treaty, as they have been waged against the United States from abroad, NATO is frequently mentioned by all Italian political actors as an additional institutional reference for the broader context in which the country's antiterrorist action should be understood.

Other legal frameworks politicians refer to are the Italian Constitution and the UN Charter of Human Rights. The values they represent, particularly the respect for democracy and human rights, are perceived to be at the basis of the Italian national iden-tity. They are compatible with the values embodied by international organizations. This is very clearly expressed, again, by Defense Minister Martino. Italy's role within the fight against terrorism is to be interpreted through its membership of international institutions, especially NATO, the EU, and the UN, that promote a system of values:

> We live in a historical phase in which, *de facto*, we are in the process of building a new dimension of common security—up to now well-embodied by the Atlantic Alliance—which [common security] also refers to the United Nations and to the European Union. In relation to terrorism, international institutions indeed establish themselves as "communities of values," reference points for all Countries and peoples who place democracy as a political system, freedom, right, individual development, at to the core of their own lives as well as their own social, cultural, and economic dynamics.
>
> It is within this framework that we think our participation to the struggle against terrorism should rightly be interpreted: not only as an attempt to protect a system of values that is the basis of the civilization we share with our friends and allies, but also as a defense of the interests and more specific expectations of our national Community, of our families and every one of us as an individual.[80]

The Geopolitical and Cultural References: The Italian National Identity

According to what emerges from the Italian political statements in the period under analysis, the country perceives itself in close contact with two regions. The first is the "Mediterranean's Southern shore" (*Sponda Sud del Mediterraneo*). Ruggiero refers to a *sponda sud* in an article published in *Corriere della Sera* on October 18.[81] The second is the Middle East and the Balkans. One reason for the Italian politicians' focus on these areas is the link, as established by Ruggiero, between regional crises and extremism/terrorism.[82] Another reason is the consideration of Italian physical proximity to the areas; involvement in peacekeeping operations in the Balkans; and commitment, through the EU institutions, to mediation in the Middle East peace process.

The consideration of the relatively low number of documents (speeches, interviews, articles) related to the 9/11 events and the occasional mentions of the conflict in Afghanistan could lead to concluding that geography, in this case the very distance from the World Trade Center, did play a role: for the Italian government the 9/11 events and the following war in Afghanistan were not relevant to the country's priorities. A comparison of the Italian political discourse with the French, however, totally reverses the assessment. Geography is important, but geographical location, rather than a fixed given, is a position *constructed* by each country within the international system. France and Italy are geographically neighbors, and one could argue, are positioned virtually at the same distance from both New York and Kabul. Despite this, Italy perceives itself as a local actor within the Mediterranean area. France, instead, clearly regards itself as a world player, supported in this perception by the pursuance of a permanent international agenda. French authorities often refer in their statements to *les grands thèmes de la politique étrangère,* "the great themes of the [French] foreign policy." The positions the two countries take at the international level, in turn, shaped by the sense of identity their political actors have constructed over time, thus do affect the development of their respective political discourses.

The fact that the position of each country is constructed is confirmed by the observation that in the geographical understanding of the world that emerges from the Italian political discourse there are also recurrent associations (and conversely, relationships of opposition) among countries. A significant one is the coupling of the United States with Israel. This implies an opposition between Palestine and the United States and an assumption that the terrorism behind 9/11 has a Middle Eastern origin. As seen in the section about the French political statements, this is extremely different from what happens in France, where even the slightest hint to equating terrorism with the Arab world is regarded as falling into the terrorists' "trap" *(piège).* In the French view, the aim of the perpetrators is precisely creating a "clash of civilizations."

The Italian political statements about 9/11 and the war in Afghanistan also contain cultural references. They are broad references to Italy's historical past, religious background, and shared values. The struggle against terrorism and its barbarity is interpreted within the tradition of liberal thought, Humanism, Renaissance, and Catholicism. It is seen, for the values it aims to defend, as part of the post-WWII legacy, particularly the fight for a democratic Constitution at the basis of the Italian Republic. Such issues are particularly emphasized by the president, but are a recurrent feature of all political actors. Also Martino, in a message to the armed forces, links the struggle against terrorism to WWII, the Risorgimento, the Liberation from the Nazi occupation, and the more recent Italian involvement in international peacekeeping missions.[83]

The values political actors refer to are those shared by Italy and the international organizations to which the country belongs. They are mentioned, as an example, by Berlusconi:

> We should be proud of the values in which we believe: tolerance; pluralism; political and economic freedoms; the protection of the rights of the individual and of minorities; women equality; cultural freedom; press freedom; teaching freedom [*libertà di insegnamento*]; religious freedom; legal guarantees in the exercise of justice; universal suffrage with free and secret vote.[84]

These examples show how national identity, an aspect of political culture, affects the country's political discourse.

PAKISTAN: 9/11 AND NATIONAL INTEREST

The analysis of Pakistani political statements relies mostly on declarations made by General Musharraf.[85] The consistency between statements by other ministers, whose official records were not available, and Musharraf's speeches was assessed on the basis of the quotes by officials identified in Pakistani news reports. A characteristic of the Pakistani political discourse is the marked difference between the framing of the 9/11 issue and the framing of the intervention in Afghanistan. This not only applies to the volume of contents, but also to how actively the construction of each issue is pursued by the Pakistani government.

The framing of 9/11 is mainly constituted by ideas related to the treatment recommendation of the issue. The Pakistani portrayal of 9/11, in fact, builds heavily on the U.S. administration's definition of the events. It is limited to elaborating why joining the coalition against terrorism is useful in terms of the Pakistani national interest. The idea of joining the coalition and supporting the action the United States will take against terrorism contributes to shifting the focus of the statements to the intervention in Afghanistan. The framing of the 9/11 issue also appears to be passive: there is no attempt to propose a different interpretation of the events. This is different from what happens in France, where in order to keep on pursuing the country's existing political agenda, governmental actors purposely say—against the American "everything has changed"—that 9/11 has "changed nothing."

Almost all public statements made by General Musharraf during the period under study refer to the intervention in Afghanistan. The politician, early after September 11, actively highlights the need to deal with the humanitarian, political, and economic reconstruction in the postwar period. Such plans are not addressed by the U.S. administration but well into October (the war starts on October 7). While it is not possible to assert that it was the Pakistani framing of the issue that drove the U.S. government's policy change on Afghanistan, the consistency with which Pakistan presented the issue possibly contributed to creating an international pressure on the matter. The ideas of the Pakistani framing were, in fact, integrated into the French official discourse as result of the interaction between the political actors of the two countries during the first week of November 2001.[86] This suggests that the consistent repetition of ideas concerning the postwar situation in the theater of war did raise an international awareness of the issue.

I am going to look at these aspects in more detail, starting from a description of the way the issues of 9/11 and the military operation in Afghanistan were consistently shaped by Musharraf throughout the period. As Samina Yasmeen points out, "Since its creation in August 1947, notions of identity and perceptions of threat to its security have influenced the security discourse in Pakistan."[87] The description of the way 9/11 events and the war in Afghanistan were framed within the Pakistani political discourse therefore cannot be separated from references to the country's national identity, its national interest, and its history as a Muslim nation. I will then elaborate on the interaction between the Pakistani government and the media, particularly on Musharraf's attempt to respond to what he claimed were media distortions of the official framing of the intervention in Afghanistan. I will finally focus on the role of a country's position taking within the international system as the last aspect affecting political discourse. This variable refers to political actors' ability to construct the position of a country in relation to the rest of the world.

Selling Pakistan's Participation to the U.S.-led Coalition

Evidence of planning in the crafting of political messages to be delivered to the media and the public by the Pakistani government is offered, first, by the need to make presidential policies acceptable to both Islamist and liberal sections of the Pakistani society, and second, by the repetition of the very same ideas throughout the time span under analysis. They will now be illustrated in turn.

A televised speech by Musharraf on September 19 in order to "take the nation into confidence" about the domestic and international implications of the events is a good example of the efforts by the Pakistani government in delivering a message that could appeal to different strata of society.[88] The decision to withdraw support from the Taliban regime for joining the U.S.-led international coalition was presented, as Yasmeen points out, through the deliberate resort by the Pakistani leadership to "Islamic language."[89] The decision to join the international community in its fight against terrorism was compared by Musharraf to the treaty agreed by Prophet Muhammad with Jewish tribes during the first six years of the history of Islam. Despite being a pact established with nonbelievers, the treaty led to benefits for the Muslim community. Using the metaphor to explain to the public the situation faced by Pakistan, Musharraf says:

> We are trying our best to come out of this critical situation without any damage to Afghanistan and Taliban [sic]. This is my earnest endeavour and with the blessings of Allah I will continue to seek such a way out. We are telling the Americans too that they should be patient. Whatever their plans, they should be cautious and balanced.... At this critical juncture, we have to frustrate the evil designs of our enemies and safeguard national interests. Pakistan is considered a fortress of Islam. God forbid, if this fortress is harmed in any way it would cause damage to the cause of Islam.[90]

The purpose of the speech was presenting evidence, to the eyes of Islamist sections of society, that "the military regime was following established Islamic practice."[91] While the decision to join the coalition was the rational way to ensure "Pakistan's existence and to deny India strategic advantage,"[92] Musharraf was aware that an attack by the United States against Afghanistan would have been interpreted by Islamists as an aggression against the Ummah (the Muslim community).[93]

At the same time the speech was designed to appeal to liberal and moderate opinion in the country. Musharraf explained that Pakistan needed to adapt its policies in order to safeguard its national interests.[94] Pakistan, as he explained, was being asked to support a campaign for which the United States had the backing "of the UN Security Council and the General Assembly in the form of a resolution.... a resolution for punishing those people who support terrorism. Islamic countries have supported this resolution."[95] To avoid "unbearable losses" the country needed to take a decision in the national interest: "Pakistan comes first, everything else comes later."[96]

General Musharraf points, in particular, to the need to meet four interests/priorities: "First of all is the security of the country from external threat. Second is our economy and its revival. Third are our strategic nuclear and missile assets. And [the] Kashmir cause."[97] Particularly, the issue of Kashmir is important in the context of the relations with India, which according to the general, would like to take advantage of the situation in order to "enter into any alliance with the United States and get Pakistan declared a terrorist state."[98]

A second piece of evidence supporting the observation that an organized delivery of political messages takes place in the Pakistani political statements is the way Musharraf frames the intervention in Afghanistan. The effort takes place from very early after September 11 and is characterized by the continuous and consistent repetition of the same set of ideas.

Musharraf says that there are three elements to the operation in Afghanistan: the military action, a "political dispensation," and a rehabilitation effort.[99] From September 30 the general stresses the need to build a friendly Afghanistan by establishing a government that takes into consideration the ethnic and demographic layout of the country.[100] The objective should be achieving peace and stability in the country.[101] A political solution for the postwar settlement should also be facilitated rather than imposed and should be found in accordance with the wishes of the Afghani people.[102] Within this context the Northern Alliance, one of the factions already fighting against the Talibans before the beginning of the U.S.-led operations, should not be imposed one sidedly.[103] The government should, instead, be broad based and the ex-king Zahir Shah, as well as moderate Talibans, could have a role if the Afghani people wish so.[104] All these points are reiterated during a press conference on October 8, when more concrete measures for the postwar reconstruction are also suggested in relation to water management, revival of agriculture, infrastructure development, so that the Afghani refugees on Pakistani soil can return to their country.[105] The ideal features of the Afghani political settlement are reemphasized on a number of occasions: during a meeting with Secretary of State Powell (October 16),[106] in an interview on PTV's (Pakistani TV channel) *NewsNight* (October 22),[107] during an interview on CNN (October 23),[108] at a meeting with President Chirac (November 7),[109] in the Pakistani leader's speech at the 56th UN General Assembly in New York (November 10),[110] and later the same day in a press conference with President Bush.[111]

Changing Circumstances, National Interest, and National Identity

The decision to "side with the international community against ter-rorism" is justified by Musharraf by the need to pursue the coun-try's interest in a changing environment.[112] This notion is particularly emphasized in the Pakistani leader's interview on CNN's *Larry King Live* on October 23. This is the exchange between King, ask-ing to explain the sudden change in Pakistani foreign policy, and the general:

> *King*: You previously had supported the Taliban, Mr. President. What changed?
>
> *Musharraf*: Well, the environment changed. As I've always been say-ing, policies are made in accordance with environments prevailing. Before the 11th of September, the environment was totally differ-ent and after the 11th of September, the environment drastically changed; and, therefore, the requirement of adjusting the policy in accordance with the ground reality.[113]

The same thinking is applied, again, to the lack of opposition to Zahir Shah, former Afghan king in exile in Rome and identified by several Afghani leaders as a new reference figure for the Afghani postwar political settlement. President Musharraf, asked at a press conference on October 8 about why he is no longer opposing the former king, says that

> environments are never constant and...30 years back, he [King Zahir] was doing something and Pakistan was rightly against it because of certain reasons. He was maybe doing something against Pakistan's interests....we should not have fixated ideas....Maybe in a short while there is going to be a leadership vacuum in 90% of Afghanistan....We need to find out [a] political dispensation which will clearly fill the vacuum being created from this operation....And in this vacuum, Zahir Shah may have a role to play.[114]

National interest appears, however, to be defined by national iden-tity. The need to join the coalition is dictated not only by the fact that the country is now a "frontline state"[115] in the WOT, but also by Pakistan's role as a "fortress of Islam."[116] As Musharraf says, "[D]ecisions about national interests should be made with wisdom and rational judgement"; they "should be in conformity with Islam."[117]

Responding to the Media

Besides national interest and sense of identity of the country, another factor that shapes the contents of the framing of the Afghanistan issue in the Pakistani political discourse is the attempt by General Musharraf to rebut the international and Pakistani media framing of the military operations. The political leader's main target is the idea, within media reports, that the main cities of Afghanistan are being bombed and that, therefore, the intervention is not aimed at terrorists but is against the Afghani people. On October 8, during a press conference in Islamabad, the general says:

> This operation is not against the people of Afghanistan but against terrorist, terrorism and their sanctuaries and supporters. . . . This action is targeted and so the perception that the four cities—Kabul, Kandahar, Jalalabad and Mazar-e-Sharif—are being attacked, is not true. . . . The terrorist camps are in fact in the vicinity of these cities.[118]

The point is made again by the Pakistani leader during his speech at the UN on November 10: "Sadly enough, the civilian casualties in this action are getting projected more as an open war against the already poor, suffering and innocent people of Afghanistan. The world in general and Pakistan in particular mourns the loss of these innocent lives and sympathizes with the bereaved."[119]

Reconstructing Pakistan's Identity

The analysis of the contents of the Pakistani political statements allows integrating observations that have previously emerged in relation to the United States, France, and Italy.

The framing of an issue by political actors is limited by the boundaries set by existing systems of meanings, particularly already established political and foreign policy agendas, but also by power relationships: process tracing reveals that, initially, Pakistan is not in the position to challenge the framing of 9/11, but given the changes in the international situation after September 11, General Musharraf is later in the position to suggest a different framing for the causes of terrorism and to advance proposals for the postwar political settlement in Afghanistan. The general draws, for example, in relation to the Kashmir cause, a distinction between "state terrorism" (perpetrated by India, in his example) and "freedom struggle."[120] Musharraf also says that, in order to solve the problem of terrorism, it is necessary to address its causes. On October 8 he states: "Certainly any operation in Afghanistan will not root out terrorism"; "[w]e need to address the root causes which are giving birth to terrorism and are the causes of extremism." Such causes, as the political leader continues, are political disputes, such as those in Palestine and Kashmir.[121]

Pakistan, thus, due to its new status of key ally in the war against terrorism, also acquires bargaining power in its relations with foreign countries. This suggests that a country's position within the international system also affects political actors' degree of freedom in constructing (framing) an issue. Positioning within the international system, however, is not dictated by power, geography, or material resources alone, but is both shaped by events and actively constructed by political actors. This is suggested by two considerations. First, Pakistan's role suddenly changed because of the U.S. decision to intervene in Afghanistan—an event beyond the control of the Pakistani leader. Second, General Musharraf framed the role of Pakistan as a "frontline state" in the WOT and took the decision—this time a deliberate choice—to join the coalition against terrorism.

This finding is important because, if this variable is found to affect also the development of the news coverage, it could challenge the role of *geographical* and *cultural proximity* (see Chapter 2) in shaping the news. These aspects will be further explored in the next chapter.

CONCLUSIONS

The comparative analysis of the political discourses in the United States, Italy, France, and Pakistan leads to drawing conclusions about the relevance of a country's political culture and news management activities by political actors in shaping news coverage, as well as the possibility that news influences the political debate. They will now be assessed in turn.

Political Culture

Political culture, as it emerges from the analysis, is a constructed system of meanings created over time by political actors through their discourse and practices. It involves national identity, existing policy agendas, international relations with foreign countries—including belonging to international organizations—and positioning within the international system. They are all linked as "who we are" affects "what we do," "who we do it with," and "where we stand" in relation to the rest of the world. Political culture is, in a constructionist view of the world, a structure. It is continuously recreated, and over time, changed through the practices and discourses of political actors within and outside a country. What we are and what we do, in fact, is established and negotiated in relation to the "others," their identity and their activities.

The analysis of the political statements in the United States, France, Italy, and Pakistan leads to one main observation: the contents of political statements, even in the United States, where officials craft sophisticated messages for mass marketing purposes, are not freely established by politicians. What politicians—agents—say or do is constrained by preexisting political structures.

The comparative analysis of the way the issues of 9/11 and the intervention in Afghanistan are framed in the four countries, indeed, reveals such marked differences that it looks like political actors live, each in his own national context, in rather different worlds. Aspects of the political culture and the way they specifically drive the differentiation of the way issues are framed within the political statements across the cases are briefly re-presented here.

Position Taking in the International System
The geographical distance from the location of the 9/11 attacks plays a role in affecting the amount of attention political actors devote to the issues. This is evident when comparing the Italian political discourse with the Pakistani statements. The attention paid to the events by Italian politicians is much lower than in the Pakistani case simply because Italy is in the middle of the Mediterranean area. Pakistan, on the other hand, shares its borders with Afghanistan and is likely to be overwhelmed by the influx of refugees from the war theater if the crisis is not handled effectively.

Geography alone, however, cannot explain why the French government is more interested in the events than Italian politicians when both countries share virtually the same distance from both New York and Kabul. This has to do with *positioning* in the international system rather than with physical *position*. France has *positioned* itself (i.e. it has deliberately *constructed* its role) as a world player, whereas Italy identifies itself as the "bridge" between Europe and the Middle East. Such positions have been built in the long term through the pursuit of different foreign policy agendas.[122]

The Already Existing Political Agenda
The already existing policy agenda provides the basic perspective from which to interpret new events. In the view of the French government,

the threat of terrorism is caused by fanaticism, in turn, fed by the lack of education. This interpretation makes more urgent the pursuing of the already existing attempt at establishing a *dialogue des cultures* (dialogue of cultures). Also, the claimed need to improve the EU legal frameworks for tackling terrorism is exploited for accelerating the project of an EU defense and enlargement already on the agenda. Pakistan also describes joining the international coalition against terrorism as the best choice in the interest of the country.

Interactions with Foreign Political Actors (International Relations)

The framing of both 9/11 and the war in Afghanistan is complex and develops over time in directions that are not just defined by single national political actors. Interactions and information exchanges with foreign officials do affect a country's political discourse. This is evident in the decision by the U.S. government to extend the objectives of the war in Afghanistan: while the operation was, at the beginning, exclusively about the rooting out of Al-Qaida training camps, it later extended to nation-building activities. Also, the framing of the Afghani crisis by the French government appears to change as a result of interactions with foreign diplomats.

Both the Italian and the French political discourses are heavily shaped by their belonging to a network of international alliances. Their institutional affiliations emerge in the fact that they constantly refer to the legal frameworks of the EU, the UN Charter of Human Rights, UN Security Council Resolutions, and the NATO treaty, especially Article V and its provision that an attack against one member of the alliance is an attack against all.

National Identity

Geopolitics, position taking at the international level, belonging to international organizations feed back into the country's sense of identity. This is, as seen, what the Italian defense minister refers to when he talks of international alliances as "communities of values": countries belonging to an international organization have common goals because they have a shared identity, and this is so because they share the same values. Pakistan also sees the struggle against Al-Qaida's terrorism as a fight against a perversion of Islam. This is consistent with the country's self-perception, within the community of Muslim nations, as a "fortress of Islam."

These aspects contribute to creating shared meanings among the political actors who shape the political discourse of a country. Such meanings have been articulated through history, common values, and national legal frameworks. In France the interpretation of the very meaning of terrorism is shaped by the history of a centralized and secular republic. Terrorism is dreaded for its potential in disrupting society and the very fabric of the state (*Etat*). Terrorism is a threat to civil liberties (*libertés*). These values are enshrined in the country's *Déclaration des Droits de l'Homme*. Both the French and the Italian political statements refer to their own national Constitutions as reference points as to what is important to each country's society.

All these components of a country's political culture have affected the way political actors framed the issues of 9/11 and the intervention in Afghanistan in the aftermath of 9/11. What remains to be seen is whether they also contributed to shaping the news coverage, which will be the focus of the analysis in the next chapter.

There is another important concept to be raised here along with political culture. The articulation of the political culture in the short term, in fact, is *national interest*, particularly in terms of foreign policy priorities in relation to the rest of the world. The national interest (and the foreign policy agenda with it) develops within the boundaries constituted by the political culture and should be distinguished from it because it can change more quickly than the latter in response to events. National interest—and the way it is defined by political leaders as an adaptation to changing circumstances—explains how changes occur within the political culture's structures. Let's think again, for example, about the speed with which Pakistan, literally within 24 hours, realigned its strategic alliances after September 11, 2001. Without consideration of the way national interest—an expression of national priorities—evolves in the short term, if political actors were simply acting within the boundaries of the political culture, no change would ever occur in the political culture of a country. This, instead, is known to develop over time.

Media Influence on the Political Debate

While the analysis finds no evidence that governmental authorities substantially change the way they frame the issues under study because of media pressure, the media have some effect on political actors. As it emerges in the case of Pakistan, General Musharraf's recurrent emphasis on specific characteristics of the intervention in Afghanistan—the war is not against the Afghani people, but against terrorism; the bombing is not against civilians, rather against terrorist infrastructures—appears to be a response to some Pakistani and international media allegations. The media were reporting that the attacks were against the main towns in Afghanistan and were conveying the idea that the operation was targeting civilians. The general is trying to avoid the domestic political damage deriving from being seen as supporting an operation that is inflicting suffering on a fellow Islamic country.

Media Management

The data collected about the news management activities in the four countries is not yet conclusive about the role of planned efforts by politicians in conveying their interpretations of the issues under study to the media. What is clear is that news management is not part of the political routine for all governments and cannot be regarded as a universal variable shaping media coverage. The effort by U.S. politicians at coordinating official messages was, however, outstanding in comparison with other countries. The data leads to the expectation that if news management really has a role in shaping the news—perhaps just in the United States—such an effort should produce clear-cut, observable results. The level of correlation between the political discourse and the news coverage in the United States should be markedly greater than in the other three countries. This hypothesis is tested in chapter 5.

CHAPTER 4

Press Coverage after 9/11

This chapter presents the results of the process-tracing analysis of eight newspapers across the United States (the *New York Times* and the *Wall Street Journal*), France (*Libération* and *Le Monde*), Italy (*La Repubblica* and *Il Corriere della Sera*), and Pakistan (the *Dawn* and the *Nation*).

The main finding is that the framing of 9/11 and the war in Afghanistan in the news is much more fragmented than in the political statements: incoherent, sometimes even contradictory ideas co-exist within the coverage. This happens because it is not "the media," as a conscious actor, that frames the issues in question. The media is rather more like a stage on which different sources "speak," thus providing different interpretations of the events. Understanding the way media contents are shaped—that is, how issues are framed—therefore translates into comprehending what affects the choice of the sources by journalists and editors in the first place. This means finding what determines the sources' newsworthiness, their number and identity, and the amount of "talking space" they are given on the newspapers' pages. The analysis shows that there is no evidence of a global journalistic culture common to all case studies. Not only does journalistic culture vary along national lines, but it is also further shaped at the level of the single media organization by editorial policy. Editors set the newspapers' agendas—the focus of interest of the newspaper—which can be more or less internationally oriented. They also affect the level of comment (individual bias) their journalists are allowed to express within the news. Editorial policy therefore affects the implementation, within each media organization, of the national journalistic culture. Despite this, there is overall very little evidence that editors exercise a strict control on first-page news so that it reflects a single stance—their own or a newspaper's "collective" point of view—on the issues under study. Another aspect that was found to play a role in shaping newspaper coverage was the political culture of each country. This emerges not as a direct and short-term influence by political actors on the news. Political culture is rather the broader system of meanings established over history by national politicians, often through interactions with their foreign counterparts. Such system of meanings is the context in which both journalists and editors understand the unfolding of local and international political events.

I will illustrate the results, distinguishing them per country and per newspaper, starting with the United States, then moving on to France, Italy, and Pakistan. The chapter will conclude with an assessment of the variables that were found to shape the coverage.

THE UNITED STATES

American journalistic culture is characterized by its aspiration to objective reporting.[1] This means that news, understood as fact-oriented information, tends to be kept distinct from comment and that journalists try to abstain from expressing personal views.[2] This tradition of news writing was established through the journalistic practices of American newspapers in the late nineteenth century.[3] On August 19, 1896, Adolf Simon Ochs, publisher of the *New York Times* at the time, wrote a declaration of principles in the editorial pages in which he expressed his "sincere desire to conduct a high-standard newspaper, clean, dignified, and trustworthy."[4] As he continued, he emphasized the values of neutrality and the commitment to reporting more than one side to a story which, over time, became the norm of Anglo-Saxon journalism:

> It will be my earnest aim that The New-York [*sic*] Times give the news, all the news, in concise and attractive form, in language that is parliamentary in good society, and give it as early, if not earlier, than it can be learned through any other reliable medium; to give the news impartially, without fear or favor, regardless of any party, sect or interest involved; to make the columns of The New-York Times a forum for the consideration of all questions of public importance, and to that end to invite intelligent discussion from all shades of opinion.[5]

The *Wall Street Journal* was founded in 1889 as a business publication also "committed to separating news and views."[6] As the comparison between the *New York Times* and the *Wall Street Journal* will point out, however, the very same journalistic culture can be interpreted differently. The *New York Times* appears to be "more objective" than the *Wall Street Journal*. On the *Wall Street Journal* dissenting voices, or "the other side of a story," might be present but they are marginalized or outnumbered by opinions consonant with the editorial take on the issues, showing the possibility—the only case among eight newspapers, though—that editorial policy does take the form of a manipulation of first-page news.

Journalists, in the *Wall Street Journal*'s coverage, are allowed to express comments within first-page articles, which appear to match a stance by the whole organization on the issues of 9/11 and Afghanistan. The editorial policy materializes there by shaping the limits of journalistic objectivity. The framing of the issues under study is also affected by the newspaper agenda: in the *Wall Street Journal* the focus of the coverage is mostly economics rather than politics, or to a lesser extent, foreign policy unlike that of the *New York Times*. The newspaper agenda therefore limits the scope of the coverage of 9/11 and the war in Afghanistan in the *Wall Street Journal* in comparison with the *New York Times*.

The New York Times

The *New York Times*'s framing of both 9/11 and the war in Afghanistan tends to be very different depending on whether we look at first-page articles or editorials. The framing of the two issues in first pages tends to be almost exclusively contained in quotes by sources. Since each actor is trying to impose his or her own interpretation of the events, this creates a general fragmentation of contents. Incompatible idea elements (IEs)—"this is a war"/"this is not a war," for instance—as will be illustrated in examples later on, coexist within the same articles. Editorials, instead, are richer in contents and, from the point of view of the way IEs relate to each other, generally provide a more coherent framing of the issues under study. The difference between first-page news and editorial framing of 9/11 and the war in Afghanistan suggests that editorial policy does not translate into a tight control of first-page contents. To illustrate these aspects I will first describe the variety of sources contributing to "fragmenting" first-page news, then I will turn to showing the generally consistent and supportive stance of the editorials in relation to the administration. Both points support the observation, presented in the analysis of the relationship between news and editorials, that the framing of 9/11 and the war in Afghanistan in first-page news is not consistent with the editorial line on the issues.

News

News articles tend to contain less IEs than editorials. Whereas editorials take the form of comments, reflections, often specifically focusing on either the 9/11 events or the intervention in Afghanistan, news articles mainly report facts and their details. The information provided, such as the chronology of the 9/11 events or witnesses' accounts of what happened, tends not to cover the aspects framing is related to: What do the events mean (problem definition)? What are their causes (causal interpretation)? How should the events be judged (moral evaluation)? What should be done (treatment recommendation)?

Within the 64 days of coverage under study there are no instances in which a journalist directly frames the issues by expressing his or her own opinion within a first-page article. All contributions toward framing of the issues are, instead, contained within statements by quoted sources. Most of the statements are by U.S. sources, mainly politicians, and they do tend to reproduce the governmental framing of the issues, as the Indexing hypothesis would lead to expect. There are, however, also dissenting voices, some domestic, other international.

As an example of alternative national voice, on September 28 the article "In Patriotic Times, Dissent Is Muted" reports the controversial opinion by Bill Maher, a TV presenter:

> One of the most visible examples of this burgeoning debate involved a scuffle between the White House and Bill Maher, host of the late-night talk show "Politically Incorrect." Last week, Mr. Maher said that the hijackers were not cowards but that it was cowardly for the United States to launch cruise missiles on targets thousands of miles away.[7]

Most of the alternative framing to U.S. political actors', however, originates from statements by foreign officials. They introduce inconsistent views with those expressed by national authorities. On September 17, for example, the Taliban leader Mullah Mohammed Omar suggests that even handing in Osama bin Laden to the United States would not spare Afghanistan from being attacked;[8] Al-Jazeera reports a statement by Osama bin Laden in which he rejects any responsibility for the attacks.[9] On September 18, Taliban leaders also question Osama bin Laden's culpability.[10]

The fact that most of the IEs in the news come from U.S. officials does not mean that alternative views cannot be placed prominently within the coverage. This is the case on September 30: the only IEs contributing to the framing of the 9/11 issues are from Pakistani religious groups. They provide a very different framing from the U.S. authorities' by supporting the ideas that 9/11 is a punishment inflicted on the United States by Allah ("Allah took out his sword"), that the events have triggered a clash of civilizations, and that Jewish people are responsible for the attacks.[11] As the *New York Times* article reports: "Newspapers in Karachi have promised yet more 'Death to America,' and warned that the attacks in New York and Washington were a trick by the Jews to plunge the United States and Islam into war."[12]

Editorials
While the news contains a variety of conflicting IEs, editorials present a more coherent framing of both issues. Despite this, rather than critical comments on the current political situation, possibly from a consistent angle, editorial articles often limit themselves to summarizing the news. The article "The Battle for Mazar-i-Sharif" on November 10 is an example of a piece that reproduces the official framing of the situation in Afghanistan: "[T]he first important military victory of the war against terrorism," "a psychological and political boost to the American-led campaign to drive the Taliban from power and bring Osama bin Laden to justice." The article simply describes the country at war as it emerges from the rest of the coverage without proposing an alternative view of the situation.[13]

The contents of the editorials can be located well within the sphere of debate among the political elites under several respects. They generally tend to reproduce the administration's framing of the events. The articles tend to either support—and sometimes quite enthusiastically—the president's framing of the events or mildly criticize it without offering a different interpretation. Here are a few examples of the main trends. An excerpt from the article "Mr Bush's New Gravitas" (October 12) expresses strong support for the president at the same time as reproducing his treatment recommendation for the issue of Afghanistan:

> Using a mixture of straight talk, statesmanship and a touch of humor here and there, Mr. Bush clarified and sharpened his positions on several important issues. It was heartening to hear him say the United States and its allies will not walk away from Afghanistan once Osama bin Laden and his followers are captured or killed. His inclination to seek the assistance of the United Nations in establishing a new government in Kabul if the Taliban is ousted was wise. And his reaffirmation of the need for humanitarian aid to the people of Afghanistan—including donations from American children—seemed heartfelt. Mr. Bush may

have scrambled his stern message slightly when he offered to reconsider the military assault on Afghanistan if the Taliban leadership surrenders Mr. bin Laden, but the gesture is likely to reassure other Muslim nations that Washington is not bloody-minded.[14]

As an instance of "cosmetic criticism" the editorial "Wartime Rhetoric" on October 19 challenges the comment made by Bush about Osama bin Laden being wanted "dead or alive." The article questions the way the president expresses himself, not the decision to capture or kill the suspected terrorist through a war in Afghanistan:

> The hotter the rhetoric now, the harder President Bush will find it later if his better judgment winds up telling him to delay action, or to concentrate for a while on diplomatic and economic sanctions rather than military force. Keeping an even tone under current conditions will be difficult, but one of Mr. Bush's greatest talents as a politician is his ability to maintain a consistent message, even under extreme provocation. The country needs him to do that now.[15]

A case of more substantial policy criticism, which paradoxically reinforces the idea contained in the political statements that there is an imminent terrorist threat on the country, is the editorial published on October 22. The article comments about the meeting between President Bush and President Putin at the APEC Summit in Shanghai:

> The two sides [the United States and Russia] need to keep working on a package deal that would include offensive nuclear weapons cuts, changes in the 1972 Antiballistic Missile Treaty and more cordial ties between NATO and Russia. Washington should be more realistic about a missile shield. The Pentagon remains far from having perfected a workable defensive system and the most immediate threat to the nation comes from terrorists, not nations with intercontinental ballistic missiles.[16]

This example is particularly interesting considering that the *Wall Street Journal*'s editorial board uses the same reason—the existence of a terrorist threat to the United States—to support rather than oppose the idea of a missile shield. This suggests that even agreement with the administration's policy on some aspects of an issue (the United States is threatened by terrorists) does not automatically lead to reproducing the whole governmental framing on the matter (we need a missile shield).

Editorial articles throughout the period under analysis never really contain alternative interpretations of the issues to those of the administration. An article on September 27 recommends President Bush to be careful in relation to the issue of nation building in Afghanistan, but it does not even attempt to assess whether the latter is at all necessary or desirable. The concluding paragraph reads:

> In the presidential campaign last year, and again this week, Mr. Bush warned against the arrogance of outsiders engaging in "nation-building" in the developing world. While pondering his next move in the fight against terrorism, he should factor that caution into the military and political strategy for dealing with Afghanistan.[17]

The Contrast between News and Editorials: The Issue of Afghanistan
The framing of the intervention in Afghanistan shows that, although the newspaper tends to be openly supportive of the administration's framing in the editorials, first-page news contains a number of IEs that are incompatible with official messages. These incompatible IEs are sometimes more prominent than the contents of governmental statements. By "prominent" I mean they are given more space in the coverage or they are not balanced by the administration's perspectives. An illustration is provided by the statements made by foreign sources on October 8, first day of coverage of the war in Afghanistan. Foreign sources convey the ideas that the strikes are directed against Afghani towns and that the military intervention, apart from violating international law, is also a war against Islam. These views are indeed very far from the U.S. government's framing of Operation Enduring Freedom.

Several voices can be identified within the coverage. One is that of Dr. Abdullah, the Northern Alliance's designated foreign minister: "In a broad and confident statement, Dr. Abdullah said that [the] bombing was 'imminent' and went on to list which cities would be major targets in the attack"; "Dr. Abdullah also said that alliance forces would carry out initial attacks on Mazar-i-Sharif this evening. Within days other alliance forces will attack the city from the East from bases near the village of Khwaja Bahaouddin, he added."[18]
Another source is President Saddam Hussein:

> In Iraq, President Saddam Hussein called an emergency meeting of his inner cabinet, and a communique issued afterward said, "True believers cannot but condemn this act, not because it has been committed by America against a Muslim people but because it is an aggression perpetrated outside international law."[19]

Osama bin Laden's quotes from a tape broadcast by Al-Jazeera are also reported at length:

> Within hours of the first American bombs' dropping on Afghanistan, the world's most wanted man, Osama bin Laden, appeared in a videotape broadcast worldwide in which he taunted the United States and celebrated the Sept. 11 [sic] terrorist attacks.... "Here is America struck by Almighty God in one of its vital organs, so that its greatest buildings are destroyed," Mr. bin Laden said, referring to the attacks in which hijacked airliners rammed into the World Trade Center and the Pentagon, killing several thousand people. "Grace and gratitude to God".... "America has been filled with horror from North to South and East to West, and thanks be to God. What America is tasting now is only a copy of what we have tasted. Our Islamic nation has been tasting the same for more than 80 years, of humiliation and disgrace, its sons killed and their blood spilled, its sanctities desecrated." The reference to 80 years appeared to be invoking the Western colonization of Arab lands. The entire broadcast was infused with calls based on the argument that Islam has long been humiliated. "These events have split the whole world into two camps," he said. "The camp of belief and the camp of disbelief."[20]

Ayman al-Zawahiri, one of bin Laden's aides, also speaking on the tape, is quoted saying: "America is the head of criminals by creating this Israel, this continuous crime for 50 years. The Muslim nation shall not accept this crime."[21]

These examples, by showing the distance between editorial opinion and first-page contents, constitute evidence against the possibility that editorial policy translates into a tight control of first-page news.

The Wall Street Journal

In the *Wall Street Journal* there is less coverage of the 9/11 events and the war in Afghanistan than in the *New York Times*. The analysis suggests that this is related to two reasons. The first is the newspaper's long-established focus on business and finance rather than domestic and foreign policy.[22] Many of the purely business-oriented articles do not even mention 9/11: mergers, companies' earnings and losses seem to occur in a completely different world than the one described by the *New York Times*. On October 23, for example, right in the heat of the military operations in Afghanistan, when one would expect coverage to be at its peak, there is no relevant first-page article to be included in the sample for the study. The second reason is that the coverage presents a very consistent stance on the events. The fact that this involves mainly the editorials but also extends to first-page news articles suggests a stricter editorial control than in the *New York Times*. First-page news contains, in fact, a narrower range of opinions than can be observed in the *New York Times*. This finding is explained by the *Wall Street Journal*'s explicit commitment not only to inform readers, but also "to trying to make sense of the news."[23] The *Wall Street Journal*'s editorials, in fact, advocate a tradition of consistent "philosophy." As former editor William Grimes put it in 1951:

> On our editorial page we make no pretence of walking down the middle of the road. Or comments and interpretations are made from a definite point of view. We believe in the individual, in his [*sic*] wisdom and his decency. We oppose all infringement on individual rights, whether they stem from attempts at private monopoly, or from an overgrowing government. People will say we are conservative or even reactionary. We are not much interested in labels but if we were to choose one, we would say we are radical.[24]

I am going to address these aspects by describing first the individual biases of journalists in first-page news. I will then address the editorials, showing that the editorial line is more radical and coherent than in the *New York Times*. Then I will turn to the consistency between news and editorials and to explaining how voices that express dissonant opinions in relation to the editorial framing are marginalized within the first-page coverage.

Comments within First-Page News: Individual Biases
Whereas the *New York Times*'s journalists never directly express an opinion and the purpose of first-page articles appears to be purely informing the reader about the raw facts and "who said what," the *Wall Street Journal*'s articles contain more comment. An example is offered by what reporters David Cloug and Neil King write the day after the attacks:

> By successfully attacking the most prominent symbols of American power—Wall Street and the Pentagon—terrorists have wiped out any remaining illusions that America is safe from mass organized violence.
> That realization alone will alter the way the U.S. approaches its role in the world, as well as the way Americans travel and do business at home and abroad.[25]

Later in the same article the two journalists argue:

> The events occurred without any apparent warning, prompting imme-
> diate questions in Washington and elsewhere about a failure of U.S.
> intelligence. How did such a broad and coordinated attack on multiple
> sites occur without U.S. intelligence officials getting wind of it? How
> were so many commercial airplanes hijacked and diverted hundreds of
> miles out of their flight paths toward the nation's largest population
> centers? "Today our government failed the American people," said
> Rep. Curt Weldon, a Pennsylvania Republican.[26]

It is interesting to notice that the quote by the Republican representative appears to be *used* by the journalists to support their point, rather
than being merely reported.

A similar active use of sources' statements to frame the issue of
9/11 can be observed in another article. The claim by the reporters is this time: "Yesterday's terrorism darkened, marked and forever
altered the way Americans live their lives."[27] Again the statement is
followed by quotes emphasizing the point:

> Fear of terrorism is likely to lead Americans to tolerate more gov-
> ernment surveillance—such as overhead video cameras at sporting
> events—than they have to date. "It's very likely in the wake of today's
> events that we're going to see a greater acceptance on the public's
> part—and on the court's part—to approve certain kinds of police tac-
> tics," said William Stuntz, a Harvard Law School professor.[28]

A Firm Editorial Line

Contrary to the *New York Times*, in which editorials tend rather
passively to reproduce the administration's framing, in the *Wall
Street Journal* it is possible to observe the building of a consistent
line over the interpretations of the 9/11 events and the intervention
in Afghanistan throughout the time period under study. Editorials
make very clear points and often suggest IEs that are not present in
the governmental framing of the events. This confirms the editorial
commitment to a tradition of "vigorous and independent editorial
commentary."[29]

A more sophisticated interpretation of the causes of terrorism than
the one offered by the administration (terrorists are "flat evil") is illustrated in the editorial "A Terrorist Pearl Harbor" on September 12:

> Just as Munich led to World War II, so attempts to buy peace in the
> Middle East are surely behind this attack.... The immediate focus of

the terrorist drive is of course Israel. But as yesterday's events again show, Israel serves as a proxy for much deeper grievances against the United States and the civilization it represents. An undercurrent (or more) of resentment at the Western civilization runs through the chanceries and bazaars of the Arab world, as well as a fear of what democracy might mean for the power of local rulers.

We were glad to see that some Arab leaders denounced the attacks yesterday. Egypt's Hosni Mubarak called it "horrible and unimaginable." Even Yasser Arafat sent his condolences. But these leaders need to understand that their societies carefully nurture and inculcate resentments and hatreds against America and the non-Arab world. [30]

This view is confirmed by references on October 9 to the fact that the war on terrorism (WOT) "can't end with killing bin Laden," but must also involve peace in the Middle East.[31]

The editors clearly support the military action in Afghanistan: they agree on the fact that the terrorists have started a war and that "we" need to fight it "all the way to victory."[32] Since very early after the events the editors are not only in favor of attacking Afghanistan and toppling the Taliban regime, but also extending the military action to Saddam Hussein: "Mark us down for supporting a major military strike, not just in Afghanistan in pursuit of Osama bin Laden, but if need be against terrorist enclaves in a host of countries"; "[D]eposing Saddam has to be considered another war aim."[33] This line is kept throughout the time span of the analysis. On November 14, after the fall of Kabul, the editors further confirm it by writing that "the war moves into its next logical phase, especially into Iraq."[34]

An idea consistently present in the coverage, which challenges the administration's framing of 9/11, is the notion that the events were caused by a failure of intelligence. On September 18 the editors write that "the 'intelligence failure' so horribly on display last week is the result of political and legal attacks on our spymakers going back to the 1970s witchhunts of the Church committee."[35] On October 24 there are more references to the way the administration "clearly failed to deal with the terrorist risk."[36] More examples of new IEs introduced by the *Wall Street Journal* into the framing of the events, particularly into the category of "treatment recommendation" for the issue, are the need to have a missile shield in order to deal effectively with the threat of terrorism and the support for freedoms' restrictions.[37]

A bold stance that contributes to further distance the coverage from mainstream political discourse is taken in supporting Italian PM Berlusconi's statement about the "superiority" of Western civilization to Islamic culture:

> The Italian's point about relative levels of prosperity and religious tolerance is clearly true.... So give Mr. Berlusconi a break. The terrorists of September 11 were in part motivated by hatred of Western "civilization," including the freedom, tolerance and even secularism that that implies. The starting point in defending that civilization is believing in it.[38]

Consistency between News and Editorials

The editorial line appears to weigh more on first-page news than it is the case in the *New York Times*. This is confirmed by the reiteration on first-page coverage of ideas appearing in editorials, such as the notion of 9/11 being caused by a security failure or the need to wage a military WOT. For example, a first-page article on October 1, "In the War of Words, a Palestinian Professor Tests the Limits of Liberty," illustrates the debate between the need to restrict civic liberties and defend them. While the article does not take an explicit position, as a whole it suggests that it is better to restrict them, confirming the point made elsewhere in the editorials ("Taking Liberties," September 25, 2001).

The consistency between the news and the editorial line is also the result of a stricter selection of sources quoted in first-page articles. Their range is much more limited than in the *New York Times* as it does not extend to as many foreign voices (compare figures 5.1 and 5.2). They also appear to be selected to fit the editorial framing of the issues under analysis, as this excerpt shows: "Retaliation is another logical response. Indeed, President Bush promised as much. In an example of the country's mood, a scrawled sign outside a blood bank in New York ordered, 'Mr. Bush, bomb the bastards now.'"[39]

When dissenting voices are present in the coverage they are given less space and are placed less prominently. Some examples are provided by articles published in the immediate aftermath of the beginning of the war, when international reactions and alternative interpretations to the administration's framing by foreign actors are at their height. On a long article on October 8 critical statements by Osama bin Laden are shortly paraphrased: "[H]e didn't take responsibility for the Sept. 11 attacks"; "US attacks, he [Osama bin Laden] declared, are dividing the world into two camps, those in the Islamic world and those outside it." A very short mention is made of the Talibans' reactions: "Taliban officials called the U.S. response a terrorist attack and said the U.S wouldn't achieve its goals. Taliban Deputy Defense Minister

Mullah Noor Ali said Afghan people 'will never accept the rule of infidels.'" Additional critical quotes by Pakistani religious leaders ("a brutal attack on innocent people"), and the Afghan Defense Council (calling the strike "the aggression of America") are left to the very end of the story. This stands in sharp contrast to lengthy quotes by Bush, a number of defense officials, Defense Secretary Rumsfeld, as well as supportive comments by the journalists writing the piece ("Certainly Americans are braced for retaliation").[40]

A similar structure can be observed on another lengthy piece on October 9.[41] The space given to the Taliban's framing of the intervention amounts to the following excerpt, which also contains a rebuttal by U.S. defense officials: "The Taliban's ambassador to Pakistan said 20 civilians were killed in the strikes on the capital. But a Pentagon spokesman said it was too early to know about civilian casualties." Again quotes framing the military intervention in positive terms from several U.S. officials, the White House, President Bush, the Northern Alliance, EU allies, President Putin, even China ("[e]ven the Chinese government, a staunch foe of previous American-led military campaigns, offered a terse and tentative endorsement to the air raids") stand in sharp contrast to very few lines devoted to "less supportive" voices. Malaysia and Indonesia (angry demonstrators in Indonesia chanted "Jihad! Jihad! America is the great Satan!"), as well as Sudan (the Sudanese government declared, "[W]e reject this war on Afghanistan because it cannot be an effective means for fighting violence"), are placed at the end of the article.

FRANCE

French news is expected to contain more comment than American newspapers. Daniel Hallin and Paolo Mancini, comparing coverage by the *New York Times, Le Monde,* and *Le Figaro,* found that the French press "clearly put more emphasis on background, interpretation and opinion" and "it was more likely to involve policy advocacy or value judgments about political actions" than the American press.[42] The authors place French journalism between a Polarized Pluralist Model, characterized by political partisanship and commentary-oriented journalism—where Italy is expected to be, even more closely fitting its characteristics—and a Democratic Corporatist Model. The latter mainly characterizes Northern Europe, but stretches south to include Austria and Switzerland, and although having historically developed a strong political press, has more recently moved toward a neutral commercial journalism.[43] Both the Polarized Pluralist Model and the

Democratic Corporatist Model are different from the North Atlantic or Liberal Model, a third alternative that characterizes countries such as the United States, Britain, and Canada.[44] This last model, also referred to as Anglo-Saxon journalism, as seen with the *New York Times* and the *Wall Street Journal*, is based on a tradition of a fact-centered reporting and a stricter observance of the objectivity norm. It is characterized by a professionalization of journalism and an institutional separation between journalism and political parties, which have developed since the nineteenth century.[45]

Despite the expectation of a common mixture between facts and comment within first-page news, the analysis suggests that the way *Le Monde* and *Libération* covered the issues under study differed markedly. *Le Monde* confirms being a "newspaper of reference" rather than a "newspaper of record."[46] Jean-Marie Colombani, director of *Le Monde*, explains what the distinction means with the following words: "To say that we are a paper of reference is to say that we are not a neutral encyclopaedic mirror of events"; "[W]e are an engaged paper, engaged in the issues of the time. Our promise to the readers is that our engagement will be honest and intelligent and fair to the other side of the engagement, and that the great debates of France will be taken up in our pages."[47]

Libération, instead, is more clearly a newspaper of record. As Serge July, founder of the newspaper, put it in an interview: *Libération* is a newspaper for "information, pictures, emotions and analyses."[48] The framing of 9/11 and the war in Afghanistan on *Libération* also appears to be limited due to the newspaper's focus on national rather than international events. The opinion daily was, in fact, founded in 1973 in the wake of the protest movements following May 1968. Its purpose, as July continues in the same interview, was covering social and cultural movements' issues: they were regarded by the press of the time as "too much of a hot potato," therefore "deemed of secondary importance in the press system of the day." *Libération*'s aim was, in that context, "combining counter-culture with a radical political approach."[49]

Such difference in editorial policies is reflected in the focus of the coverage: for example, when, on October 31, *Le Monde*'s main story is "*La conduite de la guerre alarme l'Europe* (The conduct of war alarms Europe)" in *Libération* not only there is no mention of the topic, but the main title is "*Un kimono pour Renault* (A kimono for Renault)," about Nissan acquiring 15 percent of Renault. The war in Afghanistan is addressed in *Libération* more marginally than in *Le Monde*. Even at critical moments, such as the fall of Kabul, when in

Le Monde it is possible to identify a variety of different interpretations of the event by different actors, in *Libération* the range of voices is quite limited. This trend is made more extreme by *Libération*'s "*événement* formula in which a single event or trend occupies the cover and the first inside four to five pages."[50]

The differences in the ways journalism is practiced in *Libération* and *Le Monde* therefore highlights the significance of editorial policy in affecting coverage, even when the same national journalistic culture is shared. Another variable that was found significant in shaping the coverage of both newspapers, particularly editorials, was national political culture, while there was no evidence, in either outlet, that editorial policy materializes into strict editorial control on first-page news.

Libération

Libération's first-page news covers relatively more politics than *Le Monde*. The greater coverage of political issues is explained by editorial policy, particularly by the domestic focus of the newspaper's agenda and is confirmed, by contrast, by the limited attention to the issue of Afghanistan. French coverage of political reactions, however, is extremely limited if compared with reporting in the United States or Pakistan, and this is due to the presence of comment within coverage taking up space that would be attributed, in objective journalism, to political actors' quotes. As far as editorials are concerned, the analysis highlights two main aspects. First, editors raise themes that echo the contents of political authorities' statements without explicitly referring to them. The analysis of such references suggests that specific interpretations could be contained within already existing systems of meanings, particularly within the country's political culture. Second, there is no clear or single editorial line on the events: this is due to the fact that several authors contribute to the editorials. They focus on different issues over the period, depending on what is suggested by circumstances and developments at the international level. Authors themselves also develop their opinions over time. This makes a strict editorial control of first-page news unlikely. These aspects will now be analyzed in more detail.

Editorial Policy: Focus on the Domestic Dimension
The focus of interest of *Libération* is the French domestic and social dimension. This leads to a relatively greater coverage, although still limited in comparison with the American and Pakistani cases, of

domestic politics. Examples of coverage of national politicians' reactions in relation to 9/11 and the war in Afghanistan are offered, respectively, by two articles. The first, published on September 20, reports about President Chirac's visit to the United States, his meeting with President Bush, his pledge to fight terrorism with "determination without reserve" against the "absolute evil which is terrorism," as well as his doubts about whether the word "war" should be used to characterize the current situation.[51] The second, on October 4, reports about the French "action plan for Afghanistan," the speech by PM Jospin at the National Assembly, and the divergent points of view expressed by different political forces in the debate.[52] The article is accompanied by a selection of quotes from a spectrum of politicians ranging from the extreme left to the extreme right. The piece, "*Des partis divisés à la tribune* (A gallery of divided parties)," is reported here in its entirety to show the range of political positions:

> Robert Hue (PCF) [French Communist Party, left]: "I plead for the supremacy of international negotiation and politics over the strategy of using brutal force, over the spirit of vengeance."

> Valéry Giscard d'Estaing (UDF) [Union for French Democracy, right]: "There would be a thorny contradiction between the affirmation of a global policy focusing on eliminating terror and violence in the world, and the resigned acceptance of the continuation of violence in the Middle East."

> Jean-Marc Ayrault (PS) [Socialist Party, left]: "We have not entered a latent Third World War, as some reckless people have announced. This ordeal [9/11 events] is not all of a sudden going to re-draw the map of the world."

> Edouard Balladur (RPR) [Rally for the Republic, right]: "The necessity of supporting growth and consumes makes it essential to enlarge the role of the State. [But] Let's avoid making it a permanent doctrine and let's act with pragmatism."

> Jean-Pierre Chevènement (MDC) [Citizens' Movement, left]: "The best contribution France can make [to the current situation] is protecting its relationship with the countries of the Maghreb and the Middle-East in order to facilitate, when the time will come, the necessary mediations."

> Jean-François Mattéi (DL) [Liberal Democracy, right]: "We cannot tolerate any longer that weapons of war like rocket-launchers circulate freely within our country. We cannot tolerate any longer the areas of lawlessness [*non-droit*]. How can we expect exemplarity at the international level when, at home, the feeling of impunity prevails?"

> Philippe de Villiers (MPF) [Movement for France, right]: "What we are dealing with is a clash of civilizations through this new suicidal millenarism."[53]

It should be noted that the article represents the most detailed reporting of political actors' statements within the 64 days of French media coverage analyzed within the study.

The interest in the domestic dimension has also an effect on the scope of the coverage of the intervention in Afghanistan. The issue of the political scenario in Afghanistan is addressed almost exclusively in three editorials: on November 12, 13, and 14, just before and after the fall of Kabul on November 13. The issue is addressed comparatively later than in *Le Monde* and does not cover in detail the debate over the postwar political settlement.

Common Themes and Already Existing Systems of Meaning
The analysis identifies common themes within the editorials, which remind of the contents of the political statements. Since the editors are not referring to statements made by political actors, it appears that the ideas they express are part of a broader and shared system of meanings. The observation confirms the significance of French political culture in shaping the news. I will illustrate these aspects through some examples.

A first shared idea with the governmental discourse is the recurrent notion within the editorials of the need to counter terrorism through a broader approach than a military operation. The point is confirmed by the analysis of a series of editorials. The first, on September 13, is by Serge July.[54] According to the author, the 9/11 events are a "declaration of war," but "the best defense against terrorism is not war, it's justice." Within this perspective he develops the recommendation for the United States to end its isolationism policy and engage with international conflicts, particularly the one in the Middle East. Again July, in the issue published on September 15–16, writes that what is needed is a "military response, but also and above all a political response"; "The American superpower should eventually accept its responsibilities at the global level and get engaged with the problems of the world, in the name of justice, treaties and multilateralism."[55] In a piece on September 19, Gérard Dupuy argues that the Cold War had been won on the front of public opinion, and that this applies also to the current crisis. A response to the post-9/11 crisis will be most effective if the United States will be able to explain its reasons and understand the origins of Islamic extremism.

Editorial contents are also characterized by references to an already existing political agenda, particularly to the harmonization of judicial and police procedures at the EU level. Jacques Amalric on September 20 writes that improving security against the terrorist threat in the

United States—where "even identity cards are regarded as a total-itarian syndrome"—will create a cultural "revolution." In Europe, instead, there should be less debate as both the harmonization of judicial procedures and the Europeanization of justice and police (*européanisation judiciaro-policière*) have been on the agenda for a long time.[56] Gérard Dupuy also points out on November 1 that "the coordination of the European justice systems and the simplification of the expulsion procedures" would actually have existed "with or without terrorists."[57]

The attempt by Osama bin Laden at triggering a religious war is looked at with disdain. The terrorist leader is defined several times, and not always by the same author, as a *fou d'Allah* (Allah-mad).[58] The editors appear to share the same sense of rejection toward the notion of a clash of civilizations that emerged from the analysis of the French authorities' statements.

No Single Editorial Line: Unlikely Editorial Control
Since editors comment on different topics, it is not possible to iden-tify a single editorial line. July, as seen in his references to using justice against terrorism rather than war, focuses mainly on the ideo-logical aspects of the fight against terrorism. Dupuy concentrates on the interpretation of the fight against terrorism as a new kind of war. In the issue dated October 6–7, for example, he writes that pro-viding aid to civilians in Afghanistan is not contradictory with the military action. This is part of a new war in which the enemy targets civilians:

> [Terrorist attacks] are [. . .] one of the factors in the equation of the coming "war." This vulnerability of civilians, this time Western, is the least novelty in this decidedly different conflict. Not only food aid is, for the first time, overlapping with the military strategy, but the latter is against an elusive enemy who does not hesitate in using civilians as its first target.[59]

Dupuy also develops an interpretation of the international coali-tion against terrorism as a "realpolitik game." Toward the end of October he stresses the role of national interests within the alli-ance. In the issue of October 20–21 he argues that "war is a reality check" (*La guerre est une épreuve de réalité*), a "merciless evalua-tion test" (*un test d'évaluation impitoyable*) in which a country's real objectives clearly emerge. As the author eloquently puts it in the following excerpt, Afghanistan is too far from Europe to be relevant to European interests:

> The Gand summit [where the UK, France, and Germany have gathered to discuss their contributions to the U.S.-led operation in Afghanistan] with its hesitations and dissents, makes it clear why the Americans, after having requested support from NATO, have chosen, as a start, to go it alone with their close British allies [alliés de cœur]. They [the United States] do not thus have to be accountable to these many currents of European public opinions which, only just when the operations were beginning, had found that they had already lasted too long. In organizing their own summit, English, Germans and French appear to meet the assessment about America of their European colleagues. This [self-] attributed superiority will leave some bitterness within the Union. The lost bombs [les bombes perdues] of the Afghan mountains strike really very far.[60]

Editors also develop their opinions over time: an initial ambivalence toward the military operations turns into stronger opposition in the case of Dupuy and Amalric. Patrick Sabatier is, instead, more supportive of the military operations. I am going to illustrate these points with examples from the coverage.

It is not clear what Dupuy's position on the war in Afghanistan is on October 11: eradicating terrorism requires diplomacy, but a success in Afghanistan "would be a better omen. One more reason for trying to achieve it."[61] On October 30, however, his opinion becomes more critical of the conflict. He writes that "it is difficult to understand what the Americans precisely want"; what to do on the political front "remains a mystery."[62]

Amalric, instead, starts from being mildly critical of the war against terrorism. His main idea on September 22–23 is that capturing Osama bin Laden will not help in eradicating terrorism. The conflict will be long ("it could last, we are being told, between five and ten years"); "to suffocate" the Talibans "will be the easiest part of the adventure."[63] On September 25 he continues writing that freezing the terrorists' funds (financial WOT) is a useful measure, but "these Allah-mads [ces fous d'Allah] are extremely frugal and are encouraged by their mentors to finance themselves through little jobs and thefts."[64] He later turns more critical. Nobody will cry for the Talibans ("[n]obody, definitely not the Afghani people, will cry for the reversal of an obscurantist, corrupt, totalitarian and suicidal clique, which dreams about exporting its practices"), but even if the EU leaders are saying that "we" should help the poor people of Afghanistan "to live and to be finally free," "we should not add more suffering to the suffering of the survivors

and the families of the victims of 9/11" (September 27).[65] Some ambivalence in the author's opinion particularly emerges on October 8:
he says that it was clear since 9/11 that the United States would use
force. The response "to murderous folly cannot be, and mustn't be
vengeance." On the other hand, it would be "unrealistic to exclude *a
priori* the use of force against a tentacular organization which does not
rely but on violence." War is therefore "acceptable," but a "devastated"
country such as Afghanistan does not have "thousands of targets." A
prolonged bombing will only harm the civilians.[66] He finally turns
more firmly against the war on October 23: the death of civilians
is damaging the "bizarre coalition" (*la coalition heteroclite*). Civilians
who have nothing to do with international terrorism are dying: "[N]
obody really believes that it is through the bombings that bin Laden
and his men will be stopped from causing more harm and that an end
will be put to the obscurantist regime of the Talibans."[67]

Sabatier is overall more supportive of the military action, as a piece
on November 7 suggests:

> Bringing in the ground troops is the only way for the US to eliminate
> the arguments by those who, forgetting a bit too quickly 9/11, ask
> for a stop to the bombing. And to prove that they [the United States]
> are determined to win the war which has been declared against them,
> rather than getting a blind revenge. This will require time. Perhaps
> more than it took for winning against Saddam Hussein or Slobodan
> Milosevic.[68]

The lack of a clear editorial line both explains the absence of a strict
editorial control on first-page news and makes it less likely for it to
materialize.

Le Monde

The editorial on the first page of *Le Monde* was removed by Colombani
and his executive director, Edwy Plenel, soon after they took office
in 1994.[69] The critics of the practice had claimed that this "enabled
them to make the entire front page into a commentary on the day's
news."[70] The analysis confirms that, even if the editorial has been
technically removed, comment still constitutes a substantial portion
of first-page news contents: intellectuals—not just French, but also
international—contribute to framing the issues under analysis far
more than national politicians. The opening to a variety of sources,
which includes also references to foreign media, leads the coverage

to presenting a variety of ideas. The presence of comment on first-page news, the absence of political actors within the coverage, the international focus of reporting, and the way the latter contributes to introducing new ideas into the coverage will be examined in turn.

The illustration of these aspects will be followed by the analysis of editorial articles. The editorials, similar to what can be observed in the pages of *Libération*, reveal the existence of a shared system of meanings between the editorial board and the national political actors. Despite such coherent themes developing over the post-9/11 period within the coverage, there is no consistent editorial line on framing the issues of September 11 and Afghanistan, as particularly the changing editorial stance in relation to the conflict in Afghanistan proves. The fact that editorial policy does not translate into a tight control of first-page contents is confirmed by the framing dissonance, sometimes extreme, between first-page news and editorials.

Comment Articles: Increasing the Scope of First-Page Coverage

The most important feature of comment articles is that they allow coherent and alternative interpretations of the issues under study to be developed within first-page coverage. A first illustration of the very different and sophisticated ways in which a range of sources framed the aftermath of 9/11 is offered by an article written by Kofi Annan, secretary-general of the UN, on September 23–24. He explains in detail the way terrorism should be fought through UN institutions. As he writes, to triumph on the "common enemies"

> all nations should join their forces and conduct together an action that should extend to all aspects of the free and open global system so perversely exploited by those who have committed the atrocities of 11 September.
>
> The UN could not be better placed to support such action. It constitutes the essential framework for building a global coalition. It is able to provide the long term fight against terrorism with the necessary legitimacy at the international level. Furthermore, the conventions of the UN already offer a judicial framework for a number of measures to be taken in order to eradicate terrorism, including extradition, the judicial prosecution of criminals, as well as the repression of money laundering.[71]

Robert Malley, a former national security advisor to President Clinton and researcher at the Council of Foreign Relations, explains in a lengthy article on October 30 the causes of terrorism. He argues that the suggestion by Arab countries, Europe, and a handful of American intellectuals that the responsibility for the attacks belongs to American foreign policy in the Middle East is insufficient. He rather identifies the reasons of anti-Americanism and religious extremism in the lack of democracy in the Arab world:

> The absence of democracy and the repression of dissidence, together with economic imbalances, corruption, inequalities, uncontrolled urbanization, the collapse of nationalist ideologies of independence, all of this constitutes the ground of radical movements, whose most dangerous expression is religious extremism. Where, then, practicing politics in a regime that forbids it, if not in the mosque (a place that cannot be violated) and in the language of the Koran (a sacred language)? Anger has quickly arisen against the West and, particularly, the US since the American culture and goods which the local elite enjoy become a synonym of social injustice, which becomes [in turn] synonym of atheistic materialism; and since from Iraq to Iran to Palestine the American policy is felt as being intrinsically hostile to Islam and the Arab world.[72]

A totally different interpretation is presented by the French philosopher Jean Baudrillard, who, introducing original IEs into the coverage, explains that "this [9/11] is a clash neither of civilizations nor of religions"; this is "the triumphing globalization coming to terms with itself," or in other words, "the world itself that resists globalization." What the public is experiencing is a "fourth World War":

> It is really possible to talk about a World War, not a third one, but a fourth and the only one really involving the whole world, since it has as its stake globalization itself. The first two world wars reflected the classical image of war. The first put an end to the supremacy of Europe and the colonial era. The second put an end to Nazism. The third, which did happen, under the shape of a Cold War and persuasion has ended Communism. From one to the other, each time we have progressed further towards a single global order. Today the latter, virtually having reached its limit, finds itself coming to terms with the antagonist forces spread at the heart of the global, in all the current convulsions. A fractal war of all the cells [*guerre fractale de toutes les cellules*], of all the singularities which are revolting themselves under the shape of anti-bodies. A confrontation so elusive that it requires, from time to time, saving the idea of war through some spectacular staging [*mises en scène*], such as that of the Gulf war or, nowadays, that of Afghanistan. But the fourth world war is elsewhere. It is what haunts any world order, any hegemonic domination—if Islam was

dominating the world, terrorism would rise against Islam. Because it is the world itself which is resisting globalization.[73]

Baudrillard famously argued that "the Gulf War did not take place." Here the philosopher similarly develops the idea that the 9/11 terrorist violence is not real and "in a way it is worse: it is symbolic."

The article triggers a response by another French academic, Alain Minc.[74] He criticizes Baudrillard for being a "philosopher of the terrorist model." He rejects Baudrillard's interpretation ("beyond its playful dimension, his posture is pitiful"), particularly his view of the world in which "nothing is worth anything; the individual rights are an illusion; terrorist violence is the corollary to institutional totalitarianism." Instead, Minc argues, we should be acknowledging the "absolute superiority of democracy" (which is "not a unique preserve of the West") and the "right" of democracies to defend themselves.

What these examples point to is the wealth of IEs that comment articles introduce into first-page news, in contrast to more "objective" news stories.

The Absence of Political Actors

The focus of interest by *Le Monde* on comment rather than factual reporting leads to the near absence of quotes by French political actors within first-page coverage. Some main stories are devoted to national politics, but they are not related to the issues being analyzed. Two examples are leading articles on October 11, "*Chirac, président protégé, justiciable demain* (Chirac, protected president, who could be executed tomorrow)" about the debate surrounding the right of the president to judicial immunity, and October 17, "*Crise ouverte dans la cohabitation* (Open crisis in the cohabitation [difficult balance between a president and a prime minister of a different political orientation])."

On September 13, the very first day of coverage of the 9/11 events, there is virtually no first-page coverage of the reactions by French politicians. The only authority mentioned within sample is PM Jospin who expresses—the following words sum up his framing of the 9/11 issue—his "horrified sadness in front of monstrous attacks" (*tristesse horrifiée devant des attentats monstrueux*).[75] President Chirac is present in the coverage for the first time on September 20. An article reporting about his meeting with President Bush describes his support for a possible "military cooperation" and his doubts about the use of the word "war" (*je ne sais pas s'il faut parler de guerre)*.[76] Jospin is mentioned again on September 26. The coverage of two interviews the PM had with TV channels TF1 and France2 consist in the expression of a single IE in relation to the issue of 9/11: solidarity with the United States (*solidarité totale à l'égard des Etats-Unis*).[77]

References to International Media and New Ideas in the News

On September 13, in contrast to almost no framing by political actors, there is a reference to a number of reports by international media organizations. The first page contains an introduction to a review of the international press. This includes long quotes from American newspapers' editorials, but also excerpts of articles published in the Arab world. A *New York Times* editorial is reported arguing that "the best defense against terrorism is good, timely intelligence.... A concerted national effort to remake the nation's defenses must begin immediately."[78] At the same time the newspaper *Ha'aretz* from Tel-Aviv is quoted supporting the idea that "a new countdown has started yesterday, a sort of Third World War against terror."[79]

From September 18, for one week, *Le Monde* also reprints one whole page of the *New York Times* edition per day.[80] The presence of contents from a different newspaper brings new IEs into the coverage. On September 18 the page of the *New York Times* contains IEs from the administration's political statements, such as the notions of a very long struggle against terrorist organizations, but also against their state supporters, particularly in a news analysis article by Michael Gordon, "Identifying the Enemies under New Rules of War."[81]

The reporting of sources from a wider variety of countries than in the United States, or as it will be seen later, than in Italy, reveals a greater French interest in international developments. This mirrors the French political authorities' references—and actual contacts in the form of meetings with foreign diplomats—to the Arab world, the United States, European countries, and Pakistan. The contrast with the nationally focused coverage of *Libération*, however, highlights that also the different agenda of each newspaper—this time the focus on international rather than local politics—affects the shape of the coverage.

Variety of Sources and Diversity of Views within the Coverage

The focus on a wide range of international sources and the interest in their comment, combined together, produce an extremely rich picture of the issues under analysis in terms of the number of ideas present within the coverage. A very good example of the variety of interpretations present in first-page news is offered by coverage on September 19. Apart from the third upper part of the first-page cover reporting the day's news, *Enquête sur Ben Laden, la cible des Etats-Unis* (Investigation bin Laden, the target of the United States), most of the page is taken by comment articles. The first contribution to the framing of 9/11 is that of the U.S. intellectual Francis Fukuyama. He writes that

> the changes following the 11 September attacks will not make America, in my opinion, a more repressive, intolerant, xenophobic country or a country more fragmented and isolationist. On the contrary, there are reasons to believe that this tragedy could, in reality, make the American society stronger and domestically more united, and more constructively engaged at the international level.

He suggests that the United States could perhaps become "a more ordinary country [*un pays plus ordinaire*], with concrete interests and real vulnerabilities, instead of thinking of being able to decide unilaterally about the nature of the world in which it lives."[82]

A link to the reprint of a page of the *New York Times* adds the idea that, despite the attacks, life must go on and that the perpetrators are "lowlifes."[83] In the center of the cover page there is another article reporting the views of Nadia Yassine, daughter of the chief of the Moroccan Islamic movement *Justice et Bienfaisance*. She is reported saying that "globalization has a head and an address: the United States, repository of a huge economic power" (*La mondialisation a une tête et une adresse: les Etats-Unis, siège d'un pouvoir économique énorme*). This power, which "crashes the Muslims in Palestine," has had a "boomerang effect" on the United States. If the West does not want to make Islam the faith of the "underdeveloped and barbarians," then it will have to engage with the Muslims facing "either an Islamist with a knife between his [*sic*] teeth or an interlocutor within a dialogue of civilizations." Yassine also says that "for an ordinary Muslim" (*pour le musulman de base*) "bin Laden is a hero." As evidence of this point the article also reports that the weekly Moroccan *Al-Ousboue* (The Week), normally not regarded as an extremist Islamic newspaper, published in the aftermath of 9/11 a picture of the World Trade Center with the caption *Les oiseaux de Babylone qui ont frappé* ("The birds of Babylone have struck")—a reference to the Koran, precisely to a miraculous victory against the infidels.[84]

Editorials and the French Political Culture
Editorials present a number of IEs that can be found in French politicians' statements. As the analysis reveals, the articles are not merely repeating the statements by authorities. Editorials are rather raising points that "make sense" within the already existing political, legal, and historical context. Examples range from suggesting the use of legal measures for countering the terrorist threat to the refusal of the clash of civilizations thesis. I am going to illustrate these points in more detail.

The idea that terrorism should be fought through legal and diplomatic measures emerges, first, as a recommendation to wage a financial struggle against bin Laden (September 19).[85] Rather than wanting the terrorist "dead or alive," terrorism should be fought through the Organization for Economic Cooperation and Development (OECD) initiatives against money laundering. Other articles support the idea of relaunching the dialogue in the Middle East (September 20)[86] and the need to make progress on the front of a "Europe of justice" (*Europe de la justice*). In this last respect terrorism should be fought through EU-wide initiatives, particularly a common arrest mandate.[87]

The editorial *La guerre des mots* (The war of words)[88] (September 18) argues that in order to avoid creating a clash of civilizations, the fight against terrorism should not be called a "war":

> If this "war" against terrorism took a form that hurt the public opinions of the moderate Arab countries, if it had the aspect of a clash of civilizations, it would really risk to contribute realizing the objective of Osama bin Laden: a conflict between the Arab-Muslim world and the hated West. This is precisely what should be avoided.

La gaffe de Berlusconi (Berlusconi's gaffe), a critique of Italian PM Berlusconi, who had declared that Western civilization is "superior" to Islam, explains that the fight against terrorism should be "a fight 'for culture'" (*un combat 'pour la culture'*); we should not fall into the "trap" (*piège*) set by the terrorists: "Yielding to the temptation of a clash of cultures [*l'affrontement des cultures*] would mean playing the terrorists' game." The article is useful in showing that what looks like a position of the French government, is actually a common EU policy. Berlusconi's views, as the article points out, are "in contradiction with the position adopted by the European heads of state and PMs, who have rejected, during their extraordinary meeting on 21 September, 'any conflation between the groups of fanatic terrorists and the Arab Muslim world.'"[89]

The theme appears to be firmly grounded in the coverage of *Le Monde* when it surfaces again on October 10.[90] The editorial wonders about the reasons for the "silences" by Muslims, who are not "replying" to Osama bin Laden's claims about a Western aggression on Afghanistan. Within this vacuum, the article welcomes the initiative by British PM Tony Blair, who "speaks" to the terrorists on Al-Jazeera, and who declares that the West is not against Islam. The editorial continues by warning against falling into the trap set by Osama bin Laden: "The West is not against Islam. And we must not fall into the trap set by bin Laden, that of a war of civilizations." This last example highlights again that what might look like the reproduction of a statement by French politicians is, in reality, a common view shared by international allies.

Rather than through a short-term influence by authorities on the news, the presence in the editorials of the same statements as those contained in the French discourse can therefore be explained as the effect of a system of meanings developed in the long term and shared by both political actors and editors/journalists. As seen in the analysis of the French political discourse in Chapter 3, French authorities are themselves constrained in the way they frame issues by the already existing political culture, particularly by the country's foreign policy agenda and both national and international laws.

Relationship between News and Editorials: No Editorial Control
The editorial line in relation to the intervention in Afghanistan fluctuates between criticism and mild support. The analysis of the articles suggests that this is due to changing stances in accordance to developments at the international level.

On October 3 the editorial *Sauver les Afghans* (Saving the Afghans) sounds mildly against the military intervention: "The Afghans are responsible neither for the Talibans, nor for bin Laden, let alone the strikes that the previous two risk calling on the country." Later, on October 9, the first day of coverage of the conflict, however, it is possible to detect a recognition of the legitimacy of the strikes. According to the article, Osama bin Laden, in his video after the beginning of the war in Afghanistan, has revealed his responsibility. The strikes are also supported by UN Security Council Resolution 1368. Despite this, the article continues questioning current U.S. policy: there should also be a diplomatic offence on the part of the United States involving breaking the links with Saudi Arabia and Pakistan, both supporting terrorism.[91] On November 3, following the developments on the Afghani ground, the editorial opinion becomes critical again: the United States had planned to proceed simultaneously in Afghanistan on both the political and military fronts, but more energy has been put into the bombings than into diplomacy. A piece on November 14, following the fall of Kabul, is instead more encouraging and supportive of the coalition's efforts on the ground: the international community and the West should, now that Kabul has fallen, make sure that the new government is free, independent, and respectful of the rights of both men and women.[92]

The fact that the editorial position on the conflict in Afghanistan is always very cautious, both for and against it, does not hinder the publication of very different points of view in first-page news. Sometimes they are quite extreme in their critique of the U.S.-led military operation. A good example, in this respect, is offered by an article by Rony Brauman, former president of *Médecins Sans Frontières*, on September 29. Brauman argues that it is necessary to understand the political roots of terrorism and harshly criticizes the decision to bomb Afghanistan : "It is enough just slightly to change one's point of view to understand to which extent the Western discourse of the sacredness of life and the inalienable individual rights can appear as pure hypocrisy [*tartufferie*]"; "nothing can justify deliberately sentencing to death thousands of civilians" (*rien ne peu justifier la mise à mort délibérée de milliers de civils*).

A long article (apart from the beginning on the first page, it takes the whole page 15, in which it continues) by Arundhati Roy (Indian novelist and activist) is published in the issue dated October 14–15. According to the author it is the United States, through its foreign policy, that has "raised the devil." The military action in Afghanistan is described with vitriol: "Let's contemplate it, the 'infinite justice' in the 21st century: starving civilians waiting to be killed" (*Contemplons-la, la 'justice sans limites' au XXIe siècle: des civils mourant de faim en attendant d'être tués*). It should be noted that this article appears after the editorials seem to have turned slightly supportive of the intervention on October 9.

Other articles contribute to an enlargement of the debate and to adding new ideas to the coverage. One is by John Le Carré ("The Theatre of Terror") on October 18. According to the British writer, a handful of fanatics have been transformed into "something mythical" and the intervention in Afghanistan will create more terrorists.[93] Another article by French academic Jean-Claude Casanova published the following day (October 19), instead, is supportive of the United States. In his view the U.S. response is necessary and legitimate. Besides, Europeans did not have anything "concrete" to offer. The

EU can now contribute by pushing for achieving peace in the Middle East and avoiding an extension of the operations to other countries, which is precisely what Osama bin Laden wants.[94]

ITALY

A clear feature of the Italian newspapers is the presence of comment and analysis articles on the first page. The commitment to provide readers with opinions is explicitly made by both *Repubblica* and *Corriere della Sera*.

La Repubblica was born in 1976 as a newspaper in which the analysis and interpretation prevailed over the informative pages "in order to practice interventionist journalism with its own ideas and its own objectives for the modernizing of the country."[95] Eugenio Scalfari, founder of the newspaper, presented the first issue of the newspaper by writing:

> An independent daily, but not a neutral one. This newspaper is a little different from the others: it is an information newspaper which rather than parading an illusory political neutrality states explicitly that it has taken a definitive political choice. This newspaper is written by people who are part of the large field of the Italian left.[96]

Il Corriere della Sera was founded a century earlier, in 1876, by three "progressive" (*progressisti*) "young people of good will" (*tre giovani di buona volontá*).[97] According to one of them, Eugenio Torelli Viollier, the secret to the newspaper's success was the practice of good journalism, particularly the commitment to "educating and entertaining the public."[98] As he wrote:

> "I swear I am going to tell the truth, the whole truth," says the witness before making a statement in court. The journalist is like a witness; he should give the public not only the news, but all news of the day, even if he would perhaps rather not do it.[99]

While this statement echoes the *New York Times* commitment to publishing "All news that's fit to print," a more recent "Declaration of Independence" published by *Corriere* on May 29, 1973, stresses the need for the newspaper to take a more decisive stance within the public debate:

> To be great, a newspaper must beat the competition and win over readers. However, it must also be capable of expressing ideas, convictions,

projects, and feelings; it must be able to leave a mark on the society of its time. . . . Impartiality means knowing that reality is complex and that there are different points of view: journalists must take this into account, even if impartiality does not equal detachment or neutrality. Space always needs to be given to multiple "truths." But the impartiality of a newspaper (and a journalist) is a mental inclination before it is the application of a technique. To prove one's impartiality, it is not enough to place two opposing "expert" opinions on a controversial issue side-by-side on the same page.[100]

Such commitment to opinion by both newspapers is reflected by the analysis. Comment articles in both newspapers are richer in IEs than first-page factual news articles and also contain a more complete and coherent framing of the issues under study than isolated and often out-of-context quotes from politicians. The presence of comments on the first page, however, does not contribute to framing the news from a specific angle. Within the coverage there are very contrasting interpretations. They are not consistent with the editorial articles. Indeed, in both *Repubblica* and *Corriere della Sera*, it is not possible to identify a proper "editorial line" on the issues under study apart from isolating individual authors' points of view. The number of editorials, furthermore, is extremely limited.

In Italian an *editoriale* is not only an article written by the editor—*editore,* or more precisely, *direttore,* since the *editore* could be better translated into English as "publisher." Commonly speaking, an *editoriale* is also any comment and analysis piece written by an *editorialista,* essentially a columnist. While there is no lack of *editoriali* written by *editorialisti,* Italian newspapers are distinctive for the near absence of regular, proper editorials by the newspapers' editors. "Editorial," according to the selection criteria for the sample, is understood in the strict sense as a clearly labeled "comment" piece written by either the editor (*direttore*) of the paper or one of its journalists, and which expresses the point of view of the organization. For *La Repubblica* six articles were coded as editorials, for *Corriere della Sera* just four.

Editors communicate directly with the public just at specific moments, and when they do so, most of the time their article starts on the first page. In fact the very definition given by the Garzanti Italian dictionary of *editoriale* is of an article "published on the first page of a daily or a periodic publication; it is usually written by the director and reflects the ideological orientation of the newspaper."[101] Articles by the actual editors are rare. As Alberto Cavallari, editor of *Corriere della Sera* at the beginning of the 1980s, put it, either the editor has a strong idea to express or the editorial becomes "useless and boring." In his own words: "Wasted space" (*Spazio sprecato*).[102] *La Repubblica*'s editor, Ezio Mauro, writes just two relevant articles in the whole period under study (September 12 and October 31). The same can be said for Ferruccio De Bortoli, editor of *Corriere della Sera* (September 12, 15, and October 8). In *La Repubblica* editorial articles are not even labeled as "editorials."

A perhaps surprising characteristic of the Italian media coverage, considering that Italian press is regarded as highly politicized, is the scarce presence, at least on the first page, of national political actors' framing of the issues of 9/11 and the war in Afghanistan.[103] The actors dominating the framing of the first page are, instead, similar to what happens in French news coverage, intellectuals and academics (both Italian and foreign), followed by foreign politicians.

La Repubblica

La Repubblica's coverage of the aftermath of 9/11 appears more internationally oriented than that of *Corriere della Sera*. The presence of comment articles is as substantial as in *Corriere*, but there are more contributions from international scholars and writers rather than national. Coverage of political figures is scarce, and mainly involves, again underlining the greater interest in the international dimension, foreign politicians rather than national authorities. The coverage also presents more comment from reporters than in *Corriere*.

I am now going to illustrate the presence of individual reporters' biases in the news. The prominence of comment on first page, a characteristic of the national journalistic culture, leads to two points: the contribution by academics and intellectuals to shaping the coverage, and the scarce reporting of national politicians. I will then turn to showing the lack of editorial control supported by the absence of a clear editorial line on the issues under analysis. The last point stresses the relevance of the country's political culture, particularly visible in the editorial references to the importance of values in the fight against terrorism.

Individual Biases: Framing the War in Afghanistan

First-page news articles contain veiled comments by the reporters writing them, which particularly contribute to framing the intervention in Afghanistan as a "massacre of civilians" and an "inconcluding war." The idea that the war is wrong and is creating unnecessary suffering and civilians deaths emerges from several lead titles. On October 14 first page, for example, the line under the lead title reads "Kabul, bombs on the civilians" (*Kabul, bombe sui civili*).[104] The following day the main subtitle is "Rain of bombs on Kabul and Kandahar" (*Pioggia di bombe su Kabul e Kandahar*).[105] On October 22 the lead title on page 2 is "Kabul, massacre among civilians" (*Kabul, strage tra i civili*). The issue of October 25 contains almost no news of the war (one of the main stories is a fire in the alpine Gottardo tunnel causing the death of ten drivers), but a subtitle sarcastically reads "Fifteen casualties in a raid to capture two terrorists" (*Quindici vittime in un raid per catturare due terroristi*). The significant aspect of these examples is that neither are they quotes from sources, nor do they reflect an editorial position on the issue of the intervention, which, as will be illustrated later, cannot be clearly identified. Even if the individual stance of the founder of the newspaper (expressed in two articles) could be taken to represent an "editorial line," it would appear to lean toward a moderate support for the military intervention, which would still not explain the critical contents of first-page coverage.

The idea that the war is not achieving its objectives is openly expressed by commentators in November. Correspondent Guido Rampoldi, in a first-page comment article published on November 3, reports about the situation in Afghanistan and argues that a rebellion by Afghan ethnic tribes against the Taliban "could change the course of the inconcluding American war" (*cambierebbe il corso dell' inconcludente guerra Americana*).[106] A piece by another correspondent, Antonio Polito, two days later comments about the Italian official entry into the conflict. The author writes: "[A]t this stage one cannot turn back. We have committed ships, planes and troops. And in the most difficult moment of the attack against Afghanistan. The results have been up to now scarce and, which is even worse, the support of Western public opinions is beginning to crumble."[107]

First-Page Comment and Analysis: The Contribution by Italian and Foreign Intellectuals

Comments constitute most of first-page coverage contents to the point that, on some issues, they almost replace hard news. On September 17, for example, there are three relevant comment articles starting on the first page. They are by Bernardo Valli (journalist of *Repubblica*), Susan Sontag (American essayist), and Giorgio Bocca (Italian journalist and writer).[108] Three relevant comment pieces are also present on the cover of the issue dated September 19: one by Ilvo Diamanti (journalist and essayist), the second by Sandro Viola (journalist of

Repubblica), and the third by Tahar Ben Jelloun (Moroccan writer).[109] On September 20 both comment articles published on the first page are from foreign sources: "Now the US is Rediscovering Alliances" by Francis Fukuyama and "To Kill in the Name of God" by José Saramago (Portuguese Literature Nobel Prize; the article is a reprint from the Spanish daily *El Pais*).[110]

The contribution by both national and foreign writers/academics is particularly visible on the three first-page comment articles published on September 25. They are also good examples of different interpretations of the WOT. The first article, by the American sociology professor Michael Walzer, argues that what was triggered by the 9/11 events is not a "war between civilizations." It is a "war," but a "metaphorical" one, which should be pursued more on the ideological front rather than the military one.[111] The Italian philosopher Umberto Galimberti writes that indeed the "war that the West is about to start" is not different—"since good is all on one side and evil all on the other side"—from a "holy war, a 'jihad.'" The West should rather establish a dialogue with diversity.[112] Paolo Sylos Labini (Italian economist) writes, instead, about the *rogatorie*, financial measures that restrict inquiries on international capital transfers. He argues that such measures, supported by the Italian government, will play in the fight against terrorism in favor of the terrorists.[113]

The Absence of Italian Political Actors

The coverage of Italian politics is confined to first-page news, which, as seen, is almost entirely taken up by commentary. The limited coverage of national politicians involves some reporting of reactions to PM Berlusconi's controversial statements about Western civilization's "superiority."[114] The only IEs coming out of the coverage are, however, just two ("we [the West] are superior"/"we [the West] are not superior"). Even on November 8, the day on which the parliament is voting to authorize the sending of Italian soldiers to Afghanistan, the only relevant quote by an Italian politician is that of minister Giovanardi. He is reported saying: "'[W]e are not entering a war,' he spells out, 'we are taking part in an international police operation against terrorism, is this clear?'"[115]

Foreign politicians are, in comparison, given greater space. *La Repubblica*'s issue dated October 16 reports in its entirety President Chirac's speech at the General Assembly of UNESCO. In his address, Chirac refuses the idea of a clash of civilizations, explains that the terrorists want to lead us into a trap, that a dialogue of cultures, education, a fight against poverty, solidarity, and justice can defeat the fanaticism that motivates the terrorists. Fanaticism also thrives on humiliation and anger fostered by the inequalities of globalization. These are the multiple dimensions that the fight against terrorism should involve. In his long speech the French president presents a coherent interpretation of the 9/11 events and the problem of terrorism.[116]

A totally different, but as much coherent, framing of the WOT is offered on November 2 in an article by U.S. defense secretary Rumsfeld.[117] He explains at length the nature of the new terrorist threat, the identity of the enemy, the need to fight a "different war" against terrorism, and the long-term objectives of the "battle."

As in the French coverage, comment articles introduce a greater variety of IEs into the coverage than more "neutral" news stories. The analysis of the previous examples also suggests that sources from different countries carry with them different interpretations of the issues under study.

The Lack of an Editorial Line

There are no articles clearly marked as "editorials." Those written by the newspapers' director Ezio Mauro and founder of the media organization, Eugenio Scalfari, however, if they can really be taken to represent an "editorial line," do not show commonality of views on the issues of 9/11 and the war in Afghanistan. As the coverage suggests, they talk about entirely different aspects.

Scalfari makes two consistent interventions on how to tackle the problem of terrorism. In an article starting on the first page on October 14 he argues that pacifism at all costs (*porgere l'altra guancia*) "is not a political program." "We" should refuse a "total and senseless war"—rather choose "targeted and circumscribed objectives"—and pursue "a massive policy to redeem the poor as well as peace in the Middle East."[118] On November 11, on another first-page article, Scalfari writes that "neither pacifism nor war," two "great hypocrisies" (*le due grandi ipocrisie in piazza*) can solve the problem of terrorism. The war in Afghanistan is a "painful necessity imposed by international terrorism," but the real measures against terrorism are the relaunching of a peace initiative in the Middle East and "the beginning of a development, finally concrete and adequate, for the poor countries of the world."[119]

Mauro makes two contributions over the whole period: in the first, on September 12, he talks about the West being "struck at its heart" (*colpito al cuore*) by an attack targeted at democracy.[120] On October 31 the author starts from the assumption that there is a "full-blown war between the West and terrorism."[121] This, however, is just the background for further observations, which actually relate to the role of Italy within Europe. The evaluation of the country's situation extends well beyond the crisis (which is not even mentioned) and involves the nature of the government. His view is that Italy represents a "structural European anomaly" (*anomalia europea strutturale*). This status resides in the government's "populism, in its right-wing nature, in its allies, in the conflict of interests it strongly embodies, in the legality question that has obsessed it, trapped and characterized during the first one hundred days of its government, under the incredulous eyes of foreign journalists."[122]

The examples show that there is no clearly identifiable editorial line, in the form of a coherent and consistent interpretation, neither on the issue of 9/11 nor about the intervention in Afghanistan.

The Impact of the Italian Political Culture

A number of comment articles share IEs that also appear in Italian politicians' statements. They are related to the role of democratic values in the fight against terrorism. The articles are not quoting political actors and suggest that such contents belong to the country's broader political culture. They affect editorials and first-page news alike, as the examples below are going to illustrate.

Two articles strongly emphasize the idea that the 9/11 terrorist attacks are a blow against democracy, and that it is the democratic values that will protect "us" against terrorism. On September 12 the newspaper's director writes on the first page that

> there is another sentiment that Europe shares with America hit [by the attacks], and this is the sense of the fragility of democracy....but democracy is not weak....This is a different war [*questa guerra è anomala*], to the point that we don't know who the enemy is, where it will attack tomorrow, which ground it will choose for the battle, which weapon, which target. We know only that democracy is stronger until it is true to itself, and for this reason we want to defend it.[123]

Carlo de Benedetti (entrepreneur, politician, and shareholder of *Repubblica*), on September 20, argues again on first page that, if the United States wants to win the war against terrorism, it should rediscover its democratic principles:

> One cannot, and must not, impose to anybody a single model of life and economy. Cultures, religions, traditions, must be multifaceted, original and find a balance among themselves in the wisdom of knowledge and in the culture of tolerance and cohabitation [*convivenza*]. More

than two hundred years ago a bright traveller, Alexis de Tocqueville, was surprised and delighted in discovering all of this in the New World settlers' communities. If the descendants of those settlers will be able to recover that spirit, the most important battle against barbarism will not be lost.[124]

A comment article by Lucio Caracciolo (editor of *Limes,* an Italian geopolitics magazine) on September 13 refers to the same "community of values" that appears in statements by Italian politicians. He writes: "Today Europe is called to rediscover the depth of the Atlantic alliance, its historical and identity-related [*identitaria*] dimension"; "we have an opportunity for recovering the meaning of a community of values and institutions."[125]

The theme emerges again on September 27. In a first-page article, "Democracy and Crusades," Paolo Garimberti (*Repubblica* journalist) writes that the fight against terrorism is a fight for "our" democratic freedoms:

> America…should remember what it is fighting for, not what it is fighting against. And this "what" has just one name…: democracy…. America will win if it will be able to promote those freedoms Bush has claimed to defend in his speech to the Congress: "Our religious freedom, our freedom of speech, our freedom to vote." These are values for which Italy, as a founder member of the united Europe, has the duty to fight for beside the United States: but to defend them, not to impose them.[126]

The connection between democratic values and the Italian European identity is also present in another editorial article by Eugenio Scalfari (October 21). He argues that European countries can contribute to the global coalition against terrorism by "moderating its excesses" (*moderandone gli eccessi*) through their "capital of experience and values," "our true and only wealth."[127]

Il Corriere Della Sera

Almost the entire analysis of the issues under study refers to the news section, since just four editorial articles, three by director De Bortoli, one from a journalist of the newspaper, were coded as editorials. The coverage of *Corriere della Sera* is more domestically oriented than news in *Repubblica*: it pays relatively greater attention to Italian authorities, and it is mainly Italian intellectuals who contribute to the first-page comment and analysis.

These aspects will now be examined in more detail. I will start from briefly describing the limited coverage of Italian politics. I will then illustrate the variety of views introduced in the coverage by intellectuals, particularly by referring to their different interpretations of terrorism. In this context, I will further elaborate on the debate that took place over several weeks after 9/11 through statements and replies among the different authors as if the newspapers' pages were a forum for discussion. It is this variety of viewpoints within the coverage that makes a strict editorial control on first-page coverage highly unlikely. Besides this, as a fourth aspect of the coverage, I will show that similar to what can be observed in *La Repubblica*, it is not possible to detect an editorial angle on the issues beyond the identification of consistent individual "lines of opinion."

A Domestic Focus

Corriere della Sera reports relatively more about national politics than *Repubblica*. Even then, the space given to politicians is quite limited. In the following example, even if reactions by a range of politicians are reported, their isolated quotes do not contribute to framing the issues as substantially and coherently as do entire articles by academics, writers, and intellectuals. The article whose excerpts are provided next is, by far, the most detailed reporting of political actors' reactions to the events within the whole Italian coverage under analysis. The article was published on September 13, and here is what it reports about Berlusconi's statements:

> "The hottest crises areas, from Pakistan to the whole Caucasus region, should be subject to an effective control and a pressure able to block any new terrorist temptation".... Italy is beside its American ally, both from the point of view of political action—the objectives are "identifying and punishing the perpetrators," eliminating their "protection networks," the construction of valid "intelligence systems"—and the use of force: "A strong military and intelligence response is necessary, but it should also be accompanied by an even stronger political initiative".... For this reason the prime minister...announces that Italy is available...to convene and host an extraordinary session of the G8 to decide all together which answers should be given to international terrorism.

In the same article Pier Ferdinando Casini (president of the lower chamber) is reported saying that "[t]he lower Chamber will form a united front in the solidarity to the United States and the fight against terrorism." Massimo D'Alema (leader of the left) is quoted arguing:

> "We should exhaust the mines of resentment [*giacimenti d'odio*]," has
> said the former premier, focusing on the "primacy of politics" which
> should inspire the response of the West to the attack at the heart of
> America…."there are moments in which the use of force is necessary,
> and we have demonstrated this in Kosovo"…about the possibility of a
> G8 [summit] in Italy…"I do not exclude it but it would be better to
> use also other tools, such as the UN."

Fausto Bertinotti (leader of the Communist Party) supports the idea
that the attacks are "crimes against humanity"; it is necessary to act
on the "causes" of terrorism, and "it is not the G8 which should find
the right answers, it is the UN, the assembly of all countries in the
world. And Europe in this has a great role [to play]."[128]

Comment by Intellectuals: Different Views on Terrorism
The articles by academics and intellectuals in the pages of *Corriere*
strongly affect the content of the coverage to the point that, on some
days, comment almost entirely replaces factual reporting. Comment
articles contribute to increasing the number of IEs within the coverage, particularly in relation to the framing of the 9/11 events.

As far as the causal interpretation of the events is concerned, for
example, Franco Venturini on September 30 argues that the terrorists' motives are "to boycott the moderate Islamic governments"
and "weaken that ethical and political community called the West":
"[W]e" should defend our freedoms in order not to cause "the
end of that West we want to defend."[129] On October 2 Giovanni
Sartori in "The False Reasons of So Much Hatred: The Roots of
Anti-Americanism" expresses the idea that terrorism is not caused
by globalization or the divide between rich and poor ("poverty
and desperation") but by religious extremism.[130] Alberto Ronchey,
just a few days later (on October 11), instead, suggests that terrorism is caused by the "mines of resentment" (*giacimenti di rancore*)
rooted in economics: "The exasperation of the Arab and non-Arab
Islamism…resides in the gap between the demographic existence of over a billion Muslims and their economical and political
inferiority."[131]

In terms of treatment recommendation in relation to the threat
of terrorism, original ideas are introduced in the coverage through
a comment article by Francesco Merlo (*Corriere*'s journalist). On
October 17 he proposes a role for Italian Muslims in neutralizing

extremists: "Italian Muslims can help us cleaning up.... They can help us isolating also our Talibans who, from some fringes of Lega Nord [Northern League] or An [National Alliance] or extremist catholics [*ultrà cattolici*], already make intolerant claims: they want to shut down mosques, send everybody away [*cacciare via tutti*]."[132] On October 21 Tommaso Padoa Schioppa, Italian banker and former member of the European central bank, suggests that "the fight against terrorism will be at the end decided by civilians, by the common people who live in the United States, in Europe, Afghanistan, Palestine, Pakistan."[133]

The Debate on the Newspaper's Forum

A provocative article by writer and journalist Oriana Fallaci on September 29 starts a debate that will rage on the pages of *Corriere* for the following 20 days and will spread to *Repubblica*, too.[134] The debate involved even more articles than were coded, but some of the pieces did not meet the selection criteria for being included in the sample. Those that did, however, are an example of the way comment articles introduce new ideas into the framing of the issues under study. They also show the unpredictable directions in which coverage contents can develop, outside of editorial control.

In the initial article, "Anger and Pride *(La rabbia e l'orgoglio)*," Fallaci supports the idea that "we" must fight for "our civilization":

> Wake up, people, wake up! Intimidated as you are by the fear of not being mainstream, that is to appear racist (by the way an inappropriate term since we are not dealing with a race but a religion), you don't understand, or you don't want to understand that what is going on here is a reversed crusade. Used as you are to double games, blinded by always looking into your own courtyard, you don't understand or you don't want to understand that what's going on here is a religious war. Wanted and declared by a fringe of that religion, perhaps, but still a religious war. A war they call Jihad. Holy War. A war that, maybe, does not aim at conquering our territory, but which certainly aims at conquering our souls. At the disappearance of our freedom and our civilization.

She attacks those who are not taking a stance against terrorism:

> They don't care about it [the possibility of new attacks]. Anyway America is far, between Europe and America there is an ocean...Eh, no, my dear. No. There is just a thread of water. Because when the stake is the destiny of the West, the survival of our civilization, New

York is us. We are America. We Italians, we French, we English, we Germans, we Austrians, we Hungarians, we Slovaks, we Poles, we Scandinavians, we Belgians, we Spanish, we Greek, we Portuguese. If America collapses, Europe collapses. The West collapses, we collapse.

She argues that "we" cannot be tolerant of or establish a dialogue with the extremists: "So shall we have this conversation about what you call contrast-between-the-Two-Cultures? Well, if you really want to know it, it annoys me even to talk about two cultures: comparing them at the same level, as if they were two parallel entities, of equal weight and equal measure."

Replies follow the article, bringing in, every time, new IEs. On October 1 Angelo Panebianco (academic) argues that we need to believe in our values.[135] On October 5 Dacia Maraini (writer) criticizes Fallaci's "recklessness": "[W]ar is not the appropriate answer to terrorism, what is needed is rather a great international police operation." She continues by redefining Fallaci's view that 9/11 is the beginning of a "reversed crusade" by Islamic extremists:

> Why don't you call it [9/11 events] for what it is: an act of fundamentalist terrorism which, as such should be judged and fought? If you transform it into the first move of a holy war, you just play their [terrorists'] game. This is a trap, Oriana, in which it seems to me you have fallen with both feet, pushed by the transport and the bravery—in this case if I may say a bit Don Quixotian—which characterize you.[136]

On October 7 Sergio Romano makes the point that what is good about Fallaci's article is the feeling of national pride: patriotism would be more effective against terrorism than any military reaction.[137] On October 15 Giovanni Sartori replies to all previously mentioned articles (including a piece by Terzani that was not included in the sample).[138] Among the points he makes, he supports concrete action against the perpetrators. As he writes:

> "It is not a matter of justifying, of forgiving, but of understanding. Understanding, because I am convinced that the problem of terrorism cannot be solved by killing terrorists, but eliminating the reasons that make them so" [quoting Terzani]. Wise words, but only words. To state that the problem of terrorism cannot be solved by killing terrorists is like stating that the problem of criminality cannot be solved by arresting and condemning criminals. True, but which would be the al-

ternative? Eliminating prisons and sending the criminals to a "Terzani studio" where they can be studied and understood?[139]

On October 17 Giuliano Zincone closes the debate by writing that, even if he does not share Fallaci's "cultural pride," he realizes that "many intellectuals of our time look at the world from the heights of an ivory tower [*molti intellettuali del nostro tempo guardano il mondo dall'alto di freschi palmizi*]." While "one cannot impose democracy on those who do not want it," we should also understand its value and defend it. The very act of taking a position within this debate can contribute to fighting the current threat, since at least we are reflecting on our values.[140]

The excerpts reveal how far the debate is going in relation to the initial issue of the 9/11 events and the way to respond to the attacks.

The Missing Editorial Line

There are just four articles that qualify as editorials. They do not appear to constitute an editorial line not only for their limited number over 64 days of coverage, but also because they do not develop a consistent interpretation of the issues under study. Three of them are written by director De Bortoli, who expresses, even if perhaps only rhetorically, some support for a military action in Afghanistan. In his first reaction to the events, on September 12, in a first-page article entitled "We Are All Americans," the director writes:

> Until yesterday we felt we were safer and citizens of a better world. It wasn't so. The awakening has been shocking, as shocking at those flames in the Twin Towers of New York (symbol of the economic power), or at the Pentagon (symbol of the military power), which were wrapping thousands of innocent victims. Now we are really at war. And what is worse, the enemy is invisible. [...] The security network has been spectacularly pierced in several points. The only surviving superpower discovers itself, in the age of Internet and multimedia created by its own technology, weak and confused.[141]

On October 8, on the first day of coverage of the newly begun war in Afghanistan, De Bortoli writes that "it is not the time of neutrality and indifference. We are all Americans: we wrote it on 12 September, we repeat it, today, even more strongly."[142] A third article contains a single IE, the notion that the 9/11 events are a "tragedy."[143] The director's stance, however, does not appear to affect first-page contents. As previous examples have shown, there are plenty of dissonant voices within the coverage.

The fourth editorial article is by Giuliano Zincone. The article, which was included in the sample for being a comment piece written by a journalist of the newspaper, does not contribute toward a consistent editorial line (if there is one at all) since it introduces different views than those of the director, such as the idea, as shown later, that the reaction to the 9/11 events should be guided by values: "In front of such a cruel challenge [posed by terrorists], it is difficult to abandon the indiscriminate wish of revenge. But it is necessary: it is imposed on us by our secular faith."[144]

PAKISTAN

Pakistan's journalistic culture, at least for what concerns the elite newspapers under analysis, appears to be closer to the objective journalism model of the United States than the interpretative journalism of Italy, and to a lesser extent, of France. Tahir, in a report on the state of the Pakistani journalism, writes in fact that one of the expected requirements of a professional journalist is "neutrality."[145] First-page news contents are largely fact oriented, and there are usually three editorials per day, positioned in the "comment" section.

Also in Pakistan, however, editorial policy affects the way national journalistic culture is lived at the level of the news organization. The *Dawn*'s coverage is more internationally oriented than news in the *Nation*. The *Nation*'s coverage is also less objective than reporting in the *Dawn*. These differences can be explained by considering the history and mission statement of each media organization.

The *Nation* is part of the Nawa-e-Waqt group,[146] founded in 1940 with a strong political commitment to Islam and a conservative orientation.[147] As the founder Hameed Nizami declared: "[W]e [Nawa-e-Waqt] represent a commitment to the ideology of Pakistan. Our tradition is to stand up for the causes we believe in and it is a tradition we intend to keep."[148] The *Dawn*, instead, carries more economic coverage than any other Pakistani elite newspaper, and according to Akhtar, appears to have tried to emulate the *Financial Times*: the *Dawn* was the first newspaper that started publishing an eight-page weekly supplement on financial matters, which, just like the British business newspaper, was pink in color.[149] The possibility that the similarity also extends to the style of reporting is again confirmed by Akhtar. According to him the Pakistani establishment has shown greater tolerance of the dissenting views expressed by the *Dawn* on the ground of its elitist readership. The newspaper "has made good use of this tolerance" to maintain "professional integrity" and "a certain level of sobriety."[150]

What distinguishes Pakistani coverage from other countries' is the wider range of sources contributing to framing the issues of 9/11 and Afghanistan, particularly Asian sources (compare, e.g., figures 5.1 and 5.2 with figures 5.7 and 5.8). Combined with views from Western sources, they introduce a great variety of ideas within first-page news coverage. Even if editorial opinion in both newspapers is firm throughout the time span under analysis, first-page news presents therefore a much wider range of views than those of the editors.

The analysis of the editorials particularly shows the impact of the country's political culture, here mainly embodied by a shared understanding by both political actors and media professionals of Pakistan's national interest. The attention by editors to national interest is supported also by considerations about the social role of journalism in Pakistan. According to Tahir in a report about the state of journalism in Pakistan, journalists are "assets of the country. It is only because of them that the problems of the downtrodden continue coming to the light. They are the only voice of the victims of injustice in society."[151] The free press "is the only forum that can effectively help solve the problems of a nation plagued by abject poverty, illiteracy, unemployment, environmental pollution, human rights violations, gender discrimination and child labour."[152] This perception of the role of journalists in developing countries is shared by supporters of "development journalism." According to Aggarwala, "[D]evelopment journalism is the use of all journalistic skills to report development processes in an interesting fashion."[153] It is based on a different definition of news than that existing in Anglo-American journalism, and it is more appropriate to the needs of societies that experience crises and conflicts. By focusing on positive developments rather than bad news, this different kind of journalism can contribute to nation building and education.[154] As Aggarwala continues, it could "help lower the walls of intense suspicion and distrust that have arisen between Third World political leaders and the media."[155]

The Dawn

The *Dawn* appears to be more "objective" than the *Nation* insofar as there are no analysis articles within first-page coverage. Its news also appears to be more internationally oriented and presents a wider range of sources than in the *Nation*, which also supports the presence of a greater variety of ideas within the coverage.

The *Dawn*'s editorials are generally supportive of the Pakistani government's decision to join the coalition against terrorism. This does not appear to occur because editors are under the influence of the country's political leader. The analysis of editorial contents suggests that editorial reproduction of the governmental framing is rather the result of editorial considerations about the country's national interest, which suggests a role by political culture in shaping the coverage. These aspects are now going to be looked at in more detail.

Variety of Sources and Contents in the Coverage
First-page coverage relies on a number of sources. They directly contribute to diversifying the framing of the issues under study. I am going to present some examples of different sources whose alternative interpretations of the Afghanistan intervention are voiced in the same issue of the newspaper.

In relation to the U.S.-led military operation in Afghanistan, on September 30 Musharraf is reported saying that "this is an issue concerning the integrity of the country [Pakistan]. It relates to peace of the region and future and survival of Afghanistan and its people.... Our priorities and basic concerns are integrity and solidarity of the country, economic revival, defence of strategic assets and promotion of [the] Kashmir cause."[156] The EU framing of the war—represented by opinions expressed by the German chancellor Gerhard Schröder, British foreign secretary Jack Straw, and Belgian PM Guy Verhofstadt—is, instead, that the intervention in Afghanistan is a "legitimate" response by the United States to the terrorist attacks of 9/11. The "retaliation," even if authorized by Resolution 1368 of the UN Security Council, should nonetheless be "proportionate" and "targeted."[157] The Afghan ambassador to Pakistan, Mullah Abdul Salam Zaeef, frames the military intervention as the result of the U.S. will to war: "Ours was the first country to condemn the terrorist attacks in the United States, we are peace loving people and never support such activities [terrorist attacks]. Providing evidence against Osama will be the best way for resolving the problem. But when we asked for evidence, their [the Americans'] reply was in negative. Instead they insisted on their demand to surrender Osama to them."[158]

Particularly the use of Afghan sources provides a very different view of the conflict than it appears in Western newspapers. In an article published on October 5, for example, a former Afghan guerrilla leader, Gulbadin Hekmatyar, states: "If Pakistan is found participating in a campaign orchestrated by our enemies to destabilise

Afghanistan and cause death and destruction to break the nerve of this brave nation, then it would have to pay a very heavy price."[159] Within the same article his spokesman in Islamabad, Ghairat Baheer, adds that "it is not only the matter of elimination of Osama bin Laden but it's the matter of replacement of a regime and installation of another regime which is supported by the United States and its Western allies."

The interest of the *Dawn* in foreign reactions is suggested, as in the case of *Le Monde*, by references to foreign media. They are important because they introduce very different ideas in the coverage. The September 15 issue, for instance, contains excerpts from Arab newspapers.[160] The London-based Saudi daily *Al-Hayat* is reported arguing that the attempt by the United States "to avenge its injured dignity" should be "backed up by diplomacy. This should include building a world order that upholds the principles of justice and rights, one that cares for the poor, weak and oppressed." An excerpt from the UAE daily *Al-Bayan* reads: "Washington should resist the temptation to take rash revenge just to vent its wrath." The Jeddah-based *Okaz*, instead, calls for the international community "to stamp out terrorism, but this must be done within the context of international laws that respect each nation's sovereignty." On September 16, the article "Afghan Adventure Will Be Difficult: NYT [*sic*]" reports excerpts from the *New York Times* editorial "War without Illusions." In yet another perspective, the excerpts suggest that the attacks have generated a "long and unpredictable war": "Mr Bush and the nation must be under no illusions about the battles ahead."[161]

Editorial Stance Shaped by National Interest

The *Dawn's* support of the government's decision to join the coalition appears to be motivated by the realization that, internationally, Pakistan does not have a choice but to comply with U.S. demands. The point emerges from the editorial "National Interest Comes First," published on September 21. The article openly praises Musharraf for his choice to protect Pakistan's interest in the post-9/11 crisis ("[t]he nation's choice should obviously come first") and continues by saying:

> Unfortunately, there are elements in the country to whom partisan and party interests matter more than national interests. Which is a pity, because the world crisis in which Pakistan finds itself trapped today demands a complete rallying of forces unmarked by any note of discordance or disharmony. One only hopes that leaders and parties that

have a soft corner for the Taliban would realize that a strong Pakistan would be in the long run of greater help to Afghanistan in the future than a Pakistan isolated or mauled by anti-terrorists military action that now seems only a matter of time.[162]

Another editorial published on September 28 emphasizes the point that the crisis can turn into an opportunity for Pakistan to improve its position in the context of international politics:

> The world's eyes today are set on Pakistan to see the course it chooses in the context of the current international drive against terrorism. This offers an opportunity for the military government to break the schism and try to form a closer and more meaningful understanding with mainstream politics parties which are broadly in agreement with its handling of the current crisis. This is the only way Pakistan can speak to the world with one unified voice, and be part of the emerging international consensus on how best to tackle global terrorism, while not compromising its own national interests.[163]

An indication that the editors perceive Pakistan's position in relation to other countries to have shifted since 9/11 comes from another piece published later, on October 24. The article looks at the India-Pakistan relationship from the point of view of the new Pakistani positioning as a member of the coalition against terrorism. As the editors shortly put it: "Pakistan is a front-line state in the current war against terrorism."[164]

The Nation

The *Nation*'s coverage is more oriented toward comment than the *Dawn*'s. This reflects the newspaper's mission of providing "firm and constructive views" to its readership.[165] The newspaper, as the attention toward a greater number of Pakistani and Afghani sources confirms, is also slightly less internationally focused than the *Dawn*. These points are going to be addressed by describing the commentary within first-page coverage. I will then illustrate the way in which the domestic agenda set by the newspaper's editorial policy translates into a different selection of sources than in the *Dawn*.

Editorials express more radical views than in the *Dawn*, in line with the newspaper's own description: "Its [the *Nation*'s] editorials are acknowledged as the boldest and most influential in the country, while the wide variety of opinion it publishes by contributing writers, including some of the country's most prominent figures, is unrivalled."[166] Apart from showing the existence of an editorial line, I will focus on the way the awareness of the Pakistani positioning within the international system affects the editorial framing of the intervention in Afghanistan. This confirms the significance of political culture in shaping the news.

First-Page Comments
A first distinctive characteristic of the *Nation*'s coverage is the presence of commentary within first-page news. This takes the form of analysis pieces, as well as evaluative statements contained within both stories and their titles. Far from being neutral, these statements decisively contribute to framing the issues under study in specific directions. For example, a first-page article labeled "News Analysis," published on October 5 and written by special correspondent Ayesha Haroon, develops critical views about the rationale behind the imminent military operation in Afghanistan:

> There are no questions being asked about whether evidence good enough only to indict an individual [Osama bin Laden] is good enough to launch a strike against a country. Even though unanswered at present, questions abound. What would constitute sufficient evidence to attack Afghanistan to get Osama and punish the Taliban?...What would constitute sufficient reason to launch an attack against Afghanistan?[167]

The piece also makes the point that Pakistan does not have a choice but to comply with U.S. demands:

> It seems the last chapter in this bizarre book of war and terror is being written as Pakistan accepts that the material provided by the US contains sufficient basis for indictment of Osama bin Laden for trial before a court of law. After the initial shock of the September 11 attacks, international events have followed an almost expected sequence— Islamabad's acceptance of the evidence too has not come as a surprise. There was hardly any possibility of Pakistan doing otherwise.[168]

Another article by the same author on October 8, labeled "Situationer," raises the point that with the newly begun war the public is "witnessing the crushing of an already ravaged country." The author's assessment is, more precisely:

> On the Afghanistan front the situation can play out in three or four likely scenarios: Osama is captured; falls into action; or manages to elude the special forces and goes underground.

In all three scenarios terrorism would not be eradicated, for prime suspect Osama is just a first step in this long war on terror. That said, all three scenarios hold untold misery and devastation for Afghanistan. That is exactly what happened in the Gulf War. It is being said in some quarters [that] the US is planning to wrap up the unfinished business in Iraq after Afghanistan is over.[169]

Another example of comment article, heavily framing the issue of Afghanistan as a failure, is the piece "Targets Unmet" by Javed Rana (November 7), again published on first page:

US-led military operation against alleged terrorists in Afghanistan completes one month today. For a coalition planning to see a different Kabul within a week of the strikes, the operation has been three weeks too long. Washington, the mightiest of the world military power, is still far away from achieving its political objectives in Afghanistan, militarily one of the weakest nations in the world.

Intelligence disaster, both regarding alleged terrorists' hideouts and of Taliban's resilience, eventually shifted the target strikes plan to carpet bombardment of innocent civilians, leaving over 600 to 1500 Afghans dead and injuring over 800 people since October 7.[170]

A Different Selection of Sources
The *Nation* presents a different range of sources than in the *Dawn*, with a higher attention toward Afghani sources. This could be explained by the greater domestic and regional focus of the newspaper, leading its interest to gravitate more toward the Pakistani/ Afghan area.

While it is common to observe the same quote by the same source (e.g., General Musharraf) in both Pakistani newspapers, the *Nation* also contains a number of statements by Afghani sources that do not appear anywhere in the *Dawn*'s coverage. This does not mean that the sources are not mentioned in the *Dawn*'s news. The *Nation*, however, quotes them more extensively and more often. This affects the contents of the coverage, particularly resulting in a negative framing of the intervention in Afghanistan, as the following examples show.

Taliban leader Mullah Omar is quoted on September 27 in a message delivered to Pakistan-based news agency Afghan Islamic Press (AIP):

Mullah Mohammed Omar said the attacks on the United States had been carried out to avenge US "cruelty" towards Muslim countries.

He also said "The American people must know that the sad events that took place recently were the result of their government's wrong policies."[171]

On October 14 he is quoted again, this time saying that 9/11 was a pretext to wage war against Islam: "The Americans have attacked Afghanistan without any proof to cover up the failure of its [sic] intelligence agencies. It [sic] is finding a pretext to finish an Islamic country."[172]

Also, the Taliban spokesman to Pakistan, Abdul Salam Zaeef, is regularly quoted. On October 8, at the beginning of the operation in Afghanistan, Zaeef states that the operation is a military assault on Afghan cities, the bombings are "horrendous terrorist attacks," "Afghanistan is a victim of American expansionism. The United States will not achieve its political goals in dismantling the Islamic Emirate of Afghanistan," "the Afghan people will raise against this new colonial attempt."[173] The same ideas reappear over and over again within the coverage: on October 10 he states that raids are against towns: "[T]his is open terrorism, this is not prosecuting so-called terrorists"; "[h]e [Zaeef] said the real motive behind the continued US military operations is to strategically capture the natural resources of neighbouring Central Asian States";[174] on October 12, "Zaeef says 100 civilians killed";[175] on October 23 Zaeef "said that more than 100 people, including doctors, nurses and patients, were 'reported to have been martyred' in a Herat hospital";[176] on October 24 Zaeef claims "American terrorist attacks on Afghanistan are continuing"; "The US administration verbally condemns terrorism but practically commits terrorism."[177]

Variety of Ideas within the Coverage
The number of sources within the coverage and the fact that they come from a range of different countries increases, similar to what happens in the *Dawn*, the range of IEs in the coverage. An example of varied IEs within the coverage is offered by news on September 25 when it is possible to detect alternative and entirely different interpretations of the fight against terrorism. The leading article claims that "the United States and United Kingdom have finalized the operational plan to track down Osama bin Laden in Afghanistan, topple the Taliban government and launch a long war against international terrorism."[178] This view is completed by the reporting of U.S. secretary of state's remarks: "Powell said on Sunday that Washington would soon present proof to the world that Osama and

his organization al-Qaeda were behind this month's attacks."[179] The same page reports Osama bin Laden's statements on Al-Jazeera: "We hope these brethren will turn out to be the first martyrs in Islam's battle...against the new crusader-Jewish campaign led by the foremost Crusader [President Bush]."[180] Mullah Omar is also quoted: "Mullah Mohammed Omar warned that terrorism would continue as long as US troops remained in the Gulf region, home to Islam's holiest places, and as long as Washington sided with Israel against Palestinians."[181]

The quotes highlight extremely different objectives of the post-9/11 mobilization—tracking down Osama bin Laden and toppling the Taliban supporters of terrorism versus conducting a crusade against Islam—and different causes of terrorism—Al-Qaeda's attack versus a U.S. invasion of the Arab world.

The Effects of Pakistan's Positioning within the International System
The idea, within the editorial coverage, that joining the coalition against terrorism is in the best interest of Pakistan appears to be motivated by the awareness of the weak international position of the country. The realization of what Pakistan can or cannot do on the international scene represents a boundary to the framing of the situation by editors and commentators. The belief that Pakistan does not really have a choice but to comply with U.S. demands emerges, for example, in an editorial dated September 15:

> It was clear even before formally naming him that the USA had decided not only that its culprit is Osama bin Laden, but that Pakistan is to play a pivotal role in ensuring that he is appropriately punished.... At this stage, the government certainly has hard choices to make, but it must keep the national interest in mind, and further, it must make the Americans understand that [the] Pakistani public is not going to stand for action against a figure who has, for better or worse, become a folk hero, not unless it is clear about the reasons for doing so....even a military government cannot totally ignore popular feelings, and the USA must not make the mistake of making impossible or over-difficult demands.[182]

The editorial is accompanied, in the "comment" section, by a cartoon with a very explicit message: "Uncle Sam" presents General Musharraf a list of demands the Pakistani leader cannot refuse. The list reads as follows: "1.The, 2.Boss, 3.Is, 4.Always, 5.Right."[183]

Another editorial piece on September 24 makes the point that Pakistan is under the heavy burden of sanctions, and even if fighting terrorism should be "motivated by principles," agreeing to cooperate with the United States is "inevitable" due to "the predicament in which Pakistan is placed."[184] The notion reappears on November 7:

> [T]he decision to join the US-led alliance was probably unavoidable, as a debt-ridden, impoverished country like Pakistan facing a hostile neighbour like India, had limited options. What is being questioned in some circles, however, is the haste with which this crucial policy decision was taken, and that too without due process of consultation.[185]

The knowledge of the international situation affects the editorial framing of the intervention in Afghanistan, as the following article on November 11 reveals: the editorial board is against the war in Afghanistan, but since there is no way to stop it, they are going to provide recommendations on how to deal with the situation on the ground:

> More important, if the US pushes swiftly to Kabul, and suspends the bombing, it would ease the suffering of the Afghan people, and re- lieve the tension in the Muslim world, making it easier for Muslim governments to support the campaign. If Kabul proves too tough for the Northern Alliance to take, the US will know it has to use its own forces, in which case bombing can be suspended until such forces are inducted, which again takes us past Ramazan [sic]. In principle, we oppose the bombing, but since the US cannot be dissuaded, at least we can ask it to do only what is militarily necessary, rather than what seems revengeful and retaliatory.[186]

CONCLUSIONS

The analysis reveals that first-page news offers a fragmented fram- ing of both the 9/11 events and the war in Afghanistan: first-page coverage is about reporting what newsworthy actors have said about the world. Rather than coherent "frames," there are therefore many conflicting and competing ideas, most of the time not part of any single, consistent interpretation, all coexisting together. The number of IEs in the coverage depends on which proportion of the news each newspaper allocates to factual reporting rather than com- ment and analysis. Commentary tends, in fact, to contain more IEs than fact-based coverage. This observation could be partly overem- phasized by the methodological choices of the study. The sample selection involved, apart from editorials, all articles starting on the first page. In the cases of Italy and France this led to coding a large number of first-page comment pieces written by intellectuals and freelance journalists. It is, however, also true that that the very fact that comment and analysis articles were on the first page, reflects specific editorial choices and the journalistic culture of the country. Italian interpretative journalism, in particular, was found to give comment and analysis the most prominent role among the cases. Comment articles, apart from containing a very high number of IEs when they were focused on 9/11 and Afghanistan, also allowed communicating more coherent interpretations of the issues under study.

The analysis reveals that different variables weigh differently on the coverage depending on the country and the newspaper. Process tracing has illuminated not only the variables that shape the coverage—national journalistic culture, each news organization's editorial policy, and national political culture—but also an important causal mechanism that had not been initially predicted. The variables produce changes in the news by affecting the selection of sources "speaking" in the newspapers' pages. These aspects will now be elaborated, starting from the role of sources, then moving on to assessing the relevance of each of the mentioned variables.

It's All About Sources

As Leon Sigal put it, what news reports "is not what happens, but what someone says has happened or will happen."[187] The analysis at this stage confirms his point. What the process tracing suggests is, first, that nothing really just "happens" in the world. There are no "events": there is just what social actors (sources in this case) *think* is happening. In other words, it is their *interpretation* (framing) of what goes on in the world that shapes the contents of the coverage. This supports the idea that media coverage does not just "contain" frames. It is social actors who continuously construct issues through a *framing process*. Second, and related to the first point, is that the presence of different interpretations in the media coverage is not the result of framing by the "media" as an agent. While in editorials it is editors (or editorial boards) who construct an issue, first-page news appears to be the result of a framing competition—most of the time without a winner, given the level of inconsistencies even within the same page—between different sources.

The study confirms therefore the importance of sources in shaping the media coverage, which emerges in several strands of the literature.[188] The findings also support the claim by Kevin Carragee and

Wim Roefs, who call for a greater attention toward framing contests within the wider political and social domains. As they write, while the results of a number of studies point at the relevance of sources in shaping the coverage, most research about framing still neglects the issue of "frame sponsorship," that is, the fact that the interpretation emerging from media coverage is shaped by wider discourses external to media organizations.[189]

It is true, however, that even if the "media" does not exist as a conscious actor, the newspaper still has, as an organization, a mediating a role in selecting which actors will have a voice on the newspaper's forum. The main way in which the editorial policy is translated into an influence on media coverage is, in fact, sources' selection. To understand what shapes this selection it is necessary to consider three variables: national journalistic culture, national political culture, and editorial policy. They will now be dealt with in more detail, together with an assessment of the other variables that were tested through the process tracing: global journalistic culture and biases of individual journalists.

National Journalistic Culture

Interpretative journalism in Italy and France produces more IEs in terms of number and variety of ideas within the coverage than objective journalism in the United States and Pakistan. This is due to the fact that besides the fact-oriented reporting—which at best contributes toward framing the issue under study by reporting newsworthy actors' latest statements—a substantial amount of space is given to comment articles. They usually contain more IEs than objective journalism's who-what-where-when-how accounts. The IEs are also more coherently organized into arguments, rather than in telegraphic, often incoherent quotes from different sources. The way in which national journalistic culture affects the coverage is therefore by leading journalists and editors to selecting some sources rather than others. In relation to the issues of 9/11 and Afghanistan, the analysis suggests that interpretative journalism leads to a selection of sources that includes commentators, academic, intellectuals rather than (or besides) mostly officials, as in objective journalism.

National Political Culture

The analysis has shown that the framing of the issues under study is shaped by a country's political culture: existing political agendas, sense of identity, evolving international relations, positioning within the international system. Particularly, coverage in France presented similar ideas to the political statements without a direct reference to authorities' declarations, suggesting a shared understanding of the situation, rooted in an already existing system of meanings. Pakistani coverage was also found to be affected by the editorial awareness of the Pakistani standing within the international system and its subordinate position in relation to the United States. Pakistani coverage, however, also showed the way this understanding changed, in parallel with Pakistan gaining a "new" position in the international system, after having joined the U.S.-led coalition against terrorism.

Also national political culture appears to affect the choice of sources in the news. In fact, even if Pakistani journalism closely resembles the American model, coverage of the *Nation* and the *Dawn* tends to be richer in IEs than coverage in the United States. The *Dawn* and the *Nation* produce, for example, respectively 241 and 198 different IEs over the whole period of analysis. The *New York Times* and the *Wall Street Journal*, respectively, 224 and 173. This appears to be explained by the interest of Pakistani newspapers in a wider range of newsworthy sources than the press in the United States. They involve, apart from American politicians, also Afghani sources, international organizations' spokespersons, EU officials, regional and international Muslim leaders, international media. The analysis suggests that this is related to Pakistan's political culture, particularly its commitment to establishing cooperative relations with developing states and its religious identity, which places the country within the greater community of Muslim countries.[190]

Editorial Policy

The way the same issues are covered, even in newspapers within the same country, is markedly different. Editorial policy is an essential factor in explaining the distinctiveness of each media organization. Editorial policy shapes the agenda of the newspaper. This affects the relative size of the newshole allocated, in the case of 9/11 and Afghanistan, to foreign policy. Within each country's journalistic culture some newspapers are more internationally oriented than others: the *New York Times*, the *Dawn*, *Le Monde*, *La Repubblica*. Editorial policy appears to affect the way each newspaper interprets the national journalistic culture. The *New York Times* and the *Wall Street Journal* belong to the same objective journalistic culture, but the *Wall Street*

Journal's journalists are freer in expressing comments within first-page stories than the *New York Times* reporters.

Editorial policy never turns into strict editorial control of first-page news contents, even where an editorial line exists (as in the *Wall Street Journal* or the *Nation*). A consistency of views between first pages and editorials was not found but in the case of the *Wall Street Journal*. The possibility of editorial control appears to be more closely related to objective rather than interpretative journalism. In fact, the variety of views within first-page coverage that characterizes the latter makes it very unlikely that ideas in the news would match a single way of interpreting issues.

In addition to this, editorial policy appears to affect the selection of sources in the coverage in two ways. It can lead to the manipulation of the voices within a story to support specific views, as in the *Wall Street Journal*. It can also affect the sources' selection by setting the very amount of space available for "talking" about a specific topic.

No Global Journalistic Culture

The analysis shows not only that coverage reflects different national models of journalism, but also that each newspaper has an individual style characterized by more or less objectivity/interpretation than the national "norm." The differences in coverage not only among countries, but also at the level of the single newspaper do not support the existence of a global journalistic culture as a homogeneous style of reporting.

Individual Biases?

Individual bias appears to be a function of the combination between national journalistic culture and each media organization's editorial policy. The extent to which journalists are allowed to express evaluative statements and comments in the news depends, in fact, not only on whether they operate within an objective (the United States and Pakistan) or interpretative (Italy and France) model of journalism, but also on whether the newspaper for which they write values comment (the *Wall Street Journal, Le Monde, Corriere della Sera*, the *Nation*) over a more neutral reporting (the *New York Times, Libération, Repubblica*, the *Dawn*).

CHAPTER 5

Testing Different Approaches to News

The purpose of this chapter is combining the previous process-tracing observations with content analysis to finally assess the extent to which the coverage of 9/11 and its aftermath can be explained by current approaches to news in Political Communications, International Communications, and News Sociology. More specifically, from the perspective of Political Communication, to what extent was coverage reflecting the views expressed by elites within each country's political debate (indexing hypothesis)? From the viewpoint of International Communications, to what extent was coverage presenting similar features across all newspapers (globalization) rather than showing differences along national lines (localization)? Alternatively, was there any evidence that there were unbalanced news flows between richer (more powerful) and poorer countries, for example, between the United States and Pakistan? Finally, within the micro perspective of News Sociology, to which degree was each newspaper's coverage shaped by the norms of conduct and the individual biases internal to each single media organization?

The testing involves a combination of both quantitative and qualitative content analysis of the way 9/11 and the war in Afghanistan were framed in the political discourses of the United States, Italy, France, and Pakistan and in their respective newspapers' coverage (September 11 to November 14, 2001). The coding generated 1,058 entries into an Access database. The analysis involved 288 days of political statements, 443 days of first-page news coverage (the same 64 days of coverage in eight different newspapers), 302 days of editorial coverage, for a total of 12,588 idea elements (IEs) recorded in relation to 9/11 and 5,594 IEs recorded in relation to the Afghanistan issue.

The testing of the Indexing hypothesis will be presented first, followed by the testing of Media Flows. The validity of the Globalization and Localization approaches will be presented together. The testing of the extent to which each newspaper's first-page coverage reflects editorial stance or is an expression of individual reporters' bias will be illustrated last. Throughout the chapter the newspapers are indicated as follows: the *New York Times* (NYT), the *Wall Street Journal* (WSJ), *Libération* (LIB), *Le Monde* (LM), *La Repubblica* (REP), *Il Corriere della Sera* (CDS), the *Dawn* (DAWN), the *Nation* (NAT).

Testing the Indexing Hypothesis

Testing the correlation between political statements and media coverage (indexing hypothesis) essentially consists in assessing the similarity between the way the issues of 9/11 and the intervention in Afghanistan are framed by political actors and the way they are framed in the newspapers' coverage, with a distinction between editorials and first-page news, in the four countries under study.

A Lack of Correlation between Political Debate and Media Coverage

The notion that the range of elite press coverage contents, here approached as number of IEs, is contained within the range of debate of the political elite is confirmed only in the United States. By comparing the most recurrent batches of IEs (framing samples) in the governmental discourse with those of the press coverage it can be observed that in the United States the news framing of 9/11 and the intervention in Afghanistan contained less IEs than in the political statements: the NYT presented 24 IEs about 9/11 against 34 by the administration; in relation to the war in Afghanistan it contained 13 IEs against 18 official ones. In both Italy and France, instead, 9/11 news coverage contained more ideas than in the political statements— REP's coverage, for example, contained 54 IEs against the official 39. In Pakistan, first-page news framing of both issues contained more ideas. DAWN, for instance, had 35 IEs against the official 20 in relation to 9/11 and 28 against 12 for the issue of Afghanistan.

The most interesting aspects of the testing of the indexing hypothesis involve the qualitative analysis of the IEs that were shared/ not shared between the political debate and the press coverage. It is true that the project focuses on the correlation of the coverage to *governmental* statements rather than to the whole debate among a country's political elites. It could be argued that the contents that are not matching the governmental statements originate from other political, but nongovernmental, actors. The analysis of the sources confirms that this is not the case.

U.S. newspapers tend to reproduce a lower proportion of the political statements than in other countries. For example, in relation to 9/11, while NYT first-page news reproduces 47.06 percent of the administration's statements, LM reproduces 54.84 percent of the ideas contained in the French governmental discourse and DAWN reproduces 65 percent of the contents of Pakistani official statements. This 47.06 percent, however, constitutes a higher proportion of the overall media coverage. In fact, for the issue of 9/11, 66.67 percent of NYT's first-page news is constituted by IEs also appearing in the political statements. NYT's editorials even present a 72.22 percent commonality with the political framing. These values are unmatched in France, Italy, or Pakistan (see table 5.1). Just to make an example, the proportion of political statements reproduced by REP in relation to the intervention in Afghanistan is 19.23 percent.

The observation suggests that a substantial range of the debate in the media coverage in the United States is shaped by the administration, supporting the inference that authorities' news management identified in the process-tracing analysis was indeed effective. This possibility appears to be confirmed by the analysis of the sources who contribute to the framing of the issues: most of them are American officials. The observation particularly applies to the WSJ, in which the only non-American source out of a range of 13 is represented by the Afghani government. The NYT, instead, despite presenting a very similar range of American sources (also sources from the Democratic Party are quoted, not mainly Republican as in the WSJ) also gives voice to the Afghani government, the Pakistani government, the Northern Alliance, Prime Minister Blair, and President Putin (compare figures 5.1 and 5.2).

From a qualitative perspective, however, even in the United States, it is not possible to detect a particularly tight fit between political statements and press coverage in at least three respects. These trends can be observed across all cases and in relation to both the issue of 9/11 and the war in Afghanistan. First, some of the key IEs in the official interpretation of the events are missing in the coverage. Despite the high proportion of governmental messages shaping the coverage, the first-page news framing of 9/11 of both the NYT and the WSJ, for example, neither reproduces the idea of "freedom" as target of the perpetrators, nor the notion that terrorism has to

Table 5.1 Similarity between news coverage and political statements in the US, France, Italy, and Pakistan

Country	Comparison	9/11			Afghanistan war		
		N of Common IEs	Which % of Political Statements? (%)	Which % of Media Coverage? (%)	N of Common IEs	Which % of Political Statements? (%)	Which % of Media Coverage? (%)
US	Political statements/ NYT 1st page news	16	47.06	66.67	7	38.89	53.85
	Political statements/ NYT editorials	13	38.23	72.22	7	38.89	41.18
	Political statements/ WSJ 1st page news	14	41.18	58.33	8	44.44	38.1
	Political statements/ WSJ editorials	15	44.12	45.45	5	27.78	38.46
France	Political statements/ LM 1st page news	17	54.84	29.82	7	26.92	43.75
	Political statements/ LM editorials	13	41.93	29.54	6	23.08	50
	Political statements/ LIB 1st page news	11	35.48	34.37	8	30.77	42.1
	Political statements/ LIB editorials	8	25.81	26.67	4	15.38	36.36

Italy	Political statements/ REP 1st page news	15	38.46	27.78	5	19.23	35.71
	Political statements/ REP editorials	7	17.95	46.67	1	3.85	33.33
	Political statements/ CDS 1st page news	15	38. 46	30	5	19.23	27.78
	Political statements/ CDS editorials	2	5.13	50	0	–	–
Pakistan	Political statements/ DAWN 1st page news	13	65	37.14	8	66.67	28.57
	Political statements/ DAWN editorials	10	50	50	5	41.67	31.25
	Political statements/ NAT 1st page news	10	50	38.46	8	66.67	34.78
	Political statements/ NAT editorials	10	50	50	5	41.67	23.81

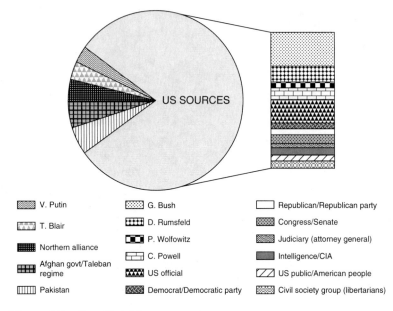

Figure 5.1 *New York Times* sources

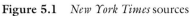

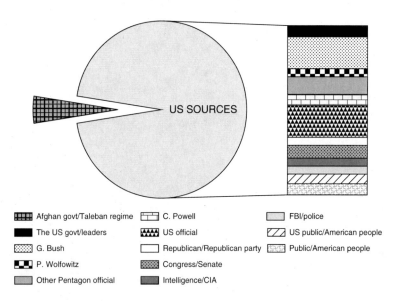

Figure 5.2 *Wall Street Journal* sources

be fought through a variety of measures, not just through military means, nor that the perpetrators should be found and brought to justice. In France political authorities explain at length that the 9/11 events are the outcome of the feelings of anger, humiliation, resentment of a part of the world, and fanaticism, but these aspects related to the framing of the causes of the attacks are not represented in the coverage of either LM or LIB. In Italy examples of contents of the political statements that are reproduced in neither REP or CDS first-page news are the ideas that the targets of the perpetrators are Western values, that dealing with terrorism involves building an international world coalition extending to Muslim countries, improving existing laws, and strengthening police forces at a national level. In the Italian authorities' discourse the response to terrorism should occur within the framework provided by Article V of the NATO treaty and should be multifaceted: diplomatic, financial, military, and judicial measures are needed. Economic development plays an important role in fighting terrorism, as do international organizations. These points are also missing from the coverage.

Second, the coverage presents IEs that do not come from the governmental framing and actually challenge official interpretations. First-page news both in the NYT and the WSJ, for example, present the notions that the current situation is a "great crisis"; the WSJ's first-page news contains the idea that the targets of the bombings are the main towns in Afghanistan. In both newspapers' coverage the idea of Osama bin Laden's responsibility coexists with the expression of doubts about his involvement, if not a rejection of his culpability. Both French newspapers present radically different IEs from the political statements, such as the notion that the intervention is against Afghani civilians (LM first-page news, LIB editorials), that the bombing is unjust (LM first-page news and editorials, LIB first-page news), that the strikes are failing to achieve their objectives (LIB first-page news and editorials). LM's editorials identify the motive of the attacks in the attempt by terrorists to divide peoples, cultures and create a "clash of civilizations," precisely the opposite of the message promoted by the French administration at the time. CDS's coverage contained challenges to the messages of solidarity expressed by national political actors. Italian authorities remarked how "awful and deadly" the events were.[1] Dario Fo, playwright and Nobel Prize winner for literature, instead, hinted at the possibility that the attacks could be almost "justified" by American policy and were not that "tragic" after all: "The great plungers [*speculatori*] wallow in an economy that kills every year tens of millions of people

through misery, what is 20 thousands dead [one of the first esti-
mates of the 9/11 casualties] in New York [in comparison]?"[2] In
Pakistan, while General Musharraf identifies political struggles as
the main reason behind terrorist acts, the DAWN's first-page news
presents the idea of resentment and anger against the United States.
The NAT simply identifies the United States as the target of the
perpetrators.

Third, media coverage does not proportionally reflect the political
debate. There is, in fact, a discrepancy of priorities attributed to different aspects of the framing. In the United States this particularly
applies to the intervention in Afghanistan. Both the NYT and the
WSJ interpret the conflict, along the political statements, as a part
of a wider war on terrorism. While the political statements mainly
develop the causal interpretation and moral evaluation aspects of
the issue, however, the coverage of both the NYT and WSJ does not
tackle the moral evaluation and deals extensively, instead, with the
treatment recommendation. In the NYT, the trend mainly develops
in the editorials and involves the suggestion of measures for a political solution to the crisis: promoting stability through a multi-
ethnic and broad-based government. The UN, in this view, has an
important role to play. A key role for the UN is envisaged also in
WSJ's editorials, although their specific recommendation involves a
full UN peacekeeping operation. Such recommendation, confirming the presence of contradictory ideas within the coverage, coexists
with the suggestion, in line with the editorial position on the 9/11
issue, of extending military operations to other countries.

The French case confirms the importance of considering both the
proportion of political discourse being reproduced in the coverage
and the proportion of coverage in common with the political discourse in the analysis: for the issue of 9/11 a higher proportion of
political discourse is reproduced within the coverage of both news
and editorials of LM than in the U.S. newspapers. The observation
that 54.84 percent of the French political statements about 9/11
is reproduced in LM against 47.06 percent of the American political statements reproduced in the NYT, for example, would lead to
draw the inference that there is "more indexing" in France than in
the United States. The common contents, however, constitute just
a fraction of the overall media coverage: this time 29.82 percent in
LM's first-page news against 66.67 percent in NYT's news (table 5.1,
9/11 issue).

The first observation is that the framing by French media is broader
and more varied than in American media. The remark begs a first

question: where does the framing that is *not* in common with the political statements come from? Looking at the sources contributing to the framing of both issues (figures 5.3 and 5.4) leads to establishing a relationship between number of sources and variety of ideas in the coverage. The number of sources is much greater than in the United States: 32 in LM and 22 in LIB. They cover U.S., French, Pakistani, Afghan, EU, Middle Eastern sources as well as international organizations and foreign media such as the American and EU press, and Al-Jazeera. The overall French media framing, thanks to such variety of sources, appears to be broader than the governmental one. The number of IEs within the press coverage therefore appears to depend on number and country of origin of sources quoted: the wider the spectrum of sources, the more varied the framing (in terms of diversity of IEs) of an issue within the coverage.

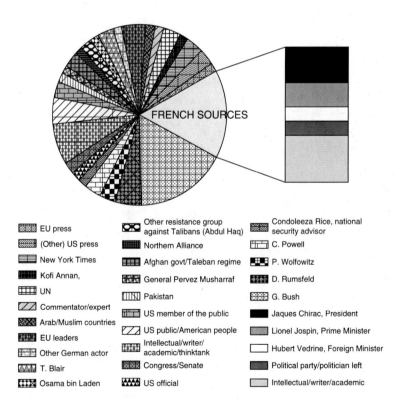

EU press	Other resistance group against Talibans (Abdul Haq)	Condoleeza Rice, national security advisor
(Other) US press	Northern Alliance	C. Powell
New York Times	Afghan govt/Taleban regime	P. Wolfowitz
Kofi Annan,	General Pervez Musharraf	D. Rumsfeld
UN	Pakistan	G. Bush
Commentator/expert	US member of the public	Jaques Chirac, President
Arab/Muslim countries	US public/American people	Lionel Jospin, Prime Minister
EU leaders	Intellectual/writer/academic/thinktank	Hubert Vedrine, Foreign Minister
Other German actor	Congress/Senate	Political party/politician left
T. Blair	US official	Intellectual/writer/academic
Osama bin Laden		

Figure 5.3 *Le Monde* sources

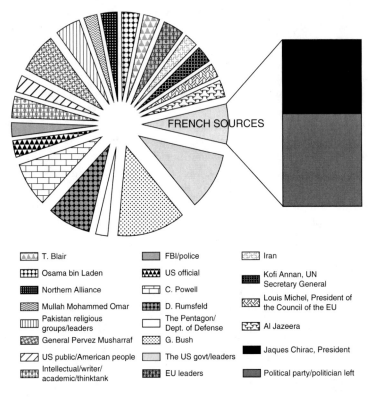

Figure 5.4 *Libération* sources

The second observation is that the relationship between the number of IEs in the political statements and the number of IEs in the coverage directly affects the prominence of governmental framing: the lower the number of IEs in the press coverage, the more prominent the political framing within it. This is supported, in the previous comparison between the American and French cases, by the fact that the whole coverage in the United States, where the official framing is more prominent, presents 272 IEs, against 311 in France. The trend is even more strongly confirmed by the Italian and Pakistani cases (respectively, presenting 288 and 362 IEs in their coverage). Both REP's and CDS's first-page news, in relation to the issue of 9/11, reproduce 38.46 percent of the political statements, which constitutes a fraction of overall media framing: 27.78 percent of REP first-page news, 30 percent of CDS first-page coverage (table 5.1). The variety of ideas within REP's coverage (297 IEs overall) derives from contributions coming from American, Italian, Pakistani, Afghan, European, Middle Eastern sources, as well as other (U.S., Italian, European) media. CDS (283 IEs overall) gives voice to an apparently smaller range of sources (12 rather than 25 as in REP) and involving U.S., Italian, Pakistani, and Afghani media, but the contribution by Italian academics, almost every single day of coverage, outnumbers the framing by any other source and introduces a wealth of alternative interpretations of the 9/11 events (figures 5.5 and 5.6).

In Pakistan first-page news coverage contains more IEs than the governmental statements. An even higher proportion of the political statements is reproduced in both Pakistani newspapers' first-page news than in the United States in relation to 9/11 (NYT 47.06 percent, WSJ 41.18 percent vs. DAWN 65 percent and NAT

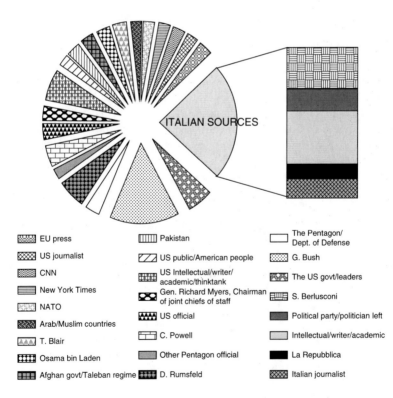

EU press
US journalist
CNN
New York Times
NATO
Arab/Muslim countries
T. Blair
Osama bin Laden
Afghan govt/Taleban regime

Pakistan
US public/American people
US Intellectual/writer/academic/thinktank
Gen. Richard Myers, Chairman of joint chiefs of staff
US official
C. Powell
Other Pentagon official
D. Rumsfeld

The Pentagon/Dept. of Defense
G. Bush
The US govt/leaders
S. Berlusconi
Political party/politician left
Intellectual/writer/academic
La Repubblica
Italian journalist

Figure 5.5 *Repubblica* sources

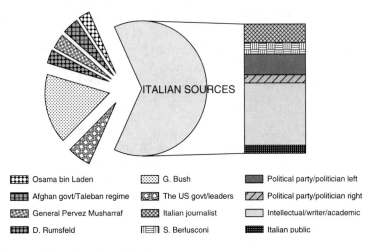

Osama bin Laden

Afghan govt/Taleban regime

General Pervez Musharraf

D. Rumsfeld

G. Bush

The US govt/leaders

Italian journalist

S. Berlusconi

Political party/politician left

Political party/politician right

Intellectual/writer/academic

Italian public

Figure 5.6 *Corriere della Sera* sources

50 percent), but again this is no evidence of indexing since the contents shared with the political statements constitute just a fraction of the overall coverage (NYT 66.67 percent, WSJ 58.33 percent vs. DAWN 37.14 percent and NAT 38.46 percent) (table 5.1). The relatively high reproduction of the political statements within the first-page news of both newspapers is explained by the growing media interest in Musharraf's statements in the context of the developing international situation.

The reason for the low proportion of contents such statements constitute within the overall press media coverage, instead, is the framing competition by voices other than the national government, as confirmed by the analysis of the sources contributing to the framing. The DAWN's sources include Pakistani religious leaders, American officials, Afghan sources, the EU, international organizations, CNN, and international news agencies. The NAT presents similar sources, with the exception of international organizations (figures 5.7 and 5.8).

This last points leads to a third observation: the number and country of origin of quoted sources varies depending on the newspaper. The differences are related to the country in which the newspaper is located, but also to the agenda of each media organization. The analysis shows that some newspapers, such as the WSJ, LIB, CDS, and the NAT appear more focused on domestic issues and rely on a

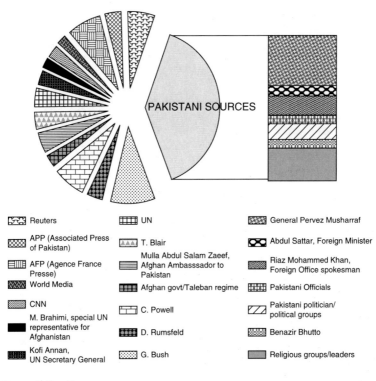

Reuters

APP (Associated Press of Pakistan)

AFP (Agence France Presse)

World Media

CNN

M. Brahimi, special UN representative for Afghanistan

Kofi Annan, UN Secretary General

UN

T. Blair

Mulla Abdul Salam Zaeef, Afghan Ambasssador to Pakistan

Afghan govt/Taleban regime

C. Powell

D. Rumsfeld

G. Bush

General Pervez Musharraf

Abdul Sattar, Foreign Minister

Riaz Mohammed Khan, Foreign Office spokesman

Pakistani Officials

Pakistani politician/ political groups

Benazir Bhutto

Religious groups/leaders

Figure 5.7 *Dawn* sources

narrower range of sources than their more internationally oriented counterparts—respectively, the NYT, LM, REP, and the DAWN. For example, while both WSJ and NYT tend to reproduce more domestic sources than Italian, French, or Pakistani newspapers, the only non-American source out of a range of 13 (representing 5 percent of all sources) in the WSJ is represented by the Afghan government. The NYT, beyond the Afghan government, also gives voice to the Pakistani government, the Northern Alliance, Prime Minister Blair, and President Putin.

Conclusions

The process-tracing analysis of the political statements in Chapter 3 had found evidence of attempts by political actors at delivering coordinated messages mainly in the United States, and to a less sophisticated

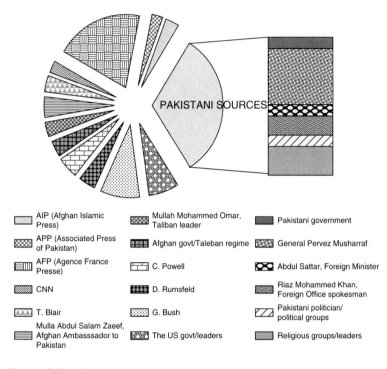

Figure 5.8 *Nation* sources

extent, in Pakistan. The expectation was that, if *news management* was a significant variable in shaping the coverage, it would produce a higher degree of correlation between news and political statements in those two countries. As the data in this chapter suggests, however, this is not the case. While the U.S. coverage tends to reproduce a higher proportion of the political statements than in foreign countries, news also contains a number of IEs that are incompatible with the administration's construction of both the 9/11 events and the intervention in Afghanistan.

A country's *form of government* as a variable in explaining the reproduction of political messages within media coverage was controlled by the choice to include in the research design both democratic and nondemocratic countries. The democracy/nondemocracy axis, however, does not produce significant variations in the level of correlation between media coverage and political statements. Pakistan reproduces a higher proportion of political statements than the United States, but this does not mean that General Musharraf dominates national media coverage. In fact, quite the contrary, such high proportion of political statements reproduced within the coverage represents a lower proportion of the media coverage than in the United States—for both the issue of 9/11 and the intervention in Afghanistan—because of the more extensive reporting of foreign sources in the Pakistani elite press.

Democracy, or the lack of it, does not therefore contribute to explaining indexing. The fact that a regime is nondemocratic leads to suspicions about the existence of rigid controls on the media. As General Musharraf writes in his memoirs, he organized a series of meetings with a cross-section of society between September 18 and October 3, 2001. Apart from tribal chiefs, students, and trade unions, he did approach "intellectuals, top editors, leading columnists, and academics."[3] It is not clear whether he demanded their support during a critical time for the country, but even if that was the case, according to the analysis of the IEs in the news, his requests did not translate into a governmental control of the coverage.

The distinction between objective and interpretative journalism is important in explaining the framing of the two issues within the media coverage. The nature of the *journalistic culture* affects the identity of the sources "speaking" on the newspapers' pages. The United States and Pakistan are examples—at least for the part of the Pakistani journalistic culture that could be observed through its most widely circulated elite newspapers—of objective journalism. They tend to reproduce the national political statements to a greater extent as they rely more on official sources. Political statements are reported less in journalistic cultures such as in Italy and France, where comment and interpretation by intellectuals/academics are given more prominence than fact-oriented reporting. Another way in which objectivity/interpretation affect the reproduction of the political statements is by having an impact on the number of IEs within the media coverage. This emerges by comparing the scope of the coverage in countries with an interpretative journalistic culture (Italy and France) with countries having an objective journalistic culture (the United States and Pakistan). The coverage in the former contains more IEs than the latter.

Even if the variables *news management*, *democratic form of government*, and *objective journalistic culture* do not individually lead to indexing, the greater correlation of the American media coverage to political statements can be explained by their *combination*. Robin

Brown, in fact, establishes a link between form of government, journalistic culture, and spin. More specifically, he argues that media management by politicians thrives in democratic countries with a culture of objective journalism. He traces the origins of political spin—the activity through which officials attempt controlling the media agenda and the way the media frame issues. He points out that the relationship between spin doctors and reporters has evolved over time and depends on "a particular configuration of economic and political forces," as well as a "historically constituted set of norms and values."[4] As he puts it: "Essentially spin emerges from the conjuncture of Anglo-American conceptions of journalistic practice with an increasingly competitive media environment."[5]

Journalists, in fact, always need sources. They might not like what they hear from officials and they might have their own opinion about it, but they still have to report it. While they may not put it exactly the way the source would have preferred, they cannot "make it up."[6] Politicians know very well how to exploit this constraint. They know that if they keep on repeating the same message, this will have to be reported because it is the only available information. The assurance that, sooner or later, what a politician says is going to end up on the newspaper pages is granted by the very objectivity of journalism.

This, however, still does not explain why Pakistani coverage, which the analysis in Chapter 4 suggests has a similar journalistic model to the United States, leads to a much lower proportion of media coverage reproducing Musharraf's statements. The reason is that there are more sources quoted in the media coverage of Pakistan. Testing the rest of the approaches to news will answer the question of *why* there is more source-competition in Pakistan than in the United States.

The possibility that the *ideological orientation of a newspaper*, either liberal or conservative, affects the framing of an issue within the coverage has to be discarded. The liberal/conservative distinction is not a predictor of the extent to which a newspaper will reproduce the contents of the political statements. As also the process tracing has suggested, in fact, the conservative WSJ is more critical of the administration than the liberal NYT. LIB in France does tend to represent the governmental statements less than LM, but this is more a result of its lack of interest in international politics, not of its ideological opposition to the authorities. CDS is more domestically oriented and quotes more Italian political sources than REP. It quotes, however, more left sources than conservative politicians, contrary to what its relatively more "conservative" stand in relation to REP would lead to expect. In Pakistan the liberal DAWN is more supportive of the government's policies than the conservative NAT. "Conservative" in Pakistan, according to Rai Akhtar, means closer to tradition and to the Islamic religious ethos of landlordism.[7] The newspaper's stance against Musharraf, a modernist, is therefore not surprising.[8] This, however, does not lead to significant differences in the two newspapers' editorial coverage of the governmental statements. The proportion of editorial ideas reproducing the political framing of 9/11 is 50 percent in both newspapers; the proportion of editorial ideas reproducing the political statements in relation to Afghanistan is 31.25 percent for the DAWN and 23.81 percent for the NAT.

TESTING MEDIA FLOWS

Testing the Media Flows hypothesis involves not only verifying the existence of flows, that is, content imbalances in the news discourses from richer toward poorer countries, but also finding evidence of a content "imperialism" by the former over the latter. The flows should materialize as varying proportions of shared IEs among news from different countries. The expectation is that the amount of shared IEs will be higher when comparing the U.S. news with the news of all other countries, lower when inverting the terms of comparison. This occurs because of the unidirectionality of the flows: the proportion of Pakistani news mirroring American news, in this perspective, should be greater than the proportion of American news mirroring Pakistani coverage. Illustrating this in an example, if the U.S. and Pakistani news discourse about 9/11 had, respectively, 100 and 80 IEs and shared 20 of them, the same 20 IEs would constitute 20 percent of the U.S. discourse and 25 percent of the Pakistani discourse. This example would confirm the hypothesis because a higher proportion of the Pakistani news mirrors the American news. The content imperialism, instead, is expected to take the form of a coherent interpretation (framing) of 9/11 being reproduced in the news coverage of another country.

The extent to which the American framing of 9/11 is reproduced in foreign news should depend on whether a country is more or less poor. Following the focus on these two main aspects, unidirectionality of flows and the extent to which news in each country reflects the American news framing of 9/11, I will now illustrate the analysis of the proportions of shared news among the different countries, together with the qualitative analysis of their content.

The Inverted Flows

What the data suggest is that news flows really tend to move in one direction, but this is exactly the opposite of that predicted by the news flows hypothesis. Flows appear to be inverted in two respects. First, in relation to the 9/11 issue the U.S. news coverage shares more ideas with the news in France (92.31 percent), then in Italy (84.61 percent) and in Pakistan (50 percent) rather than, as the hypothesis would predict on the basis of the countries' GDP rankings, first with Pakistan, then Italy and France. Second, the U.S. news has more in common with foreign news than the other way around. The U.S. and France news share, in fact, 24 IEs: they constitute 92.31 percent of the American discourse, but just 51.06 percent of the French coverage. The American and Italian coverage share 22 IEs: while they represent 84.61 percent of the American coverage, they constitute an even lower proportion of the Italian news—41.51 percent. The U.S. and Pakistani news have 13 IEs in common: as expected, they constitute a relatively low proportion of the American coverage, 50 percent, but—running entirely against expectations—they represent just 44.83 percent of the Pakistani news (table 5.2).

The main reason why such large proportions of U.S. news are in common with foreign coverage is that the scope of the U.S. news is the narrowest among the countries under study (26 IEs against 47 in France, 53 in Italy, and 29 in Pakistan) and many of the IEs constituting the U.S. coverage are most of the time "contained" within foreign media discourse. This does not mean that the U.S. media discourse somehow "dominates" foreign news. Indeed, the data suggests that the very idea of a "news imperialism" of content is flawed. The notion assumes that there is a coherent framing of an issue within the media coverage of one country and that this can shift to the media coverage of another country.

This expectation is contradicted by the analysis. Indeed, even within coverage in the same country there is no dominant interpretation of 9/11: IEs in the news are fragmented and so diverse as to often conflict with each other. For example, in France, throughout the time span under analysis, the idea that terrorism should be fought through a military action, possibly involving an intervention against Iraq in the future, coexists with the idea that a military operation should be opposed. The suggestion of restricting freedoms to improve security appears at the same time as recommendations not to restrict civil liberties. In Italy the notion that the fight against terrorism does not represent a clash of civilizations coexists with the idea that the

Table 5.2 News coverage similarity in the US, France, Italy, and Pakistan

Issue	Country	US		France		Italy		Pakistan	
		N of Common IEs	% of Shared Coverage	N of Common IEs	% of Shared Coverage	N of Common IEs	% of Shared Coverage	N of Common IEs	% of Shared Coverage
9/11	US	(26)	–	24	51.06	22	41.51	13	44.83
	France	24	92.31	(47)	–	36	67.92	18	62.07
	Italy	22	84.61	36	76.59	(53)	–	17	58.62
	Pakistan	13	50	18	38.30	17	32.07	(29)	–
Afghanistan War	US	(13)	–	8	47.06	9	69.23	7	25.92
	France	8	61.54	(17)	–	10	76.92	9	33.33
	Italy	9	69.23	10	58.82	(13)	–	6	22.22
	Pakistan	7	53.85	9	52.94	6	46.15	(27)	–

The table shows, for example, that in relation to the issue of 9/11 the U.S. and French coverage present 24 common idea elements (IEs). These 24 IEs constitute 51.06 percent of the French coverage and 92.31 percent of the U.S. coverage.

war on terrorism is a crusade by the West against Islam. In Pakistan the idea that the country should provide unstinted cooperation in the fight against terrorism coexists with the rejection of participation to the American response. The identification of Osama bin Laden as the mastermind of the attacks also appears at the same time as challenges to his responsibility.

Besides this is the fact that, even when a substantial proportion of news mirrors American coverage (51.06 percent in France), there is still a sizeable amount of ideas (at least 65 percent in Pakistan) that are *not* in common with it. Such IEs contribute to adding a greater variety of viewpoints to the news to the extent that it is not possible to detect any "American" interpretation of 9/11. Some examples of distinctive IEs are, in France, the notions that the events will have an effect on American psychology, especially on the country's sense of vulnerability, and that terrorism should not be mistaken for the Arab world. IEs that characterize the Italian news coverage include the suggestion to fight terrorism by acting in conformity with Western values and by devising a political strategy. Distinctive IEs in the Pakistani media discourse are those describing the country as a "frontline state" in the fight against terrorism, a member of the international coalition against terrorism. The issue of 9/11 should be dealt with by taking a decision in the interest of the country and the fight against terrorism should extend to all forms of terrorism.

The results related to the issue of Afghanistan are very similar. Again there is no evidence of a news imperialism by the United States on poorer countries. Pakistan presents 25.92 percent of its coverage in common with the United States (33.33 percent with France and 22.22 percent with Italy). On the contrary the proportion of coverage that the United States shares with Pakistan, 53.85 percent, is even higher than the 50 percent it presented in relation to the issue of 9/11 (table 5.2).

While negative IEs about the military campaign do not tend to appear in the U.S. coverage, French news contains the ideas that the strikes are failing to achieve their objectives, that also main towns and civilians are being bombed, and that the war is unjust. A distinctive IE in the Italian coverage is the suggestion of extending operations to other countries. The Pakistani framing of the issue is the broadest. This explains its low level of commonality with foreign news. Some distinctive and contradictory ideas within the Pakistani coverage are that operation Enduring Freedom is part of the war on terrorism, but it is also a pretext to wage war against Islam; the idea that the targets of the bombing are the Afghani people coexists with the notion that the military strikes are not directed against them. The framing also covers more extensively the suggestions about how to achieve a political solution to the crisis.

It is important to remember that these are the ideas most frequently present in the coverage. Some of them are contained in editorials, which represent a direct expression of the newspapers' directors or editorial boards, but most of the time they are contained within quotes and statements made by sources within the news text.

The Sources Shaping the News

The data suggest that there is no evidence that the American news framing of 9/11 is being imposed on news in foreign countries. What explains, then, both the similarity and diversity of ideas within the news coverage? The analysis of the actors contributing to the framing of 9/11 within the news suggests that the reason for the commonality of IEs is the quoting of the same *interpretations (framing)* of the events by the same sources. News content is not created by the "media" as if they were a conscious actor. News content is constructed and it is the result of a framing competition among different actors. At this point, understanding what shapes the news involves explaining what shapes the selection of the sources who construct it in the first place.

Sources are selected by journalists and editors according to their newsworthiness[9] and this appears to follow each country's national interest. Dennis Wu argues that media flows occur because less powerful nations are naturally interested in more powerful ones:

> ...the phenomenon of the press' concentration on the world elites perhaps is not entirely unexpected. After all, powerful players set up the game rules and dictate the repertoire of actions performed on the world stage, thus affecting the rest of the less powerful countries....Thus, it makes a lot of sense for most countries to monitor closely the moves of the few elites. In so doing, they could take necessary steps to protect their own national interests should something emergent or threatening occur.[10]

The analysis of the categories of the sources most frequently found to contribute to the framing of 9/11 confirms the fact that national interest does contribute to the selection of newsworthy sources. It shapes the range of sources quoted on newspapers' pages in terms of their country of origin. It also defines their relative importance over time. This is indicated by the frequency with which a source appears within the coverage. The closer to a country's interest, the higher the newsworthiness of a foreign country's sources. As it is possible to observe by comparing figures 5.1–5.8, in the United States there is far less interest in the outside world than in the other countries. France, Italy, and Pakistan reveal greater interest in European, Middle Eastern sources, and international organizations. It is the interest in a greater variety of sources that explains the greater diversity of ideas in these countries' news.

Another important point to note is the fact that 17 percent of Pakistani sources in the news are news agencies. The reliance on news agencies by developing countries is, in the literature, one of the common explanations for poor countries' news "dependency" on the West.[11] Poor countries, because of the lack of economic resources for gathering news through their own structures, rely on Western news agencies and this, so the argument goes, leads to news that reflects the perspective of the richer countries. This was the reasoning behind the New World Information and Communications Order (NWICO) debate in the 1970s and 1980s: "Concern about news agencies within academe was always associated with the dominance-dependency model and the NWICO debates which it fed.... Unable to control their external image, developing nations had even less control over other people's representations of them."[12]

Pakistani news coverage in the study really appears to be affected by economic constraints. DAWN's foreign correspondent in Washington, D.C. at the time of the 9/11 events, Tahir Mirza, for example, explicitly writes that most of the news gathering by Pakistani reporters in the United States is done on the Internet, by watching television, or over the phone:

> In contrast to what it may seem from afar, the life of a correspondent in Washington working for a Pakistani news organization is not easy. When it's quiet, there's the searching for morsels on the websites or in newspapers to fill the day's quota; when it's busy, as it has been this past fortnight, there's the dilemma of what to report and what to leave out.
>
> If you work for a daily newspaper, the nine-hour time difference between Washington and Pakistan means there's just about till 3 pm (midnight PST) that you can file. Often when developments are taking place as thick and fast as they have been since September 11, you have to decide whether to remain glued to the television set for updates from the cable networks or go to the various briefings....No Pakistani news organization has an office in downtown Washington, which

means that commuting time has to be taken into account. So, sometimes these days, you are forced to work from home, unshaven, ungroomed, and divide your attention between your computer and the television and the telephone. It's a highly unsatisfactory way of working, but there it is. There's no escape from it.[13]

Pakistani news marginally relies on non-Western news agencies such as the Associate Press of Pakistan (APP), the Afghani Islamic Press (AIP), the Chinese Xinhua, and the Pakistan Press International (PPI). It is, however, precisely the fact that Pakistani coverage relies mostly on Western news agencies—Agence France Presse (AFP), Associated Press (AP), Reuters—that both throws doubts on the explanatory power of a number of International Communications studies about news agencies' effects on news and confirms the importance of national interest as a guiding criterion for selecting newsworthy sources. News agencies provide huge amounts of information about what many national and international actors have said or done all over the world. It is media professionals, in this case Pakistani journalists and editors, who actively select those sources and pieces of information that are most relevant to their country's interests.

Conclusions

News "flows" exist in the sense that there are unbalanced levels of interest by each country in the foreign world depending on national priorities. This, however, translates exactly into the opposite of an imperialism of news contents. A weaker position in the international system, as the comparison between Pakistan and the United States suggests, leads to reporting more voices. The variety of voices contributes to broadening the scope of the framing, therefore making the contents of the poor country's media coverage more insulated from the possibility of a "domination" of contents from a richer country.

What is, then, the relevance of the variables identified by media flows studies as drivers of the news flows? The observation of the newsworthy sources in the coverage, as well as the previous process-tracing analysis, particularly underlines the fact that the "positioning" of a country within the international system is not dictated by *economic imbalances, cultural proximity,* or *geographical proximity* alone. The position is constructed by international political actors. France, already more attentive toward the rest of the world because of its "great power" status, engages after 9/11 in intense international negotiations.[14] This is reflected by the widening range of sources in the period following the beginning of the war in Afghanistan. Geographical and cultural proximity could therefore have a role within the broader framework of national interest. Pakistani newspapers report a range of Afghani sources. The interest of both Pakistani political actors and newspapers in Afghanistan is dictated by the fact that the developments in the war-ridden country have direct consequences, for example in terms of refugees' influx, on Pakistan. In fact, if geographical and cultural proximity had an independent role from national interest, Italy and France should be reporting about each other, but this does not occur.

It would, then, seem like news is different depending on the country under analysis: if news is constructed by sources and the selection of sources is shaped by national interests, then newspapers in the same country should present the same news. It should be possible to see a clear-cut differentiation between American, French, Italian, and Pakistani news coverage of 9/11 and its aftermath. As the testing of the Globalization and Localization hypotheses reveals, by focusing on the content of the single newspapers, however, this is not the case. There are more dynamics—and this time related to the journalistic culture of each country, as well as to the news-making process at the level of the single newspapers—that need to be taken into consideration.

TESTING GLOBALIZATION AND LOCALIZATION

This section verifies the extent to which news coverage of 9/11 across the United States, France, Italy, and Pakistan is homogeneous rather than "domesticated" along national lines. The quantitative measure of each newspaper's coverage similarity and difference with other newspapers is accompanied by a qualitative analysis of the news contents. For the domestication hypothesis to be confirmed it is not only necessary that the extent of 9/11 coverage similarity between two newspapers within the same country is greater than with foreign newspapers but also that the shared IEs constitute a coherent national—that is, either an "American," "French," "Italian," or "Pakistani"—interpretation of the 9/11 events and the war in Afghanistan. The same—this time as a shared global construction of the events among all newspapers—should be said for globalization, if the hypothesis is to be confirmed.

Neither Global nor Local

The analysis of the comparisons among the individual newspapers' framing of 9/11 largely confirm the testing of the Media Flows hypothesis. The coverage in American newspapers shares a higher proportion of news with foreign newspapers than the other way around: for example 100 percent of NYT coverage is in common with LM, but just 37.93 percent of LM's news is shared with the NYT. The NYT shares 81.82 percent of its coverage with CDS, but only 33.96 percent of CDS's news is in common with the NYT's. The WSJ shares 60 percent of its coverage with REP, but REP shares with the WSJ just 30.51 percent of its news. The WSJ shares 50 percent of its coverage with DAWN, but DAWN reflects a lower 40.54 percent of the WSJ's news. Generally, Western newspapers (in the United States, Italy, France) share fewer ideas with Pakistani news, particularly the NAT, than among themselves. The coverage of the NYT, WSJ, LIB, LM, and CDS show the lowest level of similarity, among all newspapers, with the coverage in the NAT (respectively, as proportion of each newspaper's coverage, 36.36 percent, 33.33 percent, 29.03 percent, 22.41 percent, 20.75 percent). The highest similarity of contents for news in the NYT, WSJ, LIB, and REP is with LM's coverage (respectively, as proportion of each newspaper's coverage: 100 percent, 73.33 percent, 87.1 percent, 61.02 percent) (table 5.3).

Do these values lead to the conclusion that 9/11 news is truly global? Considering that the lowest value recorded, NAT's proportion of news in common with CDS's coverage, is at least one-fifth (20.75 percent) of the entire NAT's coverage and most of the values recorded in relation to other newspapers are well above that (NYT's news contents are entirely contained within LM's coverage) would support an affirmative answer. A more in-depth qualitative look at the way the issue of 9/11 is framed, however, reveals that there are just six IEs shared by all newspapers. This means that each value expressing the extent of commonality among ideas in the news of different newspapers represents each time a different combination of IEs, not the same coherent framing of 9/11. For example when 100 percent of the 22 IEs contained within the coverage of the NYT are in common with the coverage of LM, just six are those that also are in common with all other newspapers. The other 16 IEs are specifically in common between the NYT and LM. When LIB (31 IEs) and TN (23 IEs) have in common nine IEs, it means that six are the "global" IEs, three are specific to their comparison. In addition to this, the six shared IEs

Table 5.3 News similarity among all newspapers: 9/11

Issue	Country	Newspaper	US — NYT N of common IEs	US — NYT % of shared coverage	US — WSJ N of common IEs	US — WSJ % of shared coverage	France — LIB N of common IEs	France — LIB % of shared coverage	France — LM N of common IEs	France — LM % of shared coverage	Italy — REP N of common IEs	Italy — REP % of shared coverage	Italy — CDS N of common IEs	Italy — CDS % of shared coverage	Pakistan — DAWN N of common IEs	Pakistan — DAWN % of shared coverage	Pakistan — TN N of common IEs	Pakistan — TN % of shared coverage
9/11	U.S.	NYT	(22)	–	18	60	16	51.61	22	37.93	15	25.42	18	33.96	14	37.84	8	34.78
		WSJ	18	81.81	(30)	–	18	58.06	22	37.93	18	30.51	21	39.62	15	40.54	10	43.48
	F	LIB	16	72.73	18	60	(31)	–	27	46.55	23	38.98	24	45.28	14	37.84	9	39.13
		LM	22	100	22	73.33	27	87.1	(58)	–	36	61.02	34	64.15	22	59.46	13	56.52
	I	REP	15	68.18	18	60	23	74.19	36	62.07	(59)	–	35	66.04	17	45.94	19	82.61
		CDS	18	81.82	21	70	24	77.42	34	58.62	35	59.32	(53)	–	18	48.65	11	47.83
	PK	DAWN	14	63.64	15	50	14	45.16	22	37.93	17	28.81	18	33.96	(37)	–	19	82.61
		TN	8	36.36	10	33.33	9	29.03	13	22.41	19	32.20	11	20.75	19	51.35	(23)	–

The table shows, for example, that in relation to 9/11 the coverage of the *New York Times* (NYT) and the *Wall Street Journal* (WSJ) present 18 common idea elements (IEs). These 18 IEs constitute 60 percent of the WSJ coverage and 81.81 percent of the NYT coverage.

only cover the Problem Definition and Treatment Recommendation aspects of the 9/11 issue framing: on September 11 there have been "terrorist attacks" (1), if not more generally "attacks" (2); they were orchestrated by Osama bin Laden (3), and the way to deal with the situation is making an effort (4) against terrorism (5), waging a war against it (6). "Waging a war on terrorism" refers to rejecting terrorism and its methods, rather than engaging in military action against it. Not only this interpretation is quite general, but its meaning is also changed by the addition of other IEs specific to the coverage of each newspaper. Looking again at the comparison between LIB and NAT, apart from the six mentioned IEs, the coverage of the two newspapers also presents the ideas that an international coalition should tackle the problem of terrorism through cooperation, not a military operation. Such ideas substantially distort the overall meaning of the six "global" IEs.

If no compelling evidence to confirm the hypothesis of a globalization of news exists, there is not support of a nationalization of coverage either. Only three newspapers out of eight show a higher similarity of contents with national media outlets rather than with foreign newspapers. They are LIB, having 87.1 percent of its contents in common with LM; CDS sharing 66.04 percent of its coverage with REP; NAT presenting 82.61 percent content commonality with the DAWN (table 5.3). What is interesting to notice—and this severely undermines the idea that "national perspectives" exist on the issue under study—is that such higher degree of news similarity is not reciprocal: LM shares more IEs with REP; REP with LM (here is one reciprocal similarity of contents, which cuts across national borders); the DAWN with LM.

A closer look at the ideas shared by newspapers' coverage within the same country also does not reveal anything specifically "national." For example the IEs in common between the news of LM and LIB cannot be regarded as uniquely "French." The shared idea that terrorism should be fought through financial measures also appears in coverage by the NYT, WSJ, CDS, REP, and the DAWN. The idea of improving security in order to tackle the terrorist threat is also present in the NYT, WSJ, CDS. LM and LIB, instead, individually present distinctive IEs. For example LM news contains, among IEs that appear most frequently, the ideas that "we" are at war, that the fight involves a struggle between good and evil, and that a solution to the crisis consists in killing Osama bin Laden. LIB's coverage, instead, presents the notions that the crisis should be tackled through an information war, by winning the hearts and minds of the terrorists, not through military measures.

The analysis of the results related to the war in Afghanistan appears to suggest some localization of coverage. Five newspapers out of eight show the highest similarity of coverage with another national media outlet: apart from the DAWN and the NAT, also REP and CDS show reciprocal similarity. The WSJ presents a higher degree of similarity with the NYT (72.73 percent of shared coverage) than with any other foreign newspaper (although the NYT shares just 40 percent of its coverage with the WSJ against 60 percent with foreign LM, 60 percent with REP, and 47.37 percent with CDS) (table 5.4).

The localization trend, however, is just apparent. Qualitative considerations of the IEs shared by all newspapers, in fact, rule out both the Globalization and the Localization hypotheses. The IEs shared among all newspapers are just three: what is taking place in Afghanistan is a war (1) against the Taliban regime (2) and Osama bin Laden (3). Given that the smallest framing of the issue, that of the WSJ, presents 11 IEs, while the largest by the DAWN is constituted by 27, the presence of these three IEs does not contribute to a "globalization" of contents. At the same time, by looking at the IEs within each newspaper's coverage, it is not obvious that there are "national perspectives." LM's framing contains the moral evaluation of the bombing in Afghanistan as "unjust." LIB's framing also contains the same idea, but this is negatively reinforced by the addition of other ideas that are not present in LM's coverage: the bombings are failing to achieve their objectives, they are targeting civilians and main towns. The idea of an "unjust bombing" is furthermore not exclusively "French" since it is also present in the framing by the NAT.

Conclusions

The data can be interpreted in the light of considerations made while testing the Media Flows hypothesis. As seen, news similarity and difference among newspapers is explained by different combinations of IEs: they depend on the range of sources quoted. In this perspective an explanation about newspapers' coverage similarity—which appears well grounded in the testing of previous hypotheses—is that *they are quoting the same international sources.* National interest as a factor shaping the selection of sources helps explaining why the NYT has more in common with all other Western newspapers (especially LM, CDS, REP) and less with the DAWN: Western newspapers tend

Table 5.4 News similarity among all newspapers: Afghanistan

Issue	Country	Newspaper	US				France				Italy				Pakistan			
			NYT		WSJ		LIB		LM		REP		CDS		DAWN		TN	
			N of common IEs	% of shared coverage	N of common IEs	% of shared coverage	N of common IEs	% of shared coverage	N of common IEs	% of shared coverage	N of common IEs	% of shared coverage	N of common IEs	% of shared coverage	N of common IEs	% of shared coverage	N of common IEs	% of shared coverage
Afghanistan War	U.S.	NYT	(13)	–	8	72.73	6	37.5%	9	60	9	60	9	47.37	5	18.52	8	38.1
		WSJ	8	61.54	(11)	–	3	18.75	6	40	7	46.67	7	36.84	4	14.81	5	23.8
	F	LIB	6	46.15	3	27.27	(16)	–	9	60	9	60	11	57.89	7	25.92	10	47.6
		LM	9	69.23	6	54.54	9	56.25	(15)	–	9	60	10	52.63	7	25.92	7	33.3
	I	REP	9	69.23	7	63.64	9	56.25	9	60	(15)	–	12	63.16	5	18.52	9	42.8
		CDS	9	69.23	7	63.64	11	68.75	10	66.67	12	80	(19)	–	7	25.92	9	42.8
	PK	DAWN	5	38.46	4	36.36	7	43.75	7	46.67	5	33.33	7	36.84	(27)	–	13	61.9
		TN	8	61.54	5	45.45	10	62.5	7	46.67	9	60	9	47.37	13	48.15	(21)	–

The table shows, for example, that in relation to the war in Afghanistan, the coverage of the *New York Times* (NYT) and the *Wall Street Journal* (WSJ) present 8 common idea elements (IEs). These 8 IEs constitute 72.73 percent of the WSJ coverage and 61.54 percent of the NYT coverage.

to quote the same Western leaders, particularly American political actors. The DAWN and NAT have a more similar coverage because they quote more Afghani, Asian, and Muslim sources than newspapers in the United States, Italy, or France.

Changes in national interest, as already seen in testing Media Flows, affect the newsworthiness of sources. This, however, means that the same newsworthy sources should appear in coverage by newspapers within the same country. Yet, as the analysis suggests, there is no compelling evidence that "national perspectives" on issues exist: each newspaper presents distinctive contents. Such observation rules out the possibility that *news editors gearing the news to the taste and interest of national audiences* have a major role in shaping coverage. What the data shows, instead, is that, among the potentially newsworthy sources, each media outlet privileges some over others. What remains to be seen is what drives the choice by journalists and editors at the individual newspaper's level. This is the focus in the testing of the fifth and last hypothesis.

TESTING THE ROLE OF SINGLE NEWS ORGANIZATIONS IN SHAPING COVERAGE

The purpose of this section is verifying to what extent coverage is shaped at the level of the single media outlet. The testing of the Localization hypothesis has suggested that localization occurs at a lower level than the national. An indication therefore already exists that the coverage of each newspaper is distinctive. But what exactly makes it unique? This section's aim is answering this question by quantitatively and qualitatively exploring the relationship between editorials and first-page news.

The main idea behind the planning of the comparison between first-page news and editorial contents at the beginning of the study was that a high proportion of first-page news in common with editorial articles could have suggested a tight control of coverage's contents by editors. The process-tracing analysis and the testing of the previous hypotheses, however, have highlighted the different nature of editorial and first-page news. More specifically, first-page contents, rather than the creation of one person—or the collective voice of an editorial board—are the complex result of an interaction among sources. The sources compete to impose their interpretation of an issue. Number of sources and their variety of origin contribute to create a news content outcome that can be more or less broad, diverse, fragmented, or coherent. As it will be explained, the reality of the relationship between news and editorials is far more complex to be captured than by measuring the extent to which the two sets of contents present similarities. The analysis of the data will therefore integrate previous process-tracing observations.

Interpreting the Data

The analysis of the extent of similarity between the contents of editorials and first-page news in each newspaper does not suggest clear-cut trends. One general observation is that higher proportions of commonality appear in the United States and Pakistan rather than in France: for example, in relation to 9/11, 62.5 percent of the NYT first-page coverage appears to be in common with the editorials; for the NAT the figure is a similar 53.85 percent, whereas for LIB the figure is a much lower 37.5 percent. The tentative conclusion, drawn in the light of observations made during the testing of previous hypotheses, is that it is more likely that a higher similarity between editorials and first-page news materializes where the scope of the first-page news (measured in number of IEs) is narrower. This could be related to the journalistic culture of a country. In fact, France's journalism is interpretative rather than objective, as in the United States and in Pakistan. In France, and even more strongly in Italy, comment articles on first pages tend to take off in unpredictable directions and sometimes end up far from where the discussion about an issue had started. This would explain the lower similarity between editorials and first-page news, the latter being far richer in number of IEs and sometimes including far more creative interpretations than the editorial views. An example is French philosopher Baudrillard's article on *Le Monde* describing the 9/11 events as the start of a Fourth World War,[15] or the debate among intellectuals taking place on CDS after the publication of Oriana Fallaci's article "Anger and Pride" on September 29, 2001.[16]

The fact that the measurement of the similarity between first-page and editorial contents does not suggest definite trends is actually an important finding that supports previous observations about the complex nature of first-page news as a "mosaic" of contents coming from different sources. It constitutes evidence of a lack of direct control on first-page contents by editors. Without the process-tracing analysis, however, it would be very difficult to make any further sense of the figures. If the common IEs constitute a high proportion of news—as it is the case in the NYT for the issue of Afghanistan: 69.23 percent— does this mean that there is a direct control by editors on first-page news? Perhaps editors are selecting the sources, so that they express opinions compatible with the editorial line. An alternative explanation, however, is that the high degree of similarity between news and editorials could simply reveal that editorials are not original, but simply repeating what other sources are saying, as 83.33 percent of content commonality in the NYT for the issue of 9/11 seems to confirm. Does a low value of commonality, by contrast, indicate that the editors are framing the issue in a new and alternative way to what sources might do on first-page news or rather that they do not have much interest in the issue?

The process-tracing analysis presented in Chapter 4 has found that coverage in each newspaper is directly affected by editors through the contributions they make in editorial articles. The extent of the contribution, however, greatly varies across the sample of newspapers. For example, in the case of CDS and REP only, respectively, four and six articles were coded as editorials against over 100 articles for the Pakistani newspaper NAT. The editorial content contribution by the NAT to the overall framing by the newspaper is therefore more substantial than in the Italian newspapers' case. Editorial framing does not always translate into a well-defined editorial line. In the case of the intervention in Afghanistan, for example, the NYT's editorials appear to limit themselves mainly to summarizing the news; the WSJ, instead, strongly and more actively supports a military intervention in Afghanistan and beyond; LIB's editorials are written by different people who have varying opinions on the issue: Dupuy and Amalric do not initially take a position on the conflict, but toward the end of October their ambivalence turns into opposition to the military intervention. Sabatier is, instead, more supportive of the military operation in Afghanistan. The NAT consistently and strongly opposes the war throughout the period. The two Italian newspapers reveal a low interest in the issue and it does not appear like they have an editorial line on the matter at all.

The relationship between first-page contents and editorials is not straightforward. Even where an editorial line exists, first-page news tends to present a greater number of IEs, much more varied and often contradictory than those present in the editorials. The observation, as plenty of examples have demonstrated earlier on, applies to all newspapers. It could be argued that in countries where journalistic culture is oriented toward interpretation rather than objectivity the editor could have some control on the content of the first-page news by selecting the "commentators." This is certainly true, but the qualitative analysis has revealed, first, that a contribution to the framing of an issue is often made by regular commentators (such as Enzo Biagi on CDS). They are journalists, writers, and intellectuals who have been writing for the newspaper over a long period of time. They might have a certain political orientation, but their comments about new events cannot be entirely controlled. Indeed regular contributors even change their mind within the period under analysis. Enzo Biagi, for example, writes on September 13 in CDS: "I share the pain and the fear of the Americans: may this be welcomed as a little expression of gratitude by an Italian who knows how much he owes to the American flag."[17] One week later he argues:

> Bush, in front of his people [says]: "I want bin Laden, dead or alive." And Washington starts getting ready for war, and there is somebody who, out of solidarity in the tragedy, declares: "I am American," referring to John Kennedy who, in the besieged German town [Berlin] said: "Ich bin ein Berliner." I understand and even share the emotional outburst, but I am and will always be Italian....Once [people] used sadly to say: "Dying for Dansk" [dying for some far away cause]. Dying for Afghanistan is an even more desolating perspective.[18]

Biagi also elsewhere emphasizes the need to be creative in writing for a newspaper: "Nobody has ever told me how to write. The real problem is if nobody reads you....The biggest mistake for a news writer, as Giulio De Benedetti, a great man of the trade once put it, is not being inaccurate or not very objective—it's being boring."[19] The debate among journalists, writers, and intellectuals (Oriana Fallaci, Dacia Maraini, Sergio Romano, Tiziano Terzani, Giovanni Sartori) that takes place on the pages of CDS between September 29 and October 17 expands from the issue of 9/11 to reflections about the meaningfulness (or lack of it) of comparing civilizations. The example stresses the point that comment articles can develop into unpredictable directions. This leads to the second aspect shown by the process tracing. It is often tacitly assumed that objective journalism is more neutral or balanced, while interpretative journalism is inherently and necessarily biased.[20] Indeed, the analysis openly challenges this view: since comment is so important, editors—even those, as in Italy, whose ideological allegiances are no secret—do tend to publish pieces with a variety of opinions.

As Clyde Thogmartin writes, the founder of LM, Beuve-Méry, wanted the newspaper to have opinions that were "independent and unpredictable, opinions that would make a difference in the public life of France because readers would read, value, and respect them, even if they did not agree with them."[21] Paolo Ermini, talking about what it means to write for CDS, argues that absolute objectivity does not exist ("everybody knows that"), but this does not mean that the author of an article should just express his/her own opinions.[22] A newspaper, on the other hand, should not only "*inform*, but also give its own views so that the reader can *build* his/her own opinion, even a different one from that of the newspaper he/she is reading."[23] As Giuliano Zincone confirms, being a columnist you know that "readers want to be told what they already know."[24] However, unless one is writing for a "party-newspaper," for people who just "see the world in a certain way," a journalist's function should be similar to that of a "boutique," a "luxury supermarket" providing customers (readers) with a wide range of products (opinions).[25]

These points are confirmed in the empirical study. In CDS, the editor de Bortoli writes on page 1 on October 8 that "we are all Americans."[26] His article shows that he is personally strongly supportive of the United States and its launch of Operation Enduring Freedom in Afghanistan. Just a few days earlier, however, on September 26, French academic Bruno Etienne is allowed to argue in a first-page article entitled "Behind Hatred There Isn't Only Bin Laden," that the United States has brought the attack upon itself through its policy in the Middle East.[27] On October 31 a very long article by Tiziano Terzani also expresses disgust at the military operation, which is defined as a "sea of human folly" "without limits."[28]

Other biases have been observed in the treatment of sources by WSJ's journalists. They take the form of a more or less prominent positioning of sources' quotes within first-page articles. Some sources, those in line with the orientation of the newspaper, get more space. Diverging IEs, however, are still present within the coverage. There is therefore no evidence across the sample that editors would select sources which support their opinion only. Editorial policy does translate into a selection of sources, but this operates through two intermediate steps: first it shapes the agenda of the newspaper; second, it defines the form taken by the journalistic culture of the country at the level of the single media organization. These aspects will now be approached more in detail.

The Impact of Editorial Policy

Editorial policy appears to have an impact on the coverage in two ways. First, it affects the framing of the issues under study by setting the focus of interest of the media outlet, particularly its domestic rather than international orientation. This has a great impact on the portion of newshole allocated to foreign policy issues. The WSJ, LIB, CDS, NAT are, in relative terms, more inwardly oriented. They allocate less space to the issues of international politics than their counterparts from the same country: NYT, LM, REP, and DAWN. This means that national interest shapes the newsworthiness of sources at a first level, then the newspaper agenda (its either domestic or international focus) is translated into a further selection: the amount of space allocated to international issues is a limit to how many voices can be allowed to fill the newshole. Such dynamics are intertwined with another variable affecting both the identity of the sources and the amount of IEs they can express within first-page news.

As a second point, although the journalistic culture of a country roughly shapes the ratio of news/commentary on first pages, it is the editorial policy that determines the actual shape that the journalistic culture takes at the level of the single media outlet. As seen, the NYT is, among all newspapers in the analysis, the purest version of "objective journalism." Pakistani journalistic culture, at least as far as elite newspapers are concerned, is also closer to the model of objectivity than to interpretative journalism, although it is possible to notice more commentary on the NAT than on the DAWN. French journalism is clearly more interpretative than journalism in the United States or Pakistan, but there also it is possible to make distinctions. While LM's coverage confirms its traditional notorious role as a newspaper of comment, LIB has tried from the 1970s to integrate the political focus with human interest, news features, and a more graphic presentation.[29] REP and CDS are clear examples of interpretative journalism. CDS's commentary is, however, as shown by the analysis, higher than on REP. It is therefore possible, overall, to identify newspapers that are relatively more objective—the NYT, LIB, REP, and the DAWN—from those that are less so—the WSJ, LM, CDS, and the NAT.

Conclusion: The Editor as a Bouncer Rather Than a Gatekeeper

The conclusion is that editorial influence over first-page news is really comparable to that of a "gatekeeper."[30] It is a different gatekeeper, however, than the one described by the news sociology literature. Schudson highlights the limits of the image evoked by the term:

> A problem with the metaphor is that it leaves "information" sociologically untouched, a pristine material that comes to the gate already

prepared; the journalists as "gatekeeper" simply decides which pieces of prefabricated news will be allowed through the gate.[31]

In fact the editor does not stand at a gate letting some pieces of information through and blocking others—a sort of information "goalkeeper." To be accurate it is not pieces of information travelling, as floating papers, through the "gates," but agents carrying the information walking through them: it is actually sources who contribute to shaping the coverage. The editor is therefore more similar to a person standing by a series of gates, the different sections of the newspaper, and letting crowds of people through. Each gate leads to a different room, with a different size, but the time to let people in is always the same. In order to "fill the places" on time to produce a new issue of the newspaper the person at the gate decides how wide the international issues' gate should be, to let more or less people in. He or she also has a say on the category of people who can walk through it, whether mainly politicians or also other commentators. He or she does not check individually what kind of information they carry. The editorial role could therefore be more realistically compared to that of a "bouncer," letting more ore less people into different floors of a bar depending on how crowded it is, checking that people are dressed smartly—just certain actors' categories, perhaps intellectuals rather than politicians, are allowed to voice their opinions on the newspaper's pages—but not thoroughly controlling their identity cards—the editor does not strictly control what the sources say, the opinions they carry through the gate. In other words editorial influence is not exercised in selecting contents, rather in selecting the sources speaking. The selection is not direct, but is the result of setting the editorial policy, particularly the agenda of the newspaper (domestic rather than international) and the way the national journalistic culture is implemented (whether through more or less commentary).

A Comparative Assessment of All Findings

A comparative view of all results of the testing is useful given that the relevance of either the correlation between news and political discourse, the existence of news flows, the globalization and localization of coverage, or the impact of organizational variables on journalistic outputs can be fully appreciated only when cross-compared. The purpose of the study is also establishing how a number of variables operate at different levels and how they combine.

Indexing is the correlation of news coverage to national political statements and is the newspaper-specific product of three overlapping variables: the *national interest* of a country, its *national journalistic culture*, a news organization's *editorial policy*. The testing of the hypothesis had left open the question of what affects the number of IEs within media coverage, particularly what affects the number and country of origin of sources "talking" on first-page news. Testing the Media Flows approach has illuminated the way changes in national interest, in terms of priorities toward foreign countries, translates into variations in sources' newsworthiness. More specifically, the more internationally oriented a country is, the higher the number of newsworthy foreign sources that are going to be included in its national media coverage. While limited material resources can make a country dependent on a range of foreign countries, the "shared priorities regarding relations with the rest of the world" are actively shaped by political actors.[32] The study could actually identify a shift in national priorities in the four countries under analysis within two months after the 9/11 events.

Simply put, national political actors are newsworthy in every country. This particularly applies to issues of security and foreign policy for which political actors do not face competition from alternative national sources. As an article in the *Economist* puts it, "[E]ven if Karen Hughes and company [the White House press team] were not so good at their jobs, journalists would still be scrambling for information."[33] What is regarded as "indexing" mainly by American scholars is, in reality, political actors' newsworthiness in relation to foreign policy issues. The reliance on national political actors by American newspapers is made more extreme, first, by the country's superpower status: its orientation toward the foreign world is more unilateral than multilateral. Even if a shift in American national priorities occurs within the time span of the analysis toward Afghanistan and Pakistan, this is still far from, for instance, French multilateralism. Second, the appearance of an "indexing" effect in the United States is due to an objective journalistic culture: articles contents are heavily depending on what a small range of newsworthy sources, mainly national politicians, say it happens. A third element enhancing "indexing" is the editorial policy's strict interpretation of the journalistic objectivity, which leads to a further selection of the newsworthy sources. All these variables contribute to keeping the number of IEs within the media coverage low. The relative impact of political actors decreases when the scope of the coverage (measured in number of IEs) increases, as in interpretative journalism countries France and

Italy. The framing of the issues by political actors within the coverage there shares the stage with framing by commentators, hence the lower "indexing effect."

News flows, taking the form of an unbalanced reporting across countries, exist but their effects on coverage are diametrically opposite to what the media flows perspective or dependency theory would suggest: the poorer a country, the more diverse its coverage. The United States, far from spreading a "dominant" view of the world, is indeed the country whose coverage, in terms of number of IEs, was narrowest among the international embedded cases under analysis.

The scope of a country's media coverage is defined by the position of that country in the international system, but this is not shaped by economy, culture or geography alone. The position within the international system is constructed over time by political actors through the establishment of national priorities in relation to the rest of the world (national interest). The more multilateral the foreign policy, the more diverse the coverage, since this makes a wider range of sources newsworthy. So France, even being "technically" richer than Italy, is closer to Pakistan in its being multilateral and attentive to the developing world. The study shows that a country's change in national priorities regarding the outside world, a variation in national interest, leads to a change in sources' newsworthiness.

Globalization exists as an unrestricted availability of information: advances in communication technologies make the transmission of information across the globe instantaneous. This creates what Vlahos has called an "infosphere": "the fusion of all the world's communications networks, databases, and sources of information into a vast, intertwined and heterogeneous tapestry of electronic interchange....the potential to gather all people and all knowledge together into one place."[34] The availability of information and the development of communications enable news media outlets to reach out to a variety of sources across borders. The fact that some statements by the same sources are present across most of the sample in the same form, such as President Bush's declarations immediately after the attacks, supports the conclusion that any actors' statements are available virtually instantly on the global information superhighway. While there is evidence that media around the world tend, at times, to report the opinions by the same actors, however, there is neither support for the idea of a homogenization of news, nor it is possible to conclude that coverage is localized at a national level. The framing of both 9/11 and the war in Afghanistan by newspapers within the same country do contain some common features, but the framing in each media outlet appears to be a unique combination of IEs.

The distinctive coverage in each media organization is the result of a collective contribution by many sources. The editors do not have a direct control over them, let alone over what they say. An indirect selection process is nonetheless at work: editorial policy shapes the agenda of the media outlet—whether the newspaper is going to direct its attention toward domestic rather than international issues—therefore affecting the relative size of the "newshole" devoted to issues of foreign policy. Editorial policy also affects the way the national journalistic culture is going to be interpreted at the level of the single media organization: whether the objectivity rule will be interpreted more or less strictly and whether the ratio between factual news and comment will tend more toward the former rather than the latter.

CHAPTER 6

Conclusions

This chapter covers the theoretical and methodological implications of the challenges that the study has raised against some mainstream theories in Communications. The main lesson is that we need to re-define our understanding of the role of the media in society, particularly their contribution to the life of a democracy. What threatens the quality of the contemporary democratic debate is neither an apparent inability by media professionals to fulfill their role of democratic watchdog nor the threat of a shrinking debate caused by the homogenization of news and brought about by globalization nor the spin activities of political actors. The empirical investigation suggests that the scope of the media discourse and the variety of views within it, the fuel of an informed democratic debate, are not a product of an autonomous entity called "media." While it is true that journalists and editors physically assemble the news product, their very sense of "what is news" and which sources should be allowed to "speak" within news stories are the result of a combination of influences that extend far beyond the newsroom. They cover the society in which the news organizations operate and reach further into the realm of international politics.

THEORETICAL IMPLICATIONS

Political Communications

The analysis suggests, first, that the "media" should be understood as organizations of journalists and editors operating according to their own norms and those of the broader national social and political context. Second, that understanding the relationship between political actors and the media involves the consideration of a wider set of relationships than the pure authorities-journalists interaction. At the same time and as a third point, explaining the relationship between media and political actors means also taking into account the effect of variables at a higher level than the national dimension.

The study of the 9/11 crisis and its aftermath suggests that the hypothesis of a correlation between media coverage and political debate does not apply outside the United States. On a closer qualitative scrutiny, depending on methodological choices, it might not apply to the American state-press relations either.

The point is not that a correlation between media coverage and political debate does not exist. The study of the international elite press framing of 9/11 presented here does detect *some* correlation between coverage and governmental discourse, higher in the United States than elsewhere. The fact that the media reports governmental authorities' interpretations of international crises, however, is not at all surprising. When it comes to issues of national security and terrorism, as in the case of 9/11, it is reasonable to assume that political actors are newsworthy sources in virtually every country. What is interesting, instead, is the variation across countries and newspapers, which suggests that domestic power relations between authorities and journalists are not enough to explain such patterns of correlation.

The reliance on national political actors by American newspapers is made more extreme in the United States, first, by the country's relatively lower interest in foreign countries than in France, Italy, or Pakistan. Second, by the country's objective journalistic culture: paraphrasing a well-known quote by Leon Sigal, news stories are mostly reliant on what a small range of newsworthy sources, mainly national politicians, say happens.[1] Commentators are not allowed to introduce a variety of views within the news discourse. All these elements contribute to keeping the scope of the U.S. elite press discourse narrow and generally reliant on political elite debate. The relative impact of political actors is lower where the scope of the media discourse is wider—as in Italy, France, or Pakistan—because the framing by political actors in these countries faces competition by alternative sources.

There are therefore additional and broader variables than domestic dynamics to consider, whose effects, when one analyzes the coverage from inside one's country, just cannot be seen. A country's involvement with the rest of the world (national interest), the self-perception of the role of a journalist in a society—shaping the way reporters relate to sources and write their stories (national journalistic culture)—do shape the way journalists report about foreign policy, but cannot be detected but in an international comparative dimension. Even if the role played by the editorial policies of each individual media organization can be detected within a national context, the full extent of their effects becomes visible only when journalistic practices in different parts of the world are compared.

Current conceptualizations of the media-policy relation are not able to account for differences at the cross-national level. The hypothesis of a correlation between news coverage and political discourse, however, *cannot* apply to foreign cases not only because it is a description of the interaction between political elites and the media at a domestic level. It cannot apply because it comes with a normative baggage, which is rooted into the Anglo-Saxon journalistic model. This, in turn, implies a specific idea about the way democracy should work and the role of the media within its framework. The notion is that "a strong, adversarial press must be ready to raise its own and other grass-roots voices against government officials who would exclude these voices from deliberations about the national interest."[2] It is this ideal that actually leads researchers in drawing conclusions from the data about the correlation between coverage and political debate. A high correlation (although it is not clear how high) means that the press is not doing its job. The level of correlation is used as a litmus test of the health of a democracy. The fact is that journalists' role is different in other parts of the world. In France, for example, journalists do not appear to think that their duty is to give a voice to the people. They see themselves as "high literary creators and cosmopolitan thinkers."[3] What they tend to express in their articles, to a much greater extent than in Anglo-Saxon countries, is their own voice. In developing countries, journalists might want to reproduce official views. This does not mean they are not fulfilling their democratic duties as this is precisely part of their perceived role as supporters of fragile institutions.[4] The relationship between political actors and the media, needs to be evaluated according to cultural, political, and social country-specific criteria.

Besides, the indexing hypothesis might have more accurately reflected American state-press relations in the past than in an era in which information travels instantaneously across global media networks, bypassing national boundaries and official gatekeepers. The development of communication technologies leads on the one hand to changes in the policy processes. Growing interconnections on a global scale are the root not only of a blurring between domestic and international politics. The increasing use of the term "intermestics" suggests that, to an extent, there is no longer a distinction between the two dimensions.[5] On the other hand the way in which journalists work is also changing. More specifically, the very fact that each reporter has access to a whole virtual network of information sources across different countries allows reporters to compare different, potentially contradicting, pieces of information and develop a critical attitude toward official briefings.[6]

What the study demonstrates is that some of the current paradigms in Political Communications are not only getting old. When they are applied to a different social, political, and cultural context, they are also inadequate. The media-foreign policy relation can be truly explained only in a multidisciplinary perspective. The 9/11 study suggests that a fruitful avenue is the combination between Political Communications, International Communications, and News Sociology. This needs further development but must not merely involve adding up the variables from each field. It should rather be based on reworking current paradigms completely, by starting from the elaboration of an appropriate ontological perspective, which brings together the micro interactions of journalists within news organizations and between journalists and officials (which the indexing hypothesis in its original formulation was attempting to establish) with long-term macro processes of international politics and the global changes in information production and distribution.

International Communications

The cross-national comparison of newspapers' coverage of 9/11 and the war in Afghanistan questions the widespread claim that globalization leads to a homogenization of news on a worldwide scale. Localization occurs more at the media-organizational level than at a national level. The unbalanced news exchanges denounced by the Media Flows approach really exist but lead, indeed against common assumptions, to a greater diversification of news. The U.S. reporting, far from dominating international coverage, presents the narrowest discourse in relation to both the issue of 9/11 and the war in Afghanistan than in all other cases.

The arguments supporting the notion that we are witnessing a homogenization of news on a global scale are often used to support the idea that weak and developing countries are subject to imperialism by stronger countries. Studies about the effects of new communication technologies point at the globalization of media leading to a shrinking debate rather than a proliferation of alternative views. Chris Paterson, in relation to Internet news coverage, writes that "the political economy of online news is not one of diversity but one of concentration, and the democratic potential of the medium remains mostly that—potential....despite the deluge of information available online, the most conservative (with a small c) old media sources [news agencies] remain privileged tellers of most of the stories circulating about the world."[7] The study of the international news coverage of 9/11 empirically proves that, while such statements might indeed apply to online news, as far as elite newspapers are concerned, there are no homogeneously organized and operating media outlets distributing globally homogeneous news.

Colin Sparks disagrees on a worldwide homogenization of news but argues that views in the "global public sphere" follow wealth and power.[8] Individuals, depending on their class, language skills, and country of origin can either fully or partially participate to debate in the public sphere, if not be totally excluded from it. As he puts it:

> Even full participation implies only limited active participation in the formation of global public opinion. The main fora, the newspapers and television programmes in which this process takes place, are highly capitalized and their columns and discussions are dominated by the views of the political and economic elite, either directly or as retailed through professional mediators.[9]

The views of the political elites within elite press coverage, as detected by this study, however, are limited. While the analysis cannot assess whether a global public sphere exists—it has not looked at effects that the coverage had on audiences exposed to it—indeed, the material for discussion, the news itself, was rich in ideas and varied enough to support the possibility of a healthy international debate. If economic and political interests translate into constraints on the contents of coverage, they do so through complex routes passing through the organizational routines and editorial policies of media outlets, and opinions expressed by sources debating on the newspapers' pages.

The study overall suggests that, even if communications technologies lead to the establishment of a global information space—and we might at points all read about the same issues—instead of a unique global way of covering events there are endless combinations of contents leading to very different possible interpretations.

A study conducted by George Gerbner and George Marvanyi in 1977 on 60 daily papers' coverage in nine countries (capitalist, socialist, and third world) analyzed the dimensions of foreign news coverage and the distribution of news events locations around the

world.[10] They observed that attention to foreign countries was different depending on the standing point: there were, indeed, "many
worlds." The same world looked, in other terms, different to U.S.
newspapers than to Western or Eastern European media outlets, the
Soviet block, or the third world. This led the authors to physically
draw different maps of the world on the basis of their results.[11] This
study, although much more limited in scope, certainly confirms the
existence of different worlds not only at a national, but also at a
newspaper level.

In relation to the national level the analysis confirms Hillel Nossek's
conclusions about his study of foreign news coverage in Israel:

> Despite the spectacular changes in the world of global communication,
> the role of the nation state has not ended . . . Regardless of the changes
> on the political, economic, and communication map at the end of the
> twentieth century, when it comes to politics and international rela-
> tions, foreign news is still a product of the existing frameworks of
> nationhood.[12]

The "culture" that is supposed to lead to a national interpretation
of global contents leading to their localization or "domestication"
is here pinned down as the contents of national interest: a country's
priorities toward the rest of the world. The greatest differentiation of
news, however, occurs at the level of the single media outlet. News is
shaped more by organizational constraints than by geographical contexts, no matter whether they are national or regional. The relevant
"culture" in this case is the one that develops at the level of the single
media organization in the form of editorial policy.

News Sociology

The empirical analysis clarifies and further expands the perspective
of where the social influences on elite press coverage come from.
What shaped 9/11 coverage came from beyond the last level of the
Hierarchy-of-Influences model—the national.[13] The analysis pointed,
instead, to a variable—particularly by showing the relevance of national interest—that contributes to shaping news contents from the
macro perspective of international relations. The analysis highlighted that the social interactions that start shaping media coverage are
those among international politicians, constrained in their action—
and relative rhetoric—by national identity, already existing poli-

cies, a country's membership in international organizations, and its relationships with the rest of the world.

In other terms, 9/11 news is neither "what newspapermen make it," nor is it "from nowhere."[14] In the former view news is entirely under the control of media professionals. According to the latter, news is neither entirely determined by events themselves, nor by the personal biases of journalists and editors. Richard Salant, former president of CBS News, very effectively expressed this perspective by saying: "Our reporters do not cover stories from *their* point of view. They are presenting them from *nobody's* point of view."[15] What the study concludes, instead, is that 9/11 news was the collective outcome of individual contributions, organizational constraints, and structural factors at different levels.

The understanding of the way news is shaped must involve locating media organizations within a wider social framework. Several scholars have recently turned to the application of sociology to better map the relationship between the media and the rest of society.[16] Rodney Benson explicitly calls for "bringing the sociology of media back in."[17] The author, drawing on Pierre Bourdieu's theory of fields, argues that systemic influences on journalistic discourse can be better explained by taking into account the "mezzo-level 'journalistic field.'"[18] The concept of field, a social environment shaping individuals' actions and being shaped by them, as a mediating level between the macro and the micro levels, helps in explaining how politics and economics exert an influence on the journalists working within media organizations, as well as on integrating historical and cultural analyses.[19] What the study suggests is that, while this is useful, there should be an effort to expand theoretical frameworks even further to the international dimension.

METHODOLOGICAL IMPLICATIONS

Framing and Frames

The study has shown that the framing of 9/11 and the war in Afghanistan in the statements by political authorities is the result of completely different dynamics than in media coverage. This result questions Political Communications scholars' widespread understanding of "frames" as units of content rather than processes of meaning construction. Political Communications' researchers are interested in how effectively political actors communicate with the public and the media. The assumption is that "frames" help in understanding the way messages shift from political actors (who build the frames) to media coverage. Because framing takes the shape of a coherent and relatively stable narrative in the political statements—indeed encouraging the idea that there are "frames"—the expectation of researchers is that framing will present similar characteristics within media coverage, too. Hence, the search for "media frames."[20] The very belief that there are clearly distinguishable "frames" within media coverage, however, is just a convenient guess that makes analysis more manageable and less time consuming, but that does not necessarily lead to a better understanding of the processes and factors at work in shaping media coverage.

As Daniel Hallin, talking about a study of U.S. media coverage of Central America between 1979 and 1985, puts it:

> The problem is that framing of a story can be varied and subtle, and judgments about whether a particular frame is present or absent often are quite subjective. This is particularly true in a situation where a number of competing frames share the political space, and may be mixed together within a news story, as was often the case with Central America reporting. The analyst then faces the task not merely of coding a story in one category or the other, or judging the presence or the absence of the frame, but determining whether one or the other frame is emphasized or privileged, which makes an already-subjective decision far more so.[21]

What has emerged from the analysis is that political statements and media coverage have a completely different nature. Media coverage does not present the same degree of coherence as the political statements. Framing of an issue within media coverage is fragmented, even contradictory. This occurs because news is subject to the effects of a range of variables—such as sources' interactions, journalistic culture, editorial policy—that do not weigh on political actors. Authorities, instead, construct their statements on the basis of a country's political culture: its national identity, existing policy agendas, relations with foreign countries, within the broader international system.

The study confirms the need to approach framing as a process.[22] It also underlines that an effort should be made to approach the *contents* of the framing process in a way that is coherent with the conceptualization of the nature of framing. The study suggests an inductive framing analysis that breaks down the framing process into its smallest constituent building blocks, the idea elements (IEs), and gathers them straight from the media content, without *a priori* assumptions about which "frames" are going to be present. In this way, framing really is detected as a flow of ideas through which, over time, social actors construct an issue.

International Comparative and Multidisciplinary Analysis

The study of the coverage of 9/11 at the international, national, and media-organizational levels has revealed that the five initial approaches (Indexing, Media Flows, Globalization, Localization, Hierarchy-of-Influences) were unable to fully explain the patterns of news identified in the analysis. This is due to the fact that each approach individually focuses on a single level of analysis. Political Communications approaches tend be confined to the national level.[23] International Communications leans toward relying on macro approaches.[24] News Sociology is mainly concerned with micro interactions. The study suggests that, when it comes to explaining news in an international dimension, this translates into "looking at one corner of the whole picture." It also leads to misled conclusions when it comes to identifying the variables that explain media coverage and how they shape it. As seen in the analysis, what is interpreted as "indexing" of media coverage to political elites' debate by U.S. scholars, mainly as a result of the influence by political actors on the media, is in reality the outcome of other variables, the effect of which (such as national journalistic culture or national interest) simply cannot be detected by those researchers because they have no comparative perspective to develop a sensitivity toward them. These considerations point firmly to the benefits of international comparative research designs and multidisciplinary approaches: integrating Political Communications, International Communications, and News Sociology broadens the range of theoretical and methodological tools at the disposal of the researcher for truly understanding what shapes the news in the communications age.

NOTES

INTRODUCTION

1. Tuchman, *Making News*, 1.
2. Ibid.
3. See, for example, Iyengar and Simon, "News Coverage of the Gulf Crisis and Public Opinion"; Brewer and Gross, "Values, Framing, and Citizens' Thoughts about Policy Issues."
4. Popkin, "Voter Learning in the 1992 Presidential Campaign"; Rhee, "Strategy and Issue Frames in Election Campaign Coverage."
5. Livingston and Eachus, "Humanitarian Crises and U.S. Foreign Policy"; Robinson, *The CNN Effect*.
6. Entman, *Projections of Power*, especially 162–68.
7. Campbell, *Information Age Journalism*, 15–26.
8. BMA, *Eating Disorders, Body Image and the Media*.
9. Seib, *The Global Journalist*.
10. Gitlin, *The Whole World Is Watching*; Herman and Chomsky, *Manufacturing Consent*.
11. Hallin, for instance, sees the press as a watchdog expected to put the government's policies under scrutiny, "checking the tendency of the powerful to conceal and dissemble" (Hallin, *The "Uncensored War*,*"* 5).
12. Boyd-Barrett and Rantanen, *The Globalization of News*.
13. Schlesinger, *Putting "Reality" Together*.
14. Shoemaker and Reese, *Mediating the Message*; Reese, "Understanding the Global Journalist"; Schudson, *The Sociology of News*.
15. Cohen, *The Press and Foreign Policy*; Sigal, *Reporters and Officials*; Entman, *Projections of Power*.
16. Maltese, *Spin Control;* Matalin and Carville, *All's Fair*; Graber, McQuail, and Norris, "Introduction: Political Communication in a Democracy."
17. Bennett, "Toward a Theory of Press-State Relations in the United States"; Hallin, *We Keep America on Top of the World*.
18. Boyd-Barrett and Rantanen, *The Globalization of News*.
19. Clausen, *Global News Production*.
20. Gurevitch, Levy, and Roeh, "The Global Newsroom"; Thussu, "Localising the Global."

21. From Galtung, "A Structural Theory of Imperialism"; Nordenstreng and Varis, *Television Traffic—A One-Way Street?* to, more recently, Pietiläinen, "Foreign News and Foreign Trade."
22. See, for instance, Berkowitz, *Social Meanings of News.*
23. Gurevitch and Blumler, "State of the Art of Comparative Political Communication Research."
24. Ibid., 340.
25. Hjarvard, "TV News Flows Studies Revisited."
26. Chadha and Kavoori, "Globalization and National Media Systems," 100.
27. Boyd-Barrett, "Media Imperialism Reformulated," 157.
28. Ibid.
29. Blumler and Gurevitch, "Rethinking the Study of Political Communication," 118.
30. Nacos, Shapiro, and Isernia, "Old or New Ball Game?" 1.

1 THE CONSTRUCTION OF NEWS: A MULTIDISCIPLINARY EXPLANATION

1. Giddens, *The Constitution of Society.* According to Hay, a social ontology is "a general statement of the manner in which agents are believed to appropriate their context and the consequences of that appropriation for their development as agents and for that of the context itself" (Hay, *Political Analysis,* 113).
2. Benson, "La Fin du Monde?"
3. Tuchman, *Making News,* 184.
4. Tuchman, *Making News*; Schudson, "The Sociology of News Production."
5. Schlesinger, *Putting "Reality" Together,* 165.
6. White, "The 'Gate Keeper.'"
7. Ibid., 165–66.
8. Galtung and Ruge, "The Structure of Foreign News."
9. Ibid., 70.
10. Ibid., 65–70.
11. Mellor, *The Making of Arab News,* 76, my emphasis.
12. Ibid., 81.
13. Tash (1983) cited in Mellor, *The Making of Arab News,* 82.
14. Campbell, *Information Age Journalism,* 123.
15. Ibid.
16. Nasser, "News Values Versus Ideology," 48.
17. Ibid., 49.
18. Da Costa, "New Criteria for the Selection of News in African Countries," 7.
19. Nasser, "News Values Versus Ideology," 48.
20. Lendvai, "What is Newsworthy—and What is Not—in the Communist World?" 72.

21. Beside cross-national variation, Schoenback makes the point that news values could vary over time even within the same society. As he puts it: "Western news values are not necessarily made for eternity" (Schoenback, "News in the Western World," 41).

22. Risse, "Let's Argue!"

23. Schimmelfennig, "The Community Trap."

24. Lynch, "Why Engage?"; Risse, "Let's Argue!"

25. Schultz, "Domestic Opposition and Signaling in International Crises."

26. Buzan, Waever, and de Wilde, *Security: A New Framework for Analysis.*

27. Nye, "Redefining the National Interest," 23.

28. Wilson, "The Many Voices of Political Culture," 247.

29. Reisinger, "The Renaissance of a Rubric," 334.

30. Almond and Verba, *The Civic Culture,* 12.

31. "The political culture of a society consists of the system of empirical beliefs, expressive symbols, and values which defines the situation in which political action takes place. It provides the subjective orientation to politics" (Verba, "Comparative Political Culture," 513).

32. Pye (1968) cited in Wilson, "The Many Voices of Political Culture," 247.

33. Ibid., 248.

34. Ibid., 273.

35. Almond (1990) cited in Reisinger, "The Renaissance of a Rubric," 336.

36. Hutcheson et al., "U.S. National Identity, Political Elites, and a Patriotic Press Following September 11," 28.

37. Schlesinger, "Media, the Political Order, and National Identity," 301.

38. European Union membership criteria established by the "European Council Declaration in Copenhagen."

39. Schmidt and Radaelli, "Policy Change and Discourse in Europe," 203.

40. Musharraf, "No room for extremists dispensation in Pakistan: Musharraf," October 3, 2001, available from the Government of Pakistan Information Portal, *Presidential addresses and speeches.* http://www.infopak.gov.pk/President_Addresses/presidential_addresses_index.htm (accessed February 2004).

41. Talbot, *Pakistan,* 391–92.

42. Yasmeen, "Unexpectedly at Center Stage," 197.

43. Boekle, Nadoll, and Stahl, "European Foreign Policy and National Identity," 6.

44. Ibid.

45. Musharraf, *In the Line of Fire,* 201. According to Musharraf, the Pakistani director general of Inter Services Intelligence, who was in Washington, D.C. at the time of the attacks, was told by the

U.S. deputy secretary of state Richard Armitage that, if Pakistan had chosen to side with the terrorists, it "should be prepared to be bombed back to the Stone Age" (ibid.).

46. Datta-Ray, "Asia Must Evolve Its Own Journalistic Idiom," 54.
47. Schudson, "The Objectivity Norm in American Journalism," 149.
48. Ibid.
49. Ibid.
50. Ibid., 150.
51. Ibid., 149.
52. Ibid., 150.
53. Chalaby, "Journalism As an Anglo-American Invention."
54. Schudson, "The Objectivity Norm in American Journalism," 162.
55. Ibid.
56. Ibid., 166.
57. Mancini, "Political Complexity and Alternative Models of Journalism," 268.
58. Ibid., 269–70.
59. Ibid., 270.
60. Sorrentino, *I percorsi della notizia (The news paths)*, 39.
61. Ibid., 40.
62. "Il giornale parla…*a loro*,…ma non *di loro*" (Sorrentino, *I percorsi della notizia*, 39, his emphasis).
63. Thogmartin, *The National Daily Press of France*, 273.
64. Ayish, "American-Style Journalism and Arab World Television" under "The Arab World Television Scene." His findings are also confirmed by an earlier study of the Arab press: Dajani and Donohue, "Foreign News in the Arab Press," 164.
65. Ayish, "American-Style Journalism and Arab World Television" (2001) under "Introduction."
66. Ibid., under "The Arab World Television Scene."
67. Ayish, "American-Style Journalism and Arab World Television" under "Politics As the News of All News."
68. Padioleau (1983) cited in Thogmartin, *The National Daily Press of France*, 273.
69. Gopnik, "The End of the World," 64.
70. Mellor, *The Making of Arab News*, 76–81.
71. "Ulema is the plural of [the] Arabic word *alim*, one who possesses the quality of *ilm*—knowledge, learning, science in the widest sense" (Akhtar, *Media, Religion, and Politics in Pakistan*, n.13, 53).
72. Ostgaard, "Factors Influencing the Flow of News," 44–45.
73. Soloski, "News Reporting and Professionalism," 153.
74. Thogmartin, *The National Daily Press of France*, 248.
75. Ibid., 181.
76. Sparrow also defines the *Wall Street Journal* as "more explicitly partisan and ideological" than the *New York Times* (Sparrow, "A Research Agenda for an Institutional Media," 154).
77. Dow Jones, "The Wall Street Journal Editorial Page Philosophy," n. p.

2 NEWS THEORIES:
CONFLICTING PERSPECTIVES

1. In the context of the study a theory is an explanation relating a dependent and an independent variable through a causal mechanism (King, Keohane, and Verba, *Designing Social Enquiry*, 99–100). The independent variable of the investigation is what shapes the news or—since in a socially constructed world it is agents constrained by structures who create reality—"who shapes the news under which constraints." The dependent variable is the news coverage itself.

2. For examples of front-page pictures and titles from the United States and the rest of the world see Newseum, *Archived Front Pages (September 12, 2001).* http://www.newseum.org/todaysfrontpages/archive.asp?fpArchive=091201 (accessed June 2006).

3. "Le journal télévise Irakien" in "Dans le monde musulman: rage et désolation," *Le Monde*, September 14, 2001, my translation.

4. Jean Marie Colombani, "Nous sommes tous Américains," *Le Monde*, September 13, 2001, my translation.

5. Serge July, "Le nouveau désordre mondial: Le jour où l'Amérique est devenue vulnérable," *Libération*, September 13, 2001, my translation.

6. Rogers, "Theoretical Diversity in Political Communication."

7. A few examples are the following: Cohen, *The Press and Foreign Policy*; Sigal, *Reporters and Officials*; Gans, *Deciding What's News*; Fishman, "News and Nonevents"; Berkowitz, "Who Sets the Media Agenda?"; Pfetsch, "Government News Management"; Schaefer, "Framing the US Embassy Bombings and September 11 Attacks in African and US Newspapers"; Hutcheson et al., "U.S. National Identity, Political Elites, and a Patriotic Press Following September 11."

8. Gitlin, *The Whole World Is Watching*; Hallin, "The Media, the War in Vietnam, and Political Support"; idem, *The "Uncensored War."*

9. Hallin, *We Keep America on Top of the World*, 80.

10. Hallin, "The Media, the War in Vietnam, and Political Support."

11. McCombs and Shaw, "The Evolution of Agenda-Setting Research," 61–62. For examples of literature on agenda setting, see Berkowitz, "Who Sets the Media Agenda?"; Dearing and Rogers, *Agenda-Setting*; McCombs, Shaw, and Weaver, *Communication and Democracy*; Weaver, McCombs, and Shaw, "Agenda-Setting Research."

12. McCombs and Shaw call them "set of objects" (McCombs and Shaw, "The Evolution of Agenda-Setting Research," 61).

13. Berkowitz, "Who Sets the Media Agenda?" 88.

14. Cohen, *The Press and Foreign Policy*; Sigal, *Reporters and Officials*; Gans, *Deciding What's News.*

15. Hallin, *We Keep America on Top of the World*, 12.
16. Bennett and Livingston, "A Semi-Independent Press," 359.
17. Ibid., 360.
18. For examples, see Callaghan and Schnell, "Assessing the Democratic Debate"; Althaus, "When News Norms Collide, Follow the Lead"; Livingston and Bennett, "Gatekeeping, Indexing, and Live-Event News"; Entman, "Cascading Activation"; idem, *Projections of Power.*
19. Callaghan and Schnell, "Assessing the Democratic Debate," 184.
20. Althaus, "When News Norms Collide, Follow the Lead," 388.
21. Bennett, "Toward a Theory of Press-State Relations in the United States."
22. Ibid., 106.
23. Bennett and Manheim, "Taking the Public by Storm."
24. Billeaudeaux et al., "News Norms, Indexing and a Unified Government," n.p.
25. Mermin, *Debating War and Peace.*
26. Livingston and Eachus, "Indexing News after the Cold War."
27. Ibid., 433.
28. Althaus et al., "Revising the Indexing Hypothesis."
29. Ibid.
30. Zaller and Chiu, "Government's Little Helper," 82.
31. Althaus et al., "Revising the Indexing Hypothesis," 417.
32. Ibid., 408.
33. Ibid.
34. Livingston and Eachus, "Humanitarian Crises and U.S. Foreign Policy," 425.
35. Billeaudeaux et al., "News Norms, Indexing and a Unified Government," n.p. Terms are slightly different—"voices," "themes," "symbols," "language," "viewpoints"—in Billeaudeaux et al., "Newspaper Editorials Follow Lead of Bush Administration."
36. Althaus et al., "Revising the Indexing Hypothesis," 409; Entman and Rojecki, "Freezing Out the Public," 170.
37. Bennett, "Toward a Theory of Press-State Relations," 106. Later in the article, however, he talks about "opinions" (ibid., 114).
38. Livingston and Eachus, "Humanitarian Crises and U.S. Foreign Policy," 423.
39. White, "Limits to the Indexing Hypothesis."
40. Bennett, "Toward a Theory of Press-State Relations"; Mermin, *Debating War and Peace.*
41. Zaller and Chiu, "Government's Little Helper."
42. Cohen, *The Press and Foreign Policy*; Sigal, *Reporters and Officials*; Gans, *Deciding What's News.*
43. Bennett, "Toward a Theory of Press-State Relations"; Mermin, *Debating War and Peace.*
44. Bennett, "Toward a Theory of Press-State Relations," 103.
45. Ibid.

46. Tuchman, "Objectivity as Strategic Ritual"; Sigal, *Reporters and Officials*, 69.
47. Althaus et al., "Revising the Indexing Hypothesis," 412.
48. Chalaby, "Journalism as an Anglo-American Invention"; Josephi, "Journalism in the Global Age."
49. Bennett, "Toward a Theory of Press-State Relations"; Bennett and Manheim, "Taking the Public by Storm"; Billeaudeaux et al., "News Norms, Indexing and a Unified Government."
50. White, "Limits to the Indexing Hypothesis"; Althaus et al., "Revising the Indexing Hypothesis"; Zaller and Chiu, "Government's Little Helper."
51. Zaller and Chiu, "Government's Little Helper," 63.
52. Althaus et al., "Revising the Indexing Hypothesis," 416.
53. Zaller and Chiu, "Government's Little Helper," 70.
54. Ibid., 68.
55. Ibid., 63.
56. Maltese, *Spin Control*; Matalin and Carville, *All's Fair*; Grattan, "The Politics of Spin"; Pfetsch, "Government News Management"; Gaber, "Government by Spin"; Kumar, "The Contemporary Presidency"; idem, "Source Material"; Entman, *Projections of Power*.
57. Maltese, *Spin Control*, 3.
58. Ibid., 4.
59. Gaber, "Government by Spin," 509–15.
60. Maltese, *Spin Control*, 2; Cook, *Governing with the News*, 135; Grattan, "The Politics of Spin."
61. Gaber, "Government by Spin," 510.
62. Matalin and Carville, *All's Fair*, 80, their emphasis.
63. Entman, *Projections of Power*, 9.
64. Pfetsch, "Government News Management," 82.
65. Entman, *Democracy without Citizens*, 31–36; Schaefer, "Persuading the Persuaders," 99.
66. Herman and Chomsky, *Manufacturing Consent*.
67. Page, *Who Deliberates?* 70.
68. Kahn and Kenney, "The Slant of the News."
69. Hallin and Mancini, *Comparing Media Systems*, 27.
70. Ngonyani, "Tools of Deception," 22.
71. Schiller, *Communication and Cultural Domination*, 9.
72. Tunstall, *The Media Are American*, 57.
73. Stevenson, *Communication, Development and the Third World*, 38.
74. Boyd-Barrett, "Media Imperialism," 119.
75. Ibid., 117.
76. Ibid., 119.
77. Ibid., 117.
78. Ibid., 127–28.
79. For the unidirectional flow of TV program materials see Nordenstreng and Varis, *Television Traffic—A One-Way Street?* and Varis, *International*

Flow of Television Programmes. Examples of studies about flows of foreign news are Sreberny-Mohammadi, "The 'World of News' Study"; Sreberny-Mohammadi et al., *Foreign News in the Media*.

80. Nordenstreng and Varis, *Television Traffic—A One-Way Street?* 52.
81. Varis, *International Flow of Television Programmes*, 53.
82. The lengthy list of examples include Kim and Barnett, "The Determinants of International News Flow; Ishii, "Is the U.S. Over-Reported in the Japanese Press?"; Johnson, "Predicting News Flows from Mexico"; Cunningham, Jacka, and Sinclair, "Global and Regional Dynamics of International Television Flows"; Boyd-Barrett, "Media Imperialism Reformulated"; idem, "Constructing the Global, Constructing the Local"; de Beer, "New Mirror in a New South Africa?"; Elliott, "Flows of News from the Middle Kingdom"; Lozano et al., "International News in Latin American Press"; Van Belle, "New York Times and Network TV News Coverage of Foreign Disasters"; Wu, "Systemic Determinants of International News Coverage"; idem, "Homogeneity around the World?"; Thussu, *International Communication*; idem, "Selling Neo-Imperial Conflicts"; Golan and Wanta, "International Elections on US Network News"; Swain, "Proximity and Power Factors in Western Coverage of the Sub-Saharan Aids Crisis"; Fahmy, "Emerging Alternatives or Traditional News Gates"; Pietiläinen, "Foreign News and Foreign Trade."
83. Thussu, *International Communication*, 167.
84. Thussu, "Selling Neo-Imperial Conflicts," 271.
85. Boyd-Barrett, "Media Imperialism Reformulated," 157.
86. See, for example, Giffard, "Alternative News Agencies"; Elliott, "Flows of News from the Middle Kingdom"; Seib, "Hegemonic No More."
87. Nordenstreng and Varis, *Television Traffic—A One-Way Street?*
88. Sreberny-Mohammadi et al., *Foreign News in the Media*, 123.
89. Van Belle, "New York Times and Network TV News Coverage of Foreign Disasters."
90. Kim and Barnett, "The Determinants of International News Flow."
91. Ostgaard, "Factors Influencing the Flow of News," 47.
92. Galtung, "A Structural Theory of Imperialism," 81.
93. Ibid.
94. Ibid.
95. Ibid., 91–94.
96. Nordenstreng and Varis, *Television Traffic—A One-Way Street?* 54.
97. Ibid., 55.
98. Boyd-Barrett, "Media Imperialism," 118 and 129.
99. Ibid., 119.
100. Sreberny-Mohammadi et al., *Foreign News in the Media*, 42.
101. Ibid.

102. MacBride, *Many Voices One World.*

103. Ibid.; Boyd-Barrett, "Global News Wholesalers as Agents of Globalization"; Paterson, "Global Television News Services"; idem, "Global Battlefields."

104. Boyd-Barrett, "Global News Wholesalers as Agents of Globalization," 141.

105. Van Belle, "New York Times and Network TV News Coverage of Foreign Disasters," 52.

106. Galtung and Ruge, "The Structure of Foreign News," 65.

107. Ibid.

108. Kariel and Rosenvall, "Cultural Affinity Displayed in Canadian Daily Newspapers," 435.

109. Ibid.

110. Van Belle, "New York Times and Network TV News Coverage of Foreign Disasters," 52.

111. Giddens, *The Consequences of Modernity*, 77.

112. Ibid.

113. Ibid., 77–78.

114. Giddens, *Modernity and Self-Identity*; Robertson, *Globalization*; Lash and Urry, *Economies of Signs and Space.*

115. Clausen, *Global News Production*, 8.

116. Tomlinson, *Globalization and Culture*, 20.

117. Boyd-Barrett, "Global News Wholesalers as Agents of Globalization," 143.

118. Tomlinson, "Cultural Globalization and Cultural Imperialism," 180.

119. Boyd-Barrett, "Global News Wholesalers as Agents of Globalization"; Paterson, "Global Television News Services"; idem, "Global Battlefields"; idem, "News Agency Dominance in International News on the Internet." For exceptions to the study of mainstream news agencies see Giffard, "Alternative News Agencies"; idem, "International Agencies and Global Issues."

120. Ferguson, "The Mythology about Globalization."

121. Rantanen, *The Media and Globalization*, 1, her emphasis.

122. Boyd-Barrett, "Global News Wholesalers As Agents of Globalization," 143.

123. Thussu, *International Communication*, 167.

124. Giddens, *Modernity and Self-Identity*; McLuhan and Fiore, *War and Peace in the Global Village*; Boyd-Barrett, "Global News Wholesalers As Agents of Globalization," 143; Boyd-Barrett, "Constructing the Global, Constructing the Local," 299.

125. McChesney, "Media Convergence and Globalization."

126. Paterson, "Global Television News Services"; Boyd-Barrett and Rantanen, "The Globalization of News," 2; Clausen, *Global News Production*; idem, "Localizing the Global."

127. Paterson, "Global Battlefields," 96.

128. Ibid., 82.
129. Ibid., 85.
130. Gurevitch, Levy, and Roeh, "The Global Newsroom," 202.
131. Reese, "Theorizing a Globalized Journalism," 1.
132. Ibid., 9.
133. Ibid., 10.
134. Cunningham, Jacka, and Sinclair, "Global and Regional Dynamics of International Television Flows"; Kavoori, "Trends in Global Media Reception"; Thussu, "Localising the Global."
135. Kraidy, "From Culture to Hybridity in International Communication," 252.
136. Ibid., 247.
137. For globalization as a form of imperialism see Boyd-Barrett, "Global News Wholesalers as Agents of Globalization," 143. In relation to localization as a form of resistance, the very title of a book edited by Thussu (1998) reads: *Electronic Empires: Global Media and Local Resistance*. A whole section of another book, *Media and Global Context* (1997) edited by Sreberny-Mohammady et al., is entitled "Challenge and Resistance in the Global Media System" (Part 5).
138. Clausen, *Global News Production*; idem, "Localizing the Global."
139. Gurevitch, Levy, and Roeh, "The Global Newsroom," 207.
140. Clausen, "Localizing the Global," 25.
141. Chada and Kavoori, "Globalization and National Media Systems," 100.
142. Ibid., 98.
143. Gurevitch, Levy, and Roeh, "The Global Newsroom," 202.
144. Berkowitz explains that there are also other ways of understanding news: news could be considered a "mirror" of society, a reflection of something that already exists out there, rather than the result of a social construction. He believes, however, that this perspective is "not particularly productive" for understanding news and should therefore be discarded (Berkowitz, "Overview: Why A 'Social Meanings of News' Perspective?" xi–xii). The notion of an already existing news does not fit with the constructionist stance of this book, in which all reality, including news, is constructed through human agency.
145. Gieber, "News Is What Newspapermen Make It," 7.
146. Berkowitz, "Overview: Why A 'Social Meanings of News' Perspective?" xi.
147. White, "The 'Gate Keeper'"; Gieber, "News Is What Newspapermen Make It"; Berkowitz, "Refining the Gatekeeping Metaphor for Local Television News"; Shoemaker, "A New Gatekeeping Model."
148. Shoemaker, "A New Gatekeeping Model," 57.
149. Berkowitz, *The Social Meanings of News*, 105.
150. Ettema, Whitney, and Wackman, "Professional Mass Communicators," 37.

151. Tuchman, "Objectivity As Strategic Ritual."
152. Tuchman, "Making News by Doing Work."
153. Breed, "Social Control in the Newsroom"; Sigelman, "Reporting the News"; Bantz, "News Organizations"; Soloski, "News Reporting and Professionalism."
154. Bantz, "News Organizations," 126.
155. Hallin and Mancini, "Political Structure and Representational Form in U.S. and Italian Television News"; idem, *Comparing Media Systems.*
156. Hallin and Mancini, "Political Structure and Representational Form in U.S. and Italian Television News."
157. Herman and Chomsky, *Manufacturing Consent.*
158. Altschull, "Boundaries of Journalistic Autonomy," 259.
159. Ibid., 255.
160. Schudson, "The Sociology of News Production," 16.
161. See, for example, Hallin and Mancini, "Political Structure and Representational Form in U.S. and Italian Television News"; Mancini, "Old and New Contradictions in Italian Journalism"; Chalaby, "Journalism As an Anglo-American Invention"; Wu, Weaver, and Johnson, "Professional Roles of Russian and U.S. Journalists"; Martín Algarra and González Gaitano, "The Political Role of the Spanish Journalist"; Esser, "Editorial Structures and Work Principles in British and German Newsrooms"; Mancini, "Political Complexity and Alternative Models of Journalism"; Hallin and Mancini, "Comparing Media Systems."
162. Köcher, "Bloodhounds or Missionaries."
163. Shoemaker and Reese, *Mediating the Message*; Reese, "Understanding the Global Journalist."
164. Reese, "Understanding the Global Journalist," 178–83.
165. Shoemaker, "A New Gatekeeping Model."
166. Ibid., 60.
167. Ibid., 57–62.
168. Schlesinger, *Putting "Reality" Together,* 135.
169. Ibid., 162.
170. Donohue, Olien, and Tichenor, "Structure and Constraints on Community Newspaper Gatekeepers," 95.
171. Soloski, "News Reporting and Professionalism," 150.
172. Page, *Who Deliberates?* 72 n. 6.
173. Ibid.
174. Donohue, Olien, and Tichenor, "Structure and Constraints on Community Newspaper Gatekeepers," 103.
175. Ibid.
176. Benson and Hallin, "How States, Markets and Globalization Shape the News," 5.
177. Yin, *Case Study Research.*
178. Pervez Musharraf resigned as President of Pakistan on August 18, 2008. In the following presidential elections Asif Ali Zardari of

Pakistan's People Party won by a large majority and is the President of the country at the time of writing.

179. IMF, "World Economic and Financial Surveys." The data about the gross domestic products (billions of U.S. dollars, current prices) of the four countries is, for 2001: United States 10,127.950; France 1,341.428; Italy 1,118.318; Pakistan 71.854.

180. Hester writes that a measure of cultural affinity "might include a shared language, the amount of migration between nationals, the amount of travel between them, and statuses and past-statuses such as mother country-colony, or patronage" (Hester 1973, cited in Kariel and Rosenvall, "Cultural Affinity Displayed in Canadian Daily Newspapers," 431). The greater cultural proximity of Italy and France is rooted in the fact that, applying Hester's criteria of shared language, amount of travel and a common history, the two countries speak a Latin-based language, they both belong to the EU, and have been part of its Economic Community founding members since 1957.

181. De Vreese, *Framing Europe.*

182. Entman, "Framing: Toward Clarification of a Fractured Paradigm," 52, his emphasis.

183. Ibid.

184. George Bush, "Remarks by the President after Two Planes Crash into World Trade Center," September 11, 2001, *The White House News.* http://www.whitehouse.gov/news/releases/2001/09/20010911.html (accessed September 2003).

185. George Bush, "President Building Worldwide Campaign against Terrorism," September 19, 2001, *The White House News.* http://www.whitehouse.gov/news/releases/2001/09/20010919–1.html (accessed September 2003).

186. Colin Powell, "Statement at the Special General Assembly of the Organization of American States," September 11, 2001, *U.S. Department of State Website.* http://www.state.gov/secretary/former/powell/remarks/2001/5260.htm (accessed September 2003).

187. This approach is different from that adopted by Myra Marx Ferree et al. in *Shaping Abortion Discourse* from which the study borrows the label of "idea elements." Here the purpose is gathering IEs as a dynamic flow (the "framing process") developing over time. Ferree et al., instead, group the IEs into eight "frames" derived from the legal, political, and social movements' context of the countries (the United States and Germany) involved in their study.

188. A codebook was designed for guiding the detailed content analysis of the political statements and the news coverage. The codebook provided a "9/11 datalist" and an "Afghanistan datalist." These are lists of ideas (IEs) actually identified within both the political discourses and the news coverage during a pilot study preceding the creation of the codebook. The pilot study consisted in a preliminary analysis

of all political statements and of seven days of coverage within the sample of newspaper articles. The issues covered a constructed week following 9/11. The choice of analyzing the whole sample of political statements was made on the ground that political actors' public statements were, in the two months following 9/11, more focused on the events and richer of IEs than newspaper articles. Seven issues per newspaper out of a total of 64 days of coverage constitute over 10 percent of the whole sample. The Access Database used for the analysis also allowed adding new IEs to the list while the analysis was underway. When a new IE emerged during the coding, it was added to the IEs datalists. The "9/11 datalist" eventually contained 599 IEs, the "Afghanistan datalist" 286. The codebook also provided for the recording of other variables: dates, name, and country of the political actors ("Briefers datalist"); country and names of the newspapers ("Newspapers datalist"); and distinction between first-page news and editorials. The codebook and examples of coding of both political statements and news texts can be obtained by contacting the author (c.archetti@salford.ac.uk).

189. The analysis also takes the distance from critical discourse analysis (CDA), whose approach was deliberately not applied. Despite the fact that CDA focuses on the way relationships of power shape a text (Fairclough, *Critical Discourse Analysis*)—contrary to more traditional discourse analysis that regards the text as all that exists (Potter and Wetherell, *Discourse and Social Psychology*)—its approach was judged to be excessively focused on rhetoric. CDA is most appropriate for a microanalysis of a very limited amount of texts. It is ideal to analyze the way power shapes a specific text. While the content analysis presented in the study is extremely detailed and in-depth, its purpose is drawing conclusions about more general trends affecting the shape of news. It aims answering questions such as, What shapes the news? Does news reflect the political discourse? Is news becoming "global" or "local"? Can news be regarded as mostly the product of each single media organization? The study also wants to differentiate among different possible factors shaping the news. Here the findings point at national interest, journalistic culture, editorial policy, each of them having an influence on news at either the international, national, or media-organizational level. CDA could have led to conflating such distinctions into the same "power" box.

190. Semetko and Valkenburg, "Framing European Politics."

191. The comparisons are conducted among batches of IEs: "framing samples." Framing samples are a selection of the most frequently appearing IEs within either the political statements or the media coverage (either at national level, individual newspaper level, within first-page news only, or editorials only), and which constitute at least 50 percent of all recorded IEs. Framing samples

are constituted by those IEs that would appear most salient to a hypothetical reader. The important point is that the IEs of the framing samples are selected as a *proportion* of all IEs coded in either the political statements or the media coverage. The number of IEs within each sample can therefore change and the sample can be broader or narrower depending on the characteristics of the political statements and media coverage themselves, particularly on how many IEs they present and how diverse the IEs within them are.

The selection process starts by running a query on the Access database, in which all IEs are stored, to gather all relevant IEs at the required level (e.g., either U.S. political statements or U.S. media coverage or *New York Times* first-page news coverage) including dates. The data is then exported to SPSS and entered into a table. A frequency analysis is run on the IEs by selecting from the Tool menu the option "Analyze"→"Descriptive Statistics"→"Frequencies." The analysis format is set so that the frequency is going to be ordered by descending count. The Output Sheet presents a list of IEs with relative frequencies. The list also contains the cumulative percent in relation to the whole coverage. Several trials have supported the decision to select 50 percent as proportion of the coverage to be taken as the framing sample. Here, 50 percent is a balanced option insofar as it represents both a substantial selection of the overall coverage and a large enough sample to be representative of the contents of the framing process.

192. Krippendorf, *Content Analysis,* 93.
193. Ibid., 39.
194. George and Bennett, *Case Studies and Theory Development in the Social Sciences,* 183.
195. Ibid.,153. Elsewhere Bennett and George define causal mechanisms as "the causal processes and intervening variables through which causal or exploratory variables produce causal effects" (Bennett and George, "Process Tracing in Case Study Research," 2).
196. George and Bennett, *Case Studies and Theory Development in the Social Sciences,* 210.
197. Checkel, "It's the Process Stupid!" 5, my emphasis.
198. Bennett and George, "Process Tracing in Case Study Research," 16

3   POLITICAL DISCOURSE AFTER 9/11

1. All the statements by George Bush, Colin Powell, and Donald Rumsfeld cited in this chapter have been retrieved, respectively, from White House, *News.* http://www.whitehouse.gov/news/index.html; U.S. Department of State, *Speeches and Remarks.*

http://www.state.gov/secretary/former/powell/remarks/2001; U.S. Department of Defense, *Speeches Archive 2001.* http://www. defenselink.mil/speeches/2001/index.html. All sites were accessed in September 2003.

2. Bush, "Remarks by the President in Photo Opportunity with the National Security Team," September 12, 2001.
3. Powell, "Interview by ABC News," September 12, 2001.
4. Powell, "Statement at the Special General Assembly of the Organization of American States," September 11, 2001.
5. Bush, "Remarks by the President upon Arrival," September 16, 2001.
6. Powell, "Interview on CBS Morning News," September 12, 2001.
7. Powell, "Interview by ABC News," September 12, 2001.
8. Powell, "Interview on NBC's Today Show," September 12, 2001.
9. Powell, "On-the-Record Press Briefing (1415hrs)," September 14, 2001.
10. Ibid.
11. Powell, "Remarks with Canadian Minister of Foreign Affairs John Manley," September 21, 2001.
12. Powell, "On-the-Record Briefing (1300hrs)," September 13, 2001.
13. Bush, "President: FBI Needs Tools to Track Down Terrorists," September 25, 2001.
14. Fleischer, "Press Briefing by Ari Fleischer," September 12, 2001.
15. Powell, "Interview by BBC," September 21, 2001.
16. Powell, "Interview on the News Hours with Jim Lehrer," September 13, 2001.
17. Bush, "German Leader Reiterates Solidarity with US," October 9, 2001.
18. Bush, "Presidential Address to the Nation," October 7, 2001.
19. Powell, "Remarks with His Excellency George Papandreou, Minister of Foreign Affairs of [the] Hellenic Republic," October 2, 2001.
20. Rumsfeld, "A New Kind of War," September 27, 2001.
21. Powell, "Interview by Al-Jazeerah," September 17, 2001.
22. Bush, "President Building Worldwide Campaign against Terrorism," September 19, 2001.
23. Powell, "Interview by BBC," September 21, 2001.
24. Powell, "Interview by Noah Adams of National Public Radio on 'All Things Considered,'" September 27, 2001.
25. Bush, "King of Jordan: 'We Will Stand Behind You,'" September 28, 2001.
26. Maltese, *Spin Control*; Matalin and Carville, *All's Fair*; Entman, *Projections of Power.*
27. Singh, "Superpower Response," 57.
28. Hutcheson et al., "US National Identity, Political Elites, and a Patriotic Press Following September 11."
29. Ibid., 30.

30. Roosevelt, "Address to Congress."
31. Bush, "International Campaign Against Terror Grows," September 25, 2001.
32. Powell, "Press Briefing Aboard Aircraft En Route to Shangai," October 17, 2001.
33. Bush, "Joint Statement by President Bush and President Putin," October 21, 2001.
34. Powell, "Interview on NBC's Meet the Press with Tim Russert," November 11, 2001.
35. All statements by Jacques Chirac, Lionel Jospin, Hubert Védrine, and Alain Richard cited in this chapter have been retrieved in January 2004, respectively, from Présidence de la République (The French Presidency), *Discours du Président* (Presidential Speeches). http://www.elysee.fr/rech/disc.php; Premier Ministre (The French Prime Minister), *Discours* (Speeches). http://www.premier-ministre. gouv.fr/jospin_version3/fr/ie4/index.html; Ministère des Affaires étrangères (French Ministry of Foreign Affairs), *Déclarations françaises de politique étrangère depuis 1990* (French Foreign Policy Statements since 1990). http://www.doc.diplomatie.gouv.fr/ BASIS/epic/www/doc/SF; Ministère de la Défense (The Ministry of Defense), *Archives.* http://www.defense.gouv.fr/archives/principale. html. All translations are the author's.
36. Chirac, "Point de presse conjoint de M. Jacques Chirac, président de la République, et de M. George W. Bush, président des Etats-Unis d'Amérique," September 18, 2001.
37. Védrine, "Entretien du ministre des Affaires étrangères, M. Hubert Védrine, avec 'Le grand jury RTL-LCI-Le Monde,'" September 16, 2001, 5.
38. Védrine, "Entretien du ministre des Affaires étrangères, M. Hubert Védrine, avec 'France 2' dans l'émission 'Complément d'enquête,'" September 17, 2001, 2.
39. Richard, "Point de presse de M. Alain Richard, ministre de la Défense, à l'Etat-major tactique, à Rueil Malmaison," September 13, 2001.
40. Jospin, "Intervention lors des questions d'actualité à l'Assemblée nationale au sujet de la riposte militaire en Afghanistan," October 9, 2001.
41. Schramek (2001) cited in McAllister, "Support from a Bicephalous Executive," 91.
42. Chirac, "Point de presse conjoint de Monsieur Jacques Chirac président de la République et de Monsieur Kofi Annan secrétaire général des Nations Unies," September 19, 2001.
43. McAllister, "Support from a Bicephalous Executive," 93.
44. Védrine, "Entretien du ministre des Affaires étrangères, M. Hubert Védrine, avec le quotidien 'L'Humanité,'" October 10, 2001, 2.
45. Védrine, "Entretien du ministre des Affaires étrangères, M. Hubert Védrine, avec le quotidien 'L'Humanité,'" October 10, 2001, 4.

46. Védrine, "Présentation du budget du Ministère des Affaires étrangères, Audition du ministre des Affaires étrangères, M. Hubert Védrine, et du ministre délégué à la coopération et la francophonie, M. Charles Josselin, devant la Commission des Affaires étrangères de l'Assemblée Nationale," October 18, 2001, 1.

47. Jospin, "Discours relatif à la situation consécutive aux attentats du 11 Septembre 2001," October 3, 2001.

48. Jospin, "Discours au Sénat sur la situation consécutive aux attentats perpétrés le 11 septembre aux Etats-Unis," October 10, 2001.

49. Védrine, "Entretien du ministre des Affaires étrangères, M. Hubert Védrine, avec 'Le grand jury RTL-LCI-Le Monde,'" September 16, 2001, 7.

50. Védrine, "Attentats aux Etats-Unis, Entretien du ministre des Affaires étrangères, M. Hubert Védrine, avec 'Europe 1,'" September 14, 2001, 4.

51. Védrine, "Opérations militaires en Afghanistan, Entretien du ministre des Affaires étrangères, M. Hubert Védrine, avec 'RFI-Pierre Ganz,' " October 8, 2001, 3.

52. Védrine, "Entretien du ministre des Affaires étrangères, M. Hubert Védrine, avec 'France 2' dans l'émission 'Complément d'enquête,'" September 17, 2001, 1.

53. Védrine, "Attentats aux Etats-Unis, Entretien du Ministre des Affaires étrangères, M. Hubert Védrine, avec le quotidien 'Le Monde,'" September 22, 2001, 3.

54. Richard, "Entretien avec M. Alain Richard, ministre de la Défense, concernant l'intervention française en Afghanistan, sur Europe 1," November 17, 2001.

55. Jospin, "Réponse aux Sénateurs lors de la séance exceptionnelle sur la situation consécutive aux attentats perpétrés aux Etats-Unis," October 10, 2001.

56. Chirac, "Discours de Monsieur Jacques Chirac président de la République a l'ouverture de la 31e Conférence générale de l'UNESCO," October 15, 2001.

57. Védrine, "Conseil Affaires générales, Point de presse du ministre des Affaires étrangères, M. Hubert Védrine," October 8, 2001, 5, his emphasis.

58. Védrine, "Situation Internationale, Entretien du ministre des Affaires étrangères, M. Hubert Védrine, avec la télévision Al Jazeera,'" October 26, 2001, 4.

59. Védrine, "Lutte contre le terrorisme, Réponse du ministre des Affaires étrangères, M. Hubert Védrine, a une question d'actualité à l'Assemblée Nationale," October 9, 2001.

60. Chirac, "Conférence de presse de Monsieur Jacques Chirac président de la République a l'issue de sa visite en Arabie Saoudite," November 13, 2001.

61. Védrine, "Visite en Inde, Entretien du ministre des Affaires étrangères, M. Hubert Védrine, avec la presse, " November 1, 2001, 1.

62. Védrine, "Session extraordinaire du Forum Méditerranéen, Déclaration du ministre des Affaires étrangères, M. Hubert Védrine, a son arrivée au Maroc," October 25, 2001.

63. Védrine, "Visite en Arabie Saoudite, Entretien du ministre des Affaires étrangères, M. Védrine, avec 'France 2,'" October 27, 2001.

64. Védrine, "Visite au Pakistan, Entretien du ministre des Affaires étrangères, M. Hubert Védrine, avec des radios françaises," November 2, 2001.

65. Védrine, "Entretien du ministre des Affaires étrangères, M. Hubert Védrine, avec 'France 3–France Europe Express'," November 4, 2001.

66. Chirac, "Propos de Monsieur Jacques Chirac président de la République et de Monsieur Lionel Jospin premier ministre à l'issue de la rencontre européenne sur l'Afghanistan," November 4, 2001.

67. Chirac, "Point de presse conjoint de Monsieur Jacques Chirac président de la République et de Monsieur George W. Bush président des Etats-Unis d'Amérique," November 6, 2001.

68. Védrine, "56eme session de l'Assemblée Générale des Nations Unies, Entretien du ministre des Affaires étrangères, M. Hubert Védrine, avec 'TF1,'" November 12, 2001.

69. All statements by Prime Minister Silvio Berlusconi, President Carlo Azeglio Ciampi, Foreign Minister Renato Ruggiero, Defense Minister Antonio Martino have been retrieved, respectively, from Governo Italiano–Presidenza del Consiglio dei Ministri (Italian Government–Presidency of the Ministers' Council), *Interviste ed interventi* (Interviews and interventions). http://www.governo.it/Presidente/Interventi/index.asp; *Comunicati stampa* (Press releases). http://www.governo.it/Presidente/Comunicati/index.asp; Ministro degli Affari Esteri (Ministry of Foreign Affairs), *Attualita'* (News). http://esteri.it/index.htm; Ministero della Difesa (Ministry of Defence), *Audizioni* (Speeches), *Articoli e interviste* (Articles and interviews) and *Comunicati stampa* (Press releases). http://www.difesa.it; Presidenza della Repubblica (Presidency of the Republic), *Comunicati* and *Discorsi* (Press releases and speeches). http://www.quirinale.it/homepage.asp. All documents were accessed in December 2003. All translations are the author's. Sentences may appear long winded to an English reader. This is due to the nature of Italian language. Translations were purposely kept as close as possible to the original text.

70. Daniels, "Leadership Seeking Greater Legitimacy," 113.

71. Ibid., 118.

72. Berlusconi, "Discorso del Presidente Silvio Berlusconi [al] Senato della Repubblica," October 9, 2001.

73. Ciampi, "Visita del Presidente della Repubblica Carlo Azeglio Ciampi alla Regione Basilicata," September 19, 2001.

74. Ciampi, "Cerimonia di consegna da parte del Presidente della Repubblica Carlo Azeglio Ciampi delle insegne di Cavaliere

dell'Ordine 'al merito del lavoro' ai Cavalieri del Lavoro nominati il 2 giugno 2001," October 11, 2001.

75. Daniels, "Leadership Seeking Greater Legitimacy," 114 and 120n. 1.

76. *La Repubblica* reports the following day in a window on page 2 the text of the PM's statements: "We should be aware of the superiority of our civilization, which has developed welfare and respect for human and religious rights. These are not present in Islamic countries.... We should avoid considering the two civilizations, ours and the Islamic one, at the same level. Freedom is not heritage of the Islamic civilization.... Our civilization should extend the benefits and the achievements of the West to those who are behind in history by at least 1,400 years" (*La Repubblica*, September 28, 2001, 2, my translation).

77. Daniels, "Leadership Seeking Greater Legitimacy," 114.

78. On September 28, PM Berlusconi defends himself in a speech to the Senate by saying that he has been misunderstood: "I have stated, as always, that the greatest disgrace, the greatest catastrophe that could occur would be transforming the necessary action against fanaticism, against terrorism, in a clash of civilization or, even worse, into a religious war between the West and Islam" (Berlusconi, "Resoconto stenografico dell'intervento del Presidente del Consiglio, on. Silvio Berlusconi, tenuto al Senato nella seduta del 28 settembre 2001," September 28, 2001).

79. Ruggiero, "Intervento del Ministro degli Affari Esteri, Renato Ruggiero, nell'Aula della Camera dei Deputati per riferire sulla sua missione a Washington e New York del 25–26 settembre 2001," September 28, 2001.

80. Martino, "Comunicazione sugli sviluppi della crisi internazionale del Ministro della Difesa, On.le Prof. Antonio Martino alle commissioni Esteri e della Difesa del Senato e della Camera, riunite in seduta congiunta," October 23, 2001.

81. Ruggiero, "Gli annoiati studenti di Oxford e le nuove sfide dell'Europa," *Corriere della Sera*, October 18, 2001.

82. "Now it is the time to make all possible efforts in order to eliminate the main regional crises beside which extremism and terrorism easily dwell, the Middle-East and the Balkan crises first among all" (Ruggiero, "Intervento di S.E. il Ministro degli Affari Esteri Ambasciatore Renato Ruggiero sui recenti sviluppi della situazione internazionale," October 9, 2001).

83. Martino, "Messaggio del Ministro della Difesa in Occasione del giorno dell'Unità Nazionale, Festa delle Forze Armate," November 4, 2001.

84. Berlusconi, "Resoconto stenografico dell'intervento del Presidente del Consiglio, on. Silvio Berlusconi, tenuto al Senato nella seduta del 28 settembre 2001," September 28, 2001.

85. All documents have been retrieved from Government of Pakistan info portal, *Presidential addresses and speeches.* http://www.infopak.gov.

pk/President_Addreses/presidential_addresses_index.htm (accessed February 2004), unless otherwise stated.

86. Foreign Minister Védrine visits Pakistan on November 2, 2001; President Musharraf meets President Chirac in Paris on November 7, 2001.
87. Yasmeen, "Unexpectedly at Center Stage," 188.
88. Musharraf, "Text of the Speech of President General Pervez Musharraf," September 20, 2001.
89. Yasmeen, "Unexpectedly at Center Stage: Pakistan," 188.
90. Musharraf, "Text of the Speech of President General Pervez Musharraf," September 20, 2001.
91. Yasmeen, "Unexpectedly at Center Stage," 195.
92. Ibid., 191.
93. Ibid., 189.
94. "This act of terrorism has raised a wave of deep grief, anger and retaliation in the United States. Their first target from day one is Osama bin Laden's movement Al-Qaeda about which they [the US] say that it is their first target. The second target are [the] Taliban and that is because [the] Taliban have given refuge to Osama and his network.... The third target is a long war against terrorism at the international level" (Musharraf, "Text of the Speech of President General Pervez Musharraf," September 20, 2001).
95. Ibid.
96. Ibid.
97. Ibid.
98. Ibid.
99. Musharraf, "President's Press Conference (08–10-2001)," October 8, 2001.
100. Musharraf, "President Interview to CNN (30–09-01)–Main Points," September 30, 2001.
101. Ibid.
102. Musharraf, "No Room for Extremists Dispensation in Pakistan: Musharraf," October 3, 2001.
103. Ibid.
104. Ibid.
105. Musharraf, "President's Press Conference (08–10-2001)," October 8, 2001.
106. Musharraf, "Remarks with President Pervez Musharraf of Pakistan," October 16, *U.S Department of State.* http://www.state.gov/secretary/rm/2001/5392pf.htm (accessed September 2003).
107. Musharraf, "Highlights of President Musharraf's Interview with PTV's Programme NewsNight (22–10-2001)," October 22, 2001.
108. Musharraf, "Transcript: President's Interview with CNN (23/10/2001)," October 23, 2001.

109. Musharraf, "Point de presse conjoint de Monsieur Jacques Chirac président de la République et du Général Pervez Musharraf président de la République islamique du Pakistan à l'issue de leur entretien," November 7, *Discours du Président de la République*. http://www.elysee.fr/rech/disc.php (accessed January 2004).

110. Musharraf, "President Pervez Musharraf's Speech at 56th UNGA Session (Nov 10, 2001)," November 10, 2001.

111. Musharraf, "President of Pakistan Reaffirms Commitment to Fight Terrorism," November 10, 2001, *White House News*. http://www.whitehouse.gov/news/releases/2001/11/print/20011110–6.html (accessed November 2003).

112. Musharraf, "President Interview to CNN (30–09-01)–Main Points," September 30, 2001.

113. Musharraf, "Transcript: President's Interview with CNN (23/10/2001)," October 23, 2001.

114. Musharraf, "President's Press Conference (08–10-2001)," October 8, 2001.

115. Musharraf, "No Room for Extremists Dispensation in Pakistan: Musharraf," October 3, 2001.

116. Musharraf, "Text of the Speech of President General Pervez Musharraf," September 20, 2001.

117. Ibid.

118. Musharraf, "President's Press Conference (08–10-2001)," October 8, 2001.

119. Musharraf, "President Pervez Musharraf's Speech at 56th UNGA Session (Nov 10, 2001)," November 10, 2001.

120. Musharraf, "No Room for Extremists Dispensation in Pakistan: Musharraf," October 3, 2001; idem, "President Pervez Musharraf's Speech at 56th UNGA Session (Nov 10, 2001)," November 10, 2001.

121. Musharraf, "President's Press Conference (08–10-2001)," October 8, 2001.

122. This is confirmed by an extensive comparative analysis of the national identity discourses in several European countries. For the Italian contained "European" identity see Leisenheimer, "Der italianiesche Diskurs zum NATO-Beitritt (1947–1949) (The Italian discourse at the time of joining NATO [1947–1949])," and "Der italienische Diskurs zum zweiten Golfkrieg (1990–1991) (The Italian discourse during the second Gulf War [1990–1991])." For the French "world power" identity see Stahl, "Der französische Diskurs zur Europäischen Verteidigungsgemeischaft (1952–54) (The French discourse about the European Defence Community [1952–1954])," and Stahl, "Der französische Diskurs zum Maastricht-Referendum (1992) (The French discourse about the Maastricht Referendum [1992])."

4 Press Coverage after 9/11

1. Chalaby, "Journalism As an Anglo-American Invention"; Benson, "Tearing Down the 'Wall' in American Journalism"; Hallin and Mancini, *Comparing Media Systems*, 246; Josephi, "Journalism in the Global Age."
2. For references to the "wall of separation" between news and editorials see Kahn and Kenney, "The Slant of the News," 381; Page, *Who Deliberates?* 50–51 and 76n.22; Druckman and Parkin, "The Impact of Media Bias," 1031. For references to objective journalism being fact based, see Entman, *Democracy without Citizens*, 30–31. Patterson calls American journalism "descriptive" in "Bad News, Bad Governance," 97 and 102.
3. Dicken-Garcia, *Journalistic Standards in Nineteenth-Century America*.
4. Berger, "The Story of the New York Times," 107.
5. Ibid., 107–8.
6. Dow Jones, "The Wall Street Journal."
7. "In Patriotic Time, Dissent Is Muted," *New York Times*, September 28, 2001.
8. "The Taliban leader, Mullah Mohammed Omar, has already said in a defiant, warlike radio speech on Friday that he believed that handing over Mr. bin Laden would not spare Afghanistan from an American attack" ("Pakistani Team Giving Afghans an Ultimatum," *New York Times*, September 17, 2001).
9. "As for Mr. bin Laden himself, the Qatar-based satellite television station Al Jazeera broadcast a statement on Sunday that it attributed to the world's most wanted fugitive. 'I would like to assure the world that I did not plan the recent attacks, which seem to have been planned by people for personal reasons,' read the message, whose authenticity was impossible to verify. 'I have been living in the Islamic Emirate of Afghanistan and following its leaders' rules. The current leader does not allow me to exercise such operations'" (ibid.).
10. "Taliban Refuse Quick Decision over Bin Laden," *New York Times*, September 18, 2001.
11. "Streets of Huge Pakistan City Seethe with Hatred of U.S.," *New York Times*, September 30, 2001.
12. Ibid.
13. "The Battle for Mazar-i-Sharif," *New York Times*, November 10, 2001. Examples of other editorials are "In for the Long Haul," September 16, 2001, and "Wartime Rhetoric," September 19, 2001.
14. "Mr. Bush's New Gravitas," *New York Times*, October 12, 2001, Editorial.
15. "Wartime Rhetoric," *New York Times*, September 19, 2001, Editorial.

16. "Edging Toward a Deal with Moscow," *New York Times*, October 22, 2001, Editorial.
17. "Nation-Building in Afghanistan," *New York Times*, September 27, 2001, Editorial.
18. "Thunderous Blasts and Bright Flashes Mark Kabul Strikes," *New York Times*, October 8, 2001.
19. "U.S. and Britain Strike Afghanistan, Aiming at Bases and Terrorist Camps; Bush Warns 'Taliban Will Pay a Price,'" *New York Times*, October 8, 2001.
20. "Bin Laden Taunts U.S. and Praises Hijackers," *New York Times*, October 8, 2001.
21. Ibid.
22. In 1934 the *Wall Street Journal*'s slogan was "The Newspaper for the Investor" ("History of the Wall Street Journal," available from *DowJones.com*. http://www.dowjones.com/Pressroom/PressKits/WEwsj_history.htm).
23. "The Wall Street Journal," available from *DowJones.com*. http://www.dowjones.com/Products_Services/PrintPublishing/WSJ.htm.
24. "A Newspaper's Philosophy," available from *DowJones.com*. http://www.dowjones.com/Products_Services/PrintPublishing/Grimes.htm.
25. "Terrorists Destroy World Trade Center, Hit Pentagon in Raid with Hijacked Jets—Death Toll, Source of Devastating Attacks Remain Unclear; U.S. Vows Retaliation As Attention Focuses on Bin Laden," *Wall Street Journal*, September 12, 2001.
26. Ibid.
27. "Terrorists Destroy World Trade Center, Hit Pentagon in Raid with Hijacked Jets—Hour of Horror Forever Alters American Lives—Florida Closes Universities, Baseball Is Canceled; 'It's a Test of Us,'" *Wall Street Journal*, September 12, 2001.
28. Ibid.
29. Dow Jones, "The Wall Street Journal Editorial Page Philosophy."
30. "A Terrorist Pearl Harbor," *Wall Street Journal*, September 12, 2001, Editorial.
31. "Bin Laden's Clarity," *Wall Street Journal*, October 9, 2001, Editorial.
32. "Getting Serious," *Wall Street Journal*, September 13, 2001, Editorial.
33. "War Aims," *Wall Street Journal*, September 20, 2001, Editorial.
34. "Keep Rolling," *Wall Street Journal*, November 14, 2001, Editorial.
35. "Unspooking Spooks," *Wall Street Journal*, September 18, 2001, Editorial.
36. "Ensuring Insurance," *Wall Street Journal*, October 24, 2001, Editorial.

37. "Taking Liberties," *Wall Street Journal*, September 25, 2001, Editorial.
38. "Berlusconi's Bombshell," *Wall Street Journal*, October 1, 2001, Editorial.
39. "Terrorists Destroy World Trade Center, Hit Pentagon in Raid with Hijacked Jets—Hour of Horror Forever Alters American Lives—Florida Closes Universities, Baseball Is Canceled; 'It's a Test of Us,'" *Wall Street Journal*, September 12, 2001.
40. "Counterattack: U.S. Launches Strikes on Taliban, Bin Laden with Aid of British—Targets of Nighttime Raids Include Command Posts and Antiaircraft Batteries—Bush Asks U.S. for Patience," *Wall Street Journal*, October 8, 2001.
41. "Fight Plan: On Day 2 of Bombing, U.S. Lays Groundwork for a Long Campaign—Once Air Space Is Secure, Special Forces Will Go after Bin Laden's Group—A Muted Muslim Reaction," *Wall Street Journal*, October 9, 2001.
42. Hallin and Mancini, *Comparing Media Systems,* 99.
43. Ibid., especially Chapter 4, tables 4.1 and 4.2, and figure 4.1.
44. Ibid., Chapter 7.
45. Ibid., 246.
46. Gopnik, "The End of the World," 66.
47. Ibid.
48. Rapin, "An Interview with Serge July."
49. Ibid.
50. Benson, "The Mediated Public Sphere," 33.
51. "Chirac se recueille à New York," *Libération*, September 20, 2001.
52. "L'Assemblée solidaire mais peu guerrière," *Libération*, October 4, 2001.
53. "Des partis divisés à la tribune," *Libération*, October 4, 2001.
54. July, "Le nouveau désordre mondial," *Libération*, September 13, 2001, Editorial.
55. July, "Le bouleversement américain,", *Libération*, September 15–16, 2001, Editorial.
56. Amalric, "Révolution," *Libération*, September 20, 2001, Editorial.
57. Dupuy, "Lois de circonstance," *Libération*, November 1, 2001, Editorial.
58. Amalric, October 27–28, and November 8, 2001; Dupuy, November 5, 2001.
59. Dupuy, "Double mission," *Libération*, October 6, 2001, Editorial.
60. Dupuy, "Un test d'évaluation," *Libération*, October 20–21, 2001, Editorial.
61. Dupuy, "Raison garder," *Libération*, October 11, 2001, Editorial.
62. Dupuy, "Le front de l'opinion," *Libération*, October 30, 2001, Editorial.
63. Amalric, "Tournant," *Libération*, September 22–23, 2001, Editorial.

64. Amalric, "Conversion," *Libération*, September 25, 2001, Editorial.

65. Amalric, "Peuple en otage," *Libération*, September 27, 2001, Editorial.

66. Amalric, "Prévisible," *Libération*, October 8, 2001, Editorial.

67. Amalric, "Boomerang," *Libération*, October 23, 2001, Editorial.

68. Sabatier, "Inéluctable," *Libération*, November 7, 2001, Editorial.

69. Gopnik, "The End of the World," 67.

70. Ibid.

71. Annan, "Rester unis contre le terrorisme," *Le Monde*, September 23–24, 2001.

72. Malley, "Surprises et paradoxes américains," *Le Monde*, October 30, 2001.

73. Baudrillard, "L'esprit du terrorisme," *Le Monde*, November 3, 2001.

74. Minc, "Le terrorisme de l'esprit," *Le Monde*, November 7, 2001.

75. "L'Amérique sous le choc d'un 'Pearl Harbor' terroriste," *Le Monde*, September 13, 2001.

76. "Les chefs religieux afghans et pakistanais menacent les Etats-Unis d'un djihad", *Le Monde*, September 20, 2001.

77. "Lionel Jospin refuse de céder tout le terrain diplomatique à Jacques Chirac," *Le Monde*, September 26, 2001.

78. "The War against America," *New York Times*, Editorial in "La 'troisième guerre mondiale' a commencé," *Le Monde*, September 13, 2001.

79. Oren, "Après Pearl Harbour est venu Hiroshima," *Ha'Aretz* in "La 'troisième guerre mondiale' a commencé," *Le Monde*, September 13, 2001.

80. The *New York Times* page is part of the study's sample on September 18, 19, 22, 2001.

81. Gordon, "Identifying the Enemies under New Rules of War," *New York Times*, *Le Monde*, September 18, 2001.

82. Fukuyama, "L'Etat-Uni," *Le Monde*, September 19, 2001.

83. "For One Day, Just Making Trades Meant More Than Making Money," *New York Times* in *Le Monde*, September 19, 2001.

84. Smith, "L'égérie de l'islamisme marocain: 'Si c'est Ben Laden, il nous a joué un sale tour,'" *Le Monde*, September 19, 2001.

85. "Ben Laden and Co.," *Le Monde*, September 19, 2001, Editorial.

86. "Vent de paix?" *Le Monde*, September 20, 2001, Editorial.

87. "Justice Européenne," *Le Monde*, September 22, 2001, Editorial.

88. "La guerre des mots," *Le Monde*, September 16, 2001, Editorial.

89. "La gaffe de Berlusconi," *Le Monde*, September 29, 2001, Editorial.

90. "Certains silences," *Le Monde*, October 10, 2001, Editorial.

91. "Les preuves et la cible,"*Le Monde*, October 9, 2001, Editorial.

92. "Une chance pour l'Afghanistan," *Le Monde*, November 14, 2001, Editorial.

93. Le Carré, "Le théâtre de la terreur," *Le Monde*, October 18, 2001.

94. Casanova, "Le terrorisme et l'Europe," *Le Monde*, October 19, 2001.
95. Mancini, "Political Complexity and Alternative Models of Journalism," 272.
96. Scalfari, "Un giornale indipendente ma non neutrale," *La Repubblica*, January 14, 1976.
97. Farinelli et al., *Storia del giornalismo italiano* (The History of Italian Journalism), 186.
98. Ibid., 189.
99. Torelli Viollier (1881) cited in Farinelli et al., *Storia del giornalismo italiano*, 189, his emphasis.
100. Corriere della Sera, "Declaration of Independence of the Corriere Della Sera."
101. Garzanti Linguistica, "editoriale" definition.
102. Ferrari, "Oltre la notizia (Beyond the News)," 71.
103. For the political bias of Italian journalism see Mancini, "Old and New Contradictions in Italian Journalism"; idem, "Political Complexity and Alternative Models of Journalism"; Hallin and Mancini, *Comparing Media Systems*, especially Chapter 5.
104. "Antrace, altri 5 casi in Usa," *Repubblica*, October 15, 2001.
105. "Bush: non tratto su Bin Laden,"*Repubblica*, October 15, 2001.
106. Rampoldi, "I partigiani dell'ex re," *Repubblica*, November 3, 2001.
107. Polito, "Un nuovo ruolo mentre l'ora X si avvicina," *Repubblica*, November 5, 2001.
108. Valli, "Se la guerra diventa una crociata (If the war becomes a crusade)," *Repubblica*, September 17, 2001; Sontag, "Il sostenibile peso della verità (The bearable weight of truth)," *Repubblica*, September 17, 2001; Bocca, "Dai cattivi saraceni ai piloti kamikaze (From the evil Saracens to the kamikaze pilots)," *Repubblica*, September 17, 2001.
109. Diamanti, "Come difenderci dal mondo (How to defend ourselves from the world)," *Repubblica*, September 19, 2001; Viola, "La guerra segreta (The secret war)," *Repubblica*, September 19, 2001; Ben Jelloun, "Papà, perché sono musulmana? (Dad, why am I a Muslim?)," *Repubblica*, September 19, 2001.
110. Fukuyama, "Ora gli Usa riscoprono le alleanze (Now the US re-discovers alliances)," *Repubblica*, September 20, 2001; Saramago, "Uccidere in nome di Dio (To kill in the name of God)," *Repubblica*, September 20, 2001.
111. Walzer, "Senza il campo di battaglia (Without a battlefield)," *Repubblica*, September 25, 2001.
112. Galimberti, "Quando Dio arma gli eserciti (When God arms the military)," *Repubblica*, September 25, 2001.
113. Sylos Labini, "Chi vuole impedire le rogatorie (Who wants to block the rogatorie)," *Repubblica*, September 25, 2001.
114. "Islam, bufera su Berlusconi," *Repubblica*, September 28, 2001.

115. "A Kabul, pronti ad attaccare," *Repubblica*, November 8, 2001, p. 2.
116. Chirac, "La sfida delle culture nel mondo globale (The cultural challenge in a globalized world)," *Repubblica*, October 16, 2001.
117. Rumsfeld, "Nuovi conflitti, vecchi eserciti (New conflicts, old armies)," *Repubblica*, November 2, 2001.
118. Scalfari, "Pace ai poveri guerra alla Spectre," *Repubblica*, October 14, 2001.
119. Scalfari, "Le due grandi iprocrisie in piazza", *Repubblica*, November 11, 2001.
120. Mauro, "L'Occidente colpito al cuore," *Repubblica*, September 12, 2001.
121. Mauro, "Il grande freddo tra Roma e Bruxelles," *Repubblica*, October 31, 2001.
122. Ibid.
123. Mauro, "L'Occidente colpito al cuore," *Repubblica*, September 12, 2001.
124. De Benedetti, "La fine dell'innocenza americana," *Repubblica*, September 20, 2001.
125. Caracciolo, "L'Occidente e l'identità ritrovata," *Repubblica*, September 13, 2001.
126. Garimberti, "Democrazia e crociate," *Repubblica*, September 27, 2001.
127. Scalfari, "Che può fare l'Europa per l'impero del bene," *Repubblica*, October 21, 2001.
128. Di Caro, "Berlusconi chiede una risposta militare e politica," *Corriere della Sera*, September 13, 2001.
129. Venturini, "Diritti umani e mani libere," *Corriere della Sera*, September 30, 2001.
130. Sartori, "I falsi perché di tanto odio: Alle radici dell'antiamericanismo," *Corriere della Sera*, October 2, 2001.
131. Ronchey, "Quei giacimenti di rancore," *Corriere della Sera*, October 11, 2001.
132. Merlo, "Quei fedeli che sbagliano: I musulmani e i fiancheggiatori di Bin Laden," *Corriere della Sera*, October 17, 2001.
133. Padoa Schioppa, "Alla fine decide la gente comune," *Corriere della Sera*, October 21, 2001.
134. Fallaci, "La rabbia e l'orgoglio (Anger and Pride)" *Corriere della Sera*, September 29, 2001. The article on *Repubblica*, which contributes to the debate, is by Umberto Eco, "Le guerre sante: Passione e ragione," October 5, 2001.
135. Panebianco, "Il castello delle ipocrisie: Oriana Fallaci e le cattive coscienze (The hypocrisies' castle: Oriana Fallaci and the bad consciences)," *Corriere della Sera*, October 1, 2001.
136. Maraini, "Ma il dolore non ha una bandiera (But pain does not have a flag)," *Corriere della Sera*, October 5, 2001.

137. Romano, "La bandiera italiana: Simboli trascurati e il grido della Fallaci (The Italian flag: Neglected symbols and Fallaci's scream)," *Corriere della Sera*, October 7, 2001.

138. Terzani, "Il sultano e San Francesco: Non possiamo rinunciare alla Speranza," *Corriere della Sera*, October 8, 2001.

139. Sartori, "Uditi i critici ha ragione Oriana (Having heard the critics Oriana is right)," *Corriere della Sera*, October 15, 2001. By now the articles joining the debate are even placed under the label "La rabbia e l'orgoglio: Il dibattito (Anger and pride: The debate)."

140. Zincone, "I coltivatori di dubbi e la spada di Oriana (The doubt-raisers and Oriana's sword)," *Corriere della Sera*, October 17, 2001.

141. De Bortoli, "Siamo tutti americani (We are all Americans)," *Corriere della Sera*, September 12, 2001.

142. De Bortoli, "Il terrore e la democrazia," *Corriere della Sera*, October 8, 2001.

143. De Bortoli, "La forza del silenzio," *Corriere della Sera*, September 15, 2001.

144. Zincone, "La febbre della fede," *Corriere della Sera*, September 23, 2001.

145. Tahir, "Report on the State of Journalists in Pakistan," under "The Concept of Journalism." It is important to point out that, according to Akhtar, there isn't just one media "ethos" in Pakistan. A distinction should be made between newspapers produced under a "parasitic landlordism" ethos and a "democratic ethos" (Akhtar, *Media, Religion, and Politics in Pakistan*, 78–80). "The perception of mass media in the cultural ethos of parasitic landlordism is pre-modern....landlordism and the cultural ethos evolved under it do not view the mass media as a fourth estate, and as an independent entity. For them media is 'theirs' as the land and the tenants are theirs as instruments of their political power" (ibid., 78). Newspapers produced under this ethos "would carry almost identical news stories on any given day, particularly on subjects like politics and religion mostly based on statements made by big news actors like the head of state/government, ministers, leaders of the opposition, often displayed and reported with a slant in the latter case" (ibid., 79). Newspapers produced under the democratic ethos, instead, would carry a greater variety of news, reported by "professional journalists" (ibid., 79). This study deals with the democratic ethos of Pakistani journalism only.

146. "About us," available from *The Nation on Web*. http://www.nation.com.pk/daily/jun-2007/4/about.php (accessed April 2007).

147. Akhtar, Media, Religion, and Politics in Pakistan, xxvi.

148. Ibid., xxvii.

149. Ibid., xxviii.

150. Ibid., xxviii–xxix.

151. Tahir, "Report on the State of Journalists in Pakistan," under "Critical Analysis."
152. Ibid.
153. Aggarwala, "What Is Development News?" 2181. See also Campbell, *Information Age Journalism*, 50–53.
154. Nasser, "News Values versus Ideology," 48–49.
155. Aggarwala, "What Is Development News?" 2181.
156. "CE Takes Women into Confidence on Crisis," *Dawn*, September 30, 2001.
157. "Retaliations Should Be under UN rules," *Dawn*, September 22, 2001.
158. "Taliban Say 'We Want Justice,'" *Dawn*, October 3, 2001.
159. "Pakistan Warned against Backing US," *Dawn*, October 5, 2001.
160. "Riyadh Wants End to Bias against Muslims," *Dawn*, September 15, 2001.
161. "War Without Illusions," *New York Times*, September 16, 2001.
162. "National Interest Comes First," *Dawn*, September 21, 2001, Editorial.
163. "Pleasant Contrast," *Dawn*, September 28, 2001, Editorial.
164. "Spasms of Bellicosity," *Dawn*, October 24, 2001, Editorial.
165. The Nation, "About Us."
166. Ibid.
167. Haroon, "Indictment Not Conviction," *Nation*, October 5, 2001.
168. Ibid.
169. Haroon, "How Will It Play Out?" *Nation*, October 8, 2001.
170. Rana, "Targets Unmet," *Nation*, November 7, 2001.
171. "Action against Laden on Hold," *Nation*, September 27, 2001.
172. "Omar Rejects Bush 'Second Chance' Offer," *Nation*, October 14, 2001.
173. "Laden, Omar Survive Raid," *Nation*, October 8, 2001.
174. "Osama, Omar Escape Raid," *Nation*, October 10, 2001.
175. "Kabul, Kandahar under Heavy Attacks," *Nation*, October 12, 2001.
176. "100 Killed in Raid on Herat Hospital," *Nation*, October 23, 2001.
177. "Chemical Weapons Being Used: Zaeef," *Nation*, October 24, 2001.
178. "Pakistan, US Defence Teams Open Talks," *Nation*, September 25, 2001.
179. "Taliban Mobilise 300,000 for Jehad," *Nation*, September 25, 2001.
180. "Osama Urges Pakistanis to Repel US 'Crusaders,'" *Nation*, September 25, 2001.
181. "Taliban Mobilise 300,000 for Jehad," *Nation*, September 25, 2001.
182. "Pressure on Islamabad," *Nation*, September 15, 2001, Editorial.
183. Cartoon, *Nation*, September 15, 2001.

184. "Lifting Sanction," *Nation*, September 24, 2001, Editorial.
185. "Consultative Process," *Nation*, November 7, 2001, Editorial.
186. "Mazar's Fall," *Nation*, November 11, 2001, Editorial.
187. Sigal, *Reporters and Officials*, 25.
188. On sources shaping the news see Soley, *The News Shapers*; and Kim and Weaver, "Reporting on Globalization." On the role of sources in framing an issue within the coverage see Steele, "Don't Ask, Don't Tell, Don't Explain"; Phalen and Algan, "(Ms)Taking Context for Content"; and Fahmy, "Emerging Alternatives or Traditional News Gates." On the framing competition among different sources in the coverage see Molotch and Lester, "Accidental News"; Liebler and Bendix, "Old-Growth Forests on Network News'"; Robinson and Powell, "The Postmodern Politics of Context Definition"; Gilbert, "A Response To 'Old-Growth Forests on Network News'"; Andsager, "How Interest Groups Attempt to Shape Public Opinion with Competing News Frames"; Levin, "Framing Peace Policies."
189. Carragee and Roefs, "The Neglect of Power in Recent Framing Research," 219.
190. Khan writes that, besides security, two other essential aspects of Pakistan's foreign policy are the "desire to have brotherly relations with other Islamic states and to forge affinity with the Third World countries" (Khan, "Pakistan's Foreign Policy in the Changing International Scenario," 246).

5   Testing Different Approaches to News

1. Berlusconi, "Resoconto stenografico dell'intervento del Presidente del Consiglio, on. Silvio Berlusconi, tenuto alla Camera nella seduta del 12 settembre 2001," September 12, 2001.
2. Fo's views are the object of criticism by Beppe Severgnini in "Quando l'ideologia trionfa sulla pietà: Italians (When ideology triumphs over piety: Italians)" (September 27, 2001) and Giovanni Sartori in "I falsi perché di tanto odio: Alle radici dell'antiamericanismo (The false reasons of so much hatred: The roots of antiamericanism)," (October 2, 2001). Fo's article, "Uccide di più la speculazione (Speculation kills more)," was originally published on September 15 on page 20 of *Corriere*.
3. Musharraf, *In the Line of Fire*, 206. According to an editorial published in the *Dawn*, a meeting involving "political leaders, ulema and newspaper editors" took place on Sunday, September 16, 2001, "to develop a consensus on how to face up to what is indeed a grave international crisis" ("Developing a Consensus," *Dawn*, September 18, 2001, Editorial).
4. Brown, "Rethinking Government-Media Relations," 4.
5. Ibid.
6. Ibid.

7. Akhtar, *Media, Religion, and Politics in Pakistan.*

8. According to Talbot "the Musharraf regime linked accountability with both democratic consolidation and national economic renewal; new public-spirited newcomers would replace the old greed of corrupt politicians" (Talbot, *Pakistan*, 380). The author defines as "patchy" the delivery of the government's promises of democratic empowerment and decentralization (ibid., 376–77). The leader's attitude is, nonetheless, clearly more progressive than that of the "parasitic landlordism" (Akhtar, *Media, Religion, and Politics in Pakistan*, Chapter 1).

9. Gans, *Deciding What's News*, 146–81. Newsworthiness has been discussed in greater detail in Chapter 1.

10. Wu, "Systemic Determinants of International News Coverage," 127.

11. MacBride, *Many Voices One World*; Boyd-Barrett, "International Communication and Globalization"; Boyd-Barrett and Rantanen, *The Globalization of News*; Paterson, "Global Television News Services"; idem, "Global Battlefields."

12. Oliver Boyd-Barrett, "Global News Wholesalers As Agents of Globalization," 141.

13. Mirza, "Grappling with Prejudice and Ignorance: Washington Notebook," *Dawn*, October 4, 2001, available from *Dawn: The Internet Edition*. http://www.dawn.com/2001/10/04/op.htm (accessed September 2004).

14. For references to France's past *grandeur*, see Rioux and Van Belle, "The Influence of Le Monde Coverage on French Aid Allocations," 485–86. In relation to the official meetings taking place in the aftermath of 9/11, Davison talks about a "diplomatic activism" by the French government (Davison, "French Security after 9/11," 76).

15. Baudrillard, "L'esprit du terrorisme," *Le Monde*, November 3, 2001.

16. Fallaci, "La rabbia e l'orgoglio," *Corriere della Sera*, September 29, 2001.

17. Biagi, "Manhattan, Italia," *Corriere della Sera*, September 13, 2001.

18. Biagi, "La paura globale," *Corriere della Sera*, September 20, 2001.

19. Biagi, "Il Nemico? La Noia (The Enemy? Boredom)," in *Come si scrive il Corriere della Sera* (How to write Corriere della Sera), 8.

20. For a discussion of the different perspectives see Josephi, "Journalism in the Global Age."

21. Thogmartin, *The National Daily Press of France*, 219.

22. Ermini, "Pensato, Visto, Stampato (Thought, Seen, Printed)," 27.

23. Ibid., 27–28, his emphasis.

24. Zincone, "Ipocrita lettore, simile a me... (Hypocritical reader, just like me...)," 76.

25. Ibid., 75.

26. De Bortoli, "Il terrore e la democrazia," *Corriere della Sera*, October 8, 2001, Editorial.
27. Etienne, "Dietro l'odio non c'è solo Bin Laden," *Corriere della Sera*, September 26, 2001.
28. Terzani, "Il soldato di ventura e il medico afghano," *Corriere della Sera*, October 31, 2001.
29. Hallin and Mancini, *Comparing Media Systems*, 96. The same observation is made by the authors in relation to *Repubblica* (ibid.).
30. For some examples see White, "The 'Gate Keeper'"; Gieber, "News Is What Newspapermen Make It"; Berkowitz, "Refining the Gatekeeping Metaphor for Local Television News"; Donohue, Olien, and Tichenor, "Structure and Constraints on Community Newspaper Gatekeepers"; Shoemaker, "A New Gatekeeping Model."
31. Schudson, "The Sociology of News Production," 9.
32. Nye, "Redefining the National Interest," 23.
33. "White House Discipline," *Economist*, Issue 8262, March 2, 2002, 52.
34. Vlahos, "Entering the Infosphere," 498.

6 Conclusions

1. Sigal, *Reporters and Officials*, 25.
2. Bennett, "Toward a Theory of Press-State Relations in the United States," 104.
3. Schudson, "The Objectivity Norm in American Journalism," 166.
4. Nasser, "News Values Versus Ideology," 48.
5. See Brenner, Haney, and Vanderbush, "The Confluence of Domestic and International Interests," 204, for an example.
6. Archetti and Brown, "Networks of News."
7. Paterson, "News Agency Dominance in International News on the Internet," n.p.
8. Sparks, "Is There a Global Public Sphere?" 122.
9. Ibid., 122.
10. Gerbner and Marvanyi, "International News."
11. Ibid., 58–59.
12. Nossek, "Our News and Their News," 61.
13. On the Hierarchy-of-Influences model see Shoemaker and Reese, *Mediating the Message*; Reese, "Understanding the Global Journalist."
14. Gieber, "News Is What Newspapermen Make It"; Epstein, *News From Nowhere*.
15. Epstein, *News from Nowhere*, ii, his emphasis.
16. Benson, "Field Theory in Comparative Context"; idem, "Pierre Bourdieu and the Mass Media"; idem, "The Mediated Public Sphere"; idem, "The Political/Literary Model of French Journalism";

Couldry, "Media Meta-Capital"; Benson, "Bringing the Sociology of the Media Back In"; Benson and Hallin, "How States, Markets and Globalization Shape the News"; Benson and Saguy, "Constructing Social Problems in an Age of Globalization; Hallin and Mancini, "Comparing Media Systems."

17. Benson, "Bringing the Sociology of the Media Back In."

18. Ibid., 275. For the application of Bourdieu's theory of fields to the study of media and journalism see Benson and Neveu, *Bourdieu and the Journalistic Field.*

19. Benson, "Bringing the Sociology of the Media Back In," 280.

20. For examples of studies identifying "frames" in the coverage see: Entman, "Framing US Coverage of International News"; Pan and Kosicki, "Framing Analysis"; Semetko and Valkenburg, "Framing European Politics"; De Vreese, Peter, and Semetko, "Framing Politics at the Launch of the Euro"; Entman, "Cascading Activation"; Jasperson and El-Kikhia, "CNN and Al Jazeera's Media Coverage of America's War in Afghanistan"; Rusciano, "Framing World Opinion in the Elite Press"; Schaefer, "Framing the US Embassy Bombings and September 11 Attacks in African and US Newspapers"; Entman, *Projections of Power.*

21. Hallin, *We Keep America on Top of the World,* 81.

22. De Vreese, *Framing Europe.*

23. Gurevitch and Blumler, "State of the Art of Comparative Political Communication Research."

24. Hjarvard, "TV News Flows Studies Revisited."

BIBLIOGRAPHY

Aggarwala, Narinder K. "What Is Development News?" *Journal of Communication* 29, no. 2 (1979): 2180–81.

Akhtar, Rai Shakil. *Media, Religion, and Politics in Pakistan.* Oxford: Oxford University Press, 2000.

Almond, Gabriel and Sidney Verba. *The Civic Culture: Political Attitudes and Democracy in Five Nations.* Newbury Park, CA: Sage, 1989.

Althaus, Scott L. "When News Norms Collide, Follow the Lead: New Evidence for Press Independence." *Political Communication* 20, no. 4 (2003): 381–414.

Althaus, Scott L., Jill A. Edy, Robert M. Entman, and Patricia Phalen. "Revising the Indexing Hypothesis: Officials, Media, and the Libya Crisis." *Political Communication* 13, no. 4 (1996): 407–21.

Altschull, J. Herbert. "Boundaries of Journalistic Autonomy," in D. Berkowitz (ed.) *Social Meanings of News: A Text-Reader.* London: Sage, 1997.

Andsager, Julie L. "How Interest Groups Attempt to Shape Public Opinion with Competing News Frames." *Journalism and Mass Communication Quarterly* 77, no. 3 (2000): 577–92.

Archetti, Cristina and Robin Brown. "Networks of News: News Management, Technology, and the Construction of International Relations." Paper presented at the International Studies Association annual meeting, San Francisco, CA, March 29, 2008.

Ayish, Muhammed I. "American-Style Journalism and Arab World Television: An Exploratory Study of News Selection at Six Arab World Satellite Television Channels." *Transnational Broadcasting Studies (TBS)* 6, Spring (2001). http://www.tbsjournal.com/Archives/Spring01/Ayish. html (accessed March 2007).

Bantz, Charles R. "News Organizations: Conflict As a Crafted Cultural Norm" (1985), reprint in D. Berkowitz (ed.) *Social Meanings of News: A Text-Reader.* London: Sage, 1997.

Bennett, Andrew and Alexander L. George. "Process Tracing in Case Study Research." Paper presented at the MacArthur Foundation Workshop on Case Study Methods, Belfer Center for Science and International Affairs (BCSIA), Harvard University, 1997. http://www.georgetown.edu/ faculty/bennetta/PROTCG.htm (accessed May 2006).

Bennett, Lance W. "Toward a Theory of Press-State Relations in the United States." *Journal of Communication* 40, no. 2 (1990): 103–25.

Bennett, Lance W. and Steven Livingston. "A Semi-Independent Press: Government Control and Journalistic Autonomy in the Political Construction of News." *Political Communication* 20, no. 4 (2003): 359–62.

Bennett, Lance W. and Jarol B. Manheim. "Taking the Public by Storm: Information, Cuing, and the Democratic Process in the Gulf Conflict." *Political Communication* 10 (1993): 331–51.

Benson, Rodney. "Field Theory in Comparative Context: A New Paradigm for Media Studies." *Theory and Society* 28, no. 3 (1998): 463–98.

———. "Pierre Bourdieu and the Mass Media: New Approaches for Media Sociology." Paper presented at the 95th American Sociological Association annual meeting, Washington, D.C., 2000. http://education.nyu.edu/dcc/faculty/facultypages/benson/pdfs/field_theory.pdf (accessed January 2005).

———. "The Mediated Public Sphere: A Model for Cross-National Research." Working Paper 2001–7, Center for the Study of Culture, Organizations and Politics, University of California, Berkeley, 2001. http://ist-socrates.berkeley.edu/~iir/culture/papers/Benson01_08.pdf (accessed January 2005).

———. "Tearing Down the 'Wall' in American Journalism." *Core: International Journal of the Humanities* 1, no. 1 (2001): 102–13.

———. "Bringing the Sociology of the Media Back In." *Political Communication* 21, no. 3 (2004): 275–92.

———. "La Fin Du Monde? Tradition and Change in the French Press." *French Politics, Culture and Society* 22, no. 1 (2004): 108–26.

Benson, Rodney and Daniel C. Hallin. "How States, Markets and Globalization Shape the News: The French and American National Press, 1965–1997." Paper presented at the International Communication Association annual convention, New York, 2005. http://www.allacademic.com/meta/p14185_index.html (accessed March 2006).

Benson, Rodney and Erik Neveu (eds.) *Bourdieu and the Journalistic Field.* Cambridge: Polity, 2005.

Benson, Rodney and Abigail C. Saguy. "Constructing Social Problems in an Age of Globalization: A French-American Comparison." *American Sociological Review* 71, April (2005): 233–60.

Berger, Meyer. *The Story of the New York Times: 1851–1951.* New York: Simon and Schuster, 1951.

Berkowitz, Dan. "Who Sets the Media Agenda? The Ability of Policymakers to Determine News Decisions," in D. J. Kennamer (ed.) *Public Opinion, the Press, and Public Policy.* London: Praeger, 1992.

———. "Overview: Why a 'Social Meanings of News' Perspective?" in D. Berkowitz (ed.) *Social Meanings of News: A Text-Reader.* London: Sage, 1997.

———. "Refining the Gatekeeping Metaphor for Local Television News" (1990), reprint in D. Berkowitz (ed.) *Social Meanings of News: A Text-Reader.* London: Sage, 1997.

————. (ed.) *Social Meanings of News: A Text-Reader*. London: Sage, 1997.

Biagi, Enzo. "Il nemico? La noia (The enemy? Boredom)," in BUR Fondazione Corriere della Sera (ed.) *Come si scrive Il Corriere della Sera: Dentro il quotidiano tra storia e attualità*. Milano, Italy: BUR Fondazione Corriere della Sera, 2003.

Billeaudeaux, Andre, David Domke, John S. Hutcheson, and Philip Garland. "Newspaper Editorials Follow Lead of Bush Administration." *Newspaper Research Journal* 24, no. 1 (2003): 166–84.

————. "News Norms, Indexing and a Unified Government: Reporting during the Early Stages of a Global War on Terror." Paper presented at International Communication Association annual convention, San Diego, 2003. http://lass.calumet.purdue.edu/cca/gmj/fa03/gmj-fa03-bdhg1. htm (accessed May 2005).

Blumler, Jay G. and Michael Gurevitch. "Rethinking the Study of Political Communication," in J. Curran and M. Gurevitch (eds.) *Mass Media and Society*. London: Hodder Arnold, 2005.

BMA [British Medical Association]. *Eating Disorders, Body Image and the Media*. London: BMA, 2000.

Boekle, Henning, Jörg Nadoll, and Bernhard Stahl. "European Foreign Policy and National Identity: Detecting the Link." Paper presented at the Fourth Pan-European International Relations Conference, Canterbury (UK), September 6–10, 2001. http://www.politik.uni-trier.de/forschung/pafe_canterbury.pdf (accessed May 2007).

Boyd-Barrett, Oliver. "Media Imperialism: Towards an International Framework for the Analysis of Media Systems," in J. Curran, M. Gurevitch, and J. Woollacott (eds.) *Mass Communication and Society*. London: Edward Arnold [for] Open University Press, 1977.

————. "Global News Wholesalers As Agents of Globalization," in A. Sreberny-Mohammadi et al. (eds.) *Media in Global Context: A Reader*. London: Hodder Arnold, 1997.

————. "Media Imperialism Reformulated," in D. K. Thussu (ed.) *Electronic Empires: Global Media and Resistance*. London: Arnold, 1998.

————. "Constructing the Global, Constructing the Local: News Agencies Re-Present the World," in A. Malek and A.P. Kavoori (eds.) *The Global Dynamics of News: Studies in International News Coverage and News Agendas*. Stamford, CT: Ablex Publishing, 2000.

Boyd-Barrett, Oliver and Terhi Rantanen (eds.) *The Globalization of News*. London: Sage, 1998.

————. "The Globalization of News," in O. Boyd-Barrett and T. Rantanen (eds.) *The Globalization of News*. London: Sage, 1998.

Brenner, Philip, Patrick J. Haney, and Walter Vanderbush. "The Confluence of Domestic and International Interests: U.S. Policy toward Cuba, 1998–2001." *International Studies Perspectives* 3, no. 2 (2002): 192–208.

Breed, Warren. "Social Control in the Newsroom: A Functional Analysis" (1955), reprint in D. Berkowitz (ed.) *Social Meanings of News: A Text-Reader*. London: Sage, 1997.

Brewer, Paul R. and Kimberly Gross. "Values, Framing, and Citizens' Thoughts about Policy Issues: Effects on Content and Quantity." *Political Psychology* 26, no. 6 (2005): 929–48.

Brown, Robin. "Rethinking Government-Media Relations: Towards a Theory of Spin." Paper presented at the European Consortium for Political Research (ECPR), Marburg (Germany), September 18–21, 2003.

Buckley, Mary and Rick Fawn (eds.) *Global Responses to Terrorism: 9/11, Afghanistan and Beyond*. London: Routledge, 2003.

BUR Fondazione Corriere della Sera (ed.) *Come si scrive Il Corriere della Sera: Dentro il quotidiano tra storia e attualità* (How to write Corriere della Sera: Between history and news). Milano, Italy: BUR Fondazione Corriere della Sera, 2003.

Buzan, Barry, Ole Waever, and Jaap de Wilde (eds.) *Security: A New Framework for Analysis*. London: Lynne Rienner, 1998.

Callaghan, Karen and Frauke Schnell. "Assessing the Democratic Debate: How the News Media Frame Elite Policy Discourse." *Political Communication* 18, no. 2 (2001): 183–212.

Campbell, Vincent. *Information Age Journalism: Journalism in an International Context*. London: Arnold, 2004.

Carragee, Kevin M. and Wim Roefs. "The Neglect of Power in Recent Framing Research." *Journal of Communication* 54, no. 2 (2004): 214–33.

Chadha, Kalyani and Anandan Kavoori. "Globalization and National Media Systems: Mapping Interactions in Policies Markets and Formats," in J. Curran and M. Gurevitch (eds.) *Mass Media and Society*. London: Hodder Arnold, 2005.

Chalaby, Jean K. "Journalism As an Anglo-American Invention." *European Journal of Communication* 11, no. 3 (1996): 303–26.

Checkel, Jeffrey T. "It's the Process Stupid! Process-Tracing in the Study of European and International Politics," in A. Klotz (ed.) *Qualitative Methods in International Relations*. Syracuse, NY: Syracuse University, 2005. http://www.arena.uio.no/publications/working-papers2005/papers/wp05_26.pdf (accessed June 2006).

Clausen, Lisbeth. *Global News Production*. Copenhagen: Copenhagen Business School, 2003.

———. "Localizing the Global: 'Domestication' Processes in International News Production." *Media, Culture & Society* 26, no. 1 (2004): 25–44.

Cohen, Bernard. *The Press and Foreign Policy*. Princeton, NJ: Princeton University Press, 1963.

Cook, Timothy E. *Governing with the News*. London, IL: University of Chicago Press, 1998.

Corriere della Sera. "Declaration of Independence of Corriere della Sera" (1973). *Corriere della Sera.it*. http://www.corriere.it/speciali/cdr/dichiaraENG.shtml (accessed June 2006).

Couldry, Nick. "Media Meta-Capital: Extending the Range of Bourdieu's Field Theory." *Theory and Society* 32, no. 5/6 (2003): 653–77.

Cunningham, Stuart, Elizabeth Jacka, and John Sinclair. "Global and Regional Dynamics of International Television Flows," in D. K. Thussu (ed.) *Electronic Empires: Global Media and Resistance*. London: Arnold, 1998.

Curran, James and Michael Gurevitch (eds.) *Mass Media and Society*. 4th ed. London: Hodder Arnold, 2005.

Curran, James, Michael Gurevitch, and Janet Woollacott (eds.) *Mass Communication and Society*. London: Edward Arnold [for] Open University Press, 1977.

Curran, James and Myung-Jin Park (eds.) *De-Westernizing Media Studies*. London: Routledge, 2000.

Da Costa, Alcino Louis. "New Criteria for the Selection of News in African Countries," in A. L. Da Costa et al. (eds.) *News Values and Principles of Cross-Cultural Communication*. Paris: UNESCO, 1979.

Da Costa, Alcino Louis, Yehia Aboubakr, Pran Chopra, and Fernando Reyes Matta. *News Values and Principles of Cross-Cultural Communication*. Paris: UNESCO, 1979.

Dahlgren, Peter and Colin Sparks (eds.) *Communication and Citizenship*. London: Routledge, 1991.

Dajani, Nabil and John Donohue. "Foreign News in the Arab Press: A Content Analysis of Six Arab Dailies." *Gazette* 19, no. 3 (1973): 155–70.

Daniels, Philip A. "Leadership Seeking Greater Legitimacy: Italy," in M. Buckley and R. Fawn (eds.) *Global Responses to Terrorism: 9/11, Afghanistan and Beyond*. London: Routledge, 2003.

Datta-Ray, Sunanda K. "Asia Must Evolve Its Own Journalistic Idiom," in X. Hao and S. K. Datta-Ray (eds.) *Issues and Challenges in Asian Journalism*. Singapore: Marshall Cavendish Academic, 2006.

Davison, Rémy. "French Security after 9/11: Franco-American Discord," in P. Shearman and M. Sussex (eds.) *European Security after 9/11*. Aldershot: Ashgate, 2004.

Dearing, James W. and Everett M. Rogers. *Agenda-Setting*. London: Sage, 1996.

De Beer, Arnold S. "New Mirror in a New South Africa? International News Flow and News Selection at the Afrikaans Daily, Beeld," in A. Malek and A. P. Kavoori (eds.) *The Global Dynamics of News: Studies in International News Coverage and News Agendas*. Stamford, CT: Ablex Publishing, 2000.

De Vreese, Claes H. *Framing Europe: Television News and European Integration*. Amsterdam: Aksant, 2003.

De Vreese, Claes H., Jochen Peter, and Holli A. Semetko. "Framing Politics at the Launch of the Euro: A Cross-National Comparative Study of Frames in the News." *Political Communication* 18, no. 2 (2001): 107–22.

Dexter, Lewis Anthony and David Manning White (eds.) *People, Society and Mass Communications.* London: Collier-Macmillan, 1964.

Dicken-Garcia, Hazel. *Journalistic Standards in Nineteenth-Century America.* London: University of Wisconsin Press, 1989.

Donohue, G. A., C. N. Olien, and P. J. Tichenor. "Structure and Constraints on Community Newspaper Gatekeepers" (1989), reprint in D. Berkowitz (ed.) *Social Meanings of News: A Text-Reader.* London: Sage, 1997.

Dow Jones. "A Newspaper's Philosophy." *DowJones.com.* http://www.dowjones.com/Products_Services/PrintPublishing/Grimes.htm (accessed May 2007).

———. "History of the Wall Street Journal." *DowJones.com.* http://www.dowjones.com/Pressroom/PressKits/WEwsj_history.htm (accessed May 2007).

———. "The Wall Street Journal." *DowJones.com.* http://www.dowjones.com/Products_Services/PrintPublishing/WSJ.htm (accessed May 2007).

———. "The Wall Street Journal Editorial Page Philosophy." *DowJones.com.* http://www.dowjones.com/Products_Services/PrintPublishing/EditPagePhilosophy.htm (accessed May 2007).

Druckman, James N. and Michael Parkin. "The Impact of Media Bias: How Editorial Slant Affects Voters." *Journal of Politics* 67, no. 4 (2005): 1030–49.

Elliott, Charles W. "Flows of News from the Middle Kingdom: An Analysis of International News Releases from Xinhua," in A. Malek and A. P. Kavoori (eds.) *The Global Dynamics of News: Studies in International News Coverage and News Agendas.* Stamford, CT: Ablex Publishing Corporation, 2000.

Entman, Robert M. *Democracy without Citizens: Media and the Decay of American Politics.* Oxford: Oxford University Press, 1989.

———. "Framing US Coverage of International News: Contrasts in Narratives of the KAL and Iran Air Incidents." *Journal of Communication* 41, no. 4 (1991): 6–27.

———. "Framing: Toward Clarification of a Fractured Paradigm." *Journal of Communication* 43, no. 4 (1993): 51–58.

———. "Cascading Activation: Contesting the White House's Frame after 9/11." *Political Communication* 20, no. 4 (2003): 415–32.

———. *Projections of Power: Framing News, Public Opinion, and U.S. Foreign Policy.* London: University of Chicago Press, 2004.

Entman, Robert M. and Andrew Rojecki. "Freezing Out the Public: Elite and Media Framing of the U.S. Anti-Nuclear Movement." *Political Communication* 10, no. 2 (1993): 155–73.

Epstein, Edward Jay. *News from Nowhere: Television and the News.* Chicago: Ivan R. Dee, 2000 [1973].

Ermini, Paolo. "Pensato, visto, stampato (Thought, seen, printed)," in BUR Fondazione Corriere della Sera (ed.) *Come si scrive il Corriere della Sera:*

Dentro il quotidiano tra storia e attualità. Milano, Italy: BUR Fondazione Corriere della Sera, 2003.

Esser, Frank. "Editorial Structures and Work Principles in British and German Newsrooms." *European Journal of Communication* 13, no. 3 (1998): 375–405.

Esser, Frank and Barbara Pfetsch (eds.) *Comparing Political Communication: Theories, Cases, and Challenges.* Cambridge: Cambridge University Press, 2004.

Ettema, James S., D. Charles Whitney, and Daniel B. Wackman. "Professional Mass Communicators" (1987), reprint in D. Berkowitz (ed.) *Social Meanings of News: A Text-Reader.* London: Sage, 1997.

European Council. "European Council Declaration in Copenhagen," June 2003. http://europa.eu/rapid/pressReleasesAction.do?reference=DOC/93/3&format=HTML&aged=1&language=EN&guiLanguage=en (accessed April 2008).

Fahmy, Shahira. "Emerging Alternatives or Traditional News Gates: Which News Sources Were Used to Picture the 9/11 Attack and the Afghan War?" *Gazette* 67, no. 5 (2005): 381–98.

Fairclough, Norman. *Critical Discourse Analysis.* London: Longman, 1995.

Farinelli, Giuseppe, Ermanno Paccagnini, Giovanni Santambrogio, and Angela Ida Villa. *Storia del giornalismo italiano: Dalle origini a oggi* (History of Italian journalism: From the origins to the present day). Torino: UTET Libreria, 2004.

Ferguson, Marjorie. "The Mythology about Globalization." *European Journal of Communication* 7, no. 1 (1992): 69–93.

Ferree, Myra Marx, A. William Gamson, Jürgen Gerhards, and Dieter Rucht. *Shaping Abortion Discourse: Democracy and the Public Sphere in Germany and the United States.* Cambridge: Cambridge University Press, 2002.

Fishman, Mark. "News and Nonevents: Making the Visible Invisible" (1982), reprint in D. Berkowitz (ed.) *Social Meanings of News: A Text-Reader.* London: Sage, 1997.

Gaber, Ivor. "Government by Spin: An Analysis of the Process." *Media, Culture & Society* 22, no. 4 (2000): 507–18.

Galtung, Johan. "A Structural Theory of Imperialism." *Journal of Peace Research* 8, no. 2 (1971): 81–117.

Galtung, Johan and Mari Holmboe Ruge. "The Structure of Foreign News: Presentation of the Congo, Cuba and Cyprus Crises in Four Norwegian Newspapers." *Journal of Peace Research* 2, no. 1 (1965): 64–91.

Gans, Herbert J. *Deciding What's News: A Study of CBS Evening News, NBC Nightly News, Newsweek, and Time.* Evanston, IL: Northwestern University Press, 2004 [1979].

Garzanti Linguistica. "Editoriale." http://www.garzantilinguistica.it/interna_ita.html (accessed July 2006).

George, Alexander L. and Andrew Bennett. *Case Studies and Theory Development in the Social Sciences*. London: BCSIA Studies in International Security, 2005.

Gerbner, George and George Marvanyi. "International News: The Many Worlds of the World's Press." *Journal of Communication* 27, no. 1 (1977): 52–66.

Giddens, Anthony. *The Constitution of Society: Outline of the Theory of Structuration*. Cambridge: Polity Press, 1984.

———. *The Consequences of Modernity*. Stanford, CA: Stanford University Press, 1990.

———. *Modernity and Self-Identity: Self and Society in the Late Modern Age*. Stanford, CA: Stanford University Press, 1991.

Gieber, Walter. "News Is What Newspapermen Make It," in L. A. Dexter and D. Manning White (eds.) *People, Society and Mass Communications*. London: Collier-Macmillan, 1964.

Giffard, Anthony. "Alternative News Agencies," in O. Boyd-Barrett and T. Rantanen (eds.) *The Globalization of News*. London: Sage, 1998.

———. "International Agencies and Global Issues: The Decline of the Cold War News Frame," in A. Malek and A. P. Kavoori (eds.) *The Global Dynamics of News: Studies in International News Coverage and News Agendas*. Stamford, CT: Ablex Publishing, 2000.

Gilbert, Sarah Ann. "A Response To 'Old-Growth Forests on Network News: News Sources and the Framing of an Environmental Controversy.'" *Journalism and Mass Communication Quarterly* 74, no. 4 (1997): 883–85.

Gitlin, Todd. *The Whole World Is Watching: Mass Media in the Making and Unmaking of the New Left*. London: University of California Press, 1980.

Goffman, Erving. *Frame Analysis: An Essay on the Organization of Experience*. New York: Harper and Row, 1974.

Golan, Guy and Wayne Wanta. "International Elections on US Network News: An Examination of Factors Affecting Newsworthiness." *Gazette* 65, no. 1 (2003): 25–39.

Gopnik, Adam. "The End of the World: Crisis at France's Most Venerable Newspaper." *New Yorker*, November 15, 2004.

Graber, Doris, Denis McQuail, and Pippa Norris. "Introduction: Political Communication in a Democracy," in D. Graber, D. McQuail, and P. Norris (eds.) *The Politics of News: The News of Politics*. Washington, D.C.: CQ Press, 1998.

———. (eds.) *The Politics of News: The News of Politics*. Washington, D.C.: CQ Press, 1998.

Grattan, Michelle. "The Politics of Spin." *Australian Studies in Journalism* 7 (1998): 32–45.

Gurevitch, Michael and Jay G. Blumler. "State of the Art of Comparative Political Communication Research: Poised for Maturity?" in F. Esser and B. Pfetsch (eds.) *Comparing Political Communication:*

Theories, Cases, and Challenges. Cambridge: Cambridge University Press, 2004.

Gurevitch, Michael, Mark R. Levy, and Itzhak Roeh. "The Global Newsroom: Convergences and Diversities in the Globalization of Television News," in P. Dahlgren and C. Sparks *Communication and Citizenship.* London: Routledge, 1991.

Hallin, Daniel C. "The Media, the War in Vietnam, and Political Support: A Critique of the Thesis of an Oppositional Media." *Journal of Politics* 46, no. 1 (1984): 2–24.

———. *The "Uncensored War": The Media and Vietnam.* London: University of California Press, 1989.

———. *We Keep America on Top of the World: Television Journalism and the Public Sphere.* London: Routledge, 1994.

Hallin, Daniel C. and Paolo Mancini. "Political Structure and Representational Form in U.S. and Italian Television News." *Theory and Society* 13 (1984): 829–50.

———. *Comparing Media Systems: Three Models of Media and Politics.* Cambridge: Cambridge University Press, 2004.

———. "Comparing Media Systems," in J. Curran and M. Gurevitch (eds.) *Mass Media and Society.* London: Hodder Arnold, 2005.

Hao, Xiaoming and Sunanda K. Datta-Ray (eds.) *Issues and Challenges in Asian Journalism.* Singapore: Marshall Cavendish Academic, 2006.

Herman, Edward S. and Noam Chomsky. *Manufacturing Consent: The Political Economy of the Mass Media.* London: Vintage, 1994.

Hill, Christopher. "Renationalizing or Regrouping?: EU Foreign Policy since 11 September 2001." *Journal of Common Market Studies* 42, no. 1 (2004): 143–63.

Hjarvard, Stig. "TV News Flows Studies Revisited." *Electronic Journal of Communication* 5, no. 2&3 (1995). http://www.cios.org/getfile/Hjarvard_V5N2395 (accessed April 2005).

Hutcheson, John, David Domke, Andre Billeaudeaux, and Philip Garland. "U.S. National Identity, Political Elites, and a Patriotic Press Following September 11." *Political Communication* 21, no. 1 (2004): 27–50.

IMF. "World Economic and Financial Surveys: World Economic Outlook Database." http://www.imf.org/external/pubs/ft/weo/2006/02/data/index.aspx (accessed July 2006).

Ishii, Kenichi. "Is the U.S. Over-Reported in the Japanese Press?" *Gazette* 57, no. 2 (1996): 135–44.

Iyengar, Shanto and Adam Simon. "News Coverage of the Gulf Crisis and Public Opinion: A Study of Agenda Setting, Priming, and Framing," in S. Iyengar and R. Reeves (eds.) *Do the Media Govern? Politicians, Voters, and Reporters in America.* London: Sage, 1997.

Iyengar, Shanto and Richard Reeves (eds.) *Do the Media Govern? Politicians, Voters, and Reporters in America.* London: Sage, 1997.

Jasperson, Amy E. and Mansour O. El-Kikhia. "CNN and Al Jazeera's Media Coverage of America's War in Afghanistan," in P. Norris,

K. Montague, and M. Just (eds.) *Framing Terrorism: The News Media, the Government, and the Public.* London: Routledge, 2003.

Joerissen, Britta and Bernhard Stahl (eds.) *Europäische Außenpolitik und nationale Identität: Vergleichende Diskurs- und Verhaltenstudien zu Dänemark, Deutschland, Frankreich, Griechenland, Italien und den Niederlanden* (European foreign policy and national identity: Comparing discourses and policy behaviours in Denmark, Germany, France, Greece, Italy and the Netherlands). Münster, Germany: LIT, 2003.

Johnson, Melissa A. "Predicting News Flows from Mexico." *Journalism and Mass Communication Quarterly* 74, no. 2 (1997): 315–30.

Josephi, Beate. "Journalism in the Global Age." *Gazette* 67, no. 6 (2005): 575–90.

Kahn, Kim Fridkin and Patrick J. Kenney. "The Slant of the News: How Editorial Endorsements Influence Campaign Coverage and Citizens' Views of Candidates." *American Political Science Review* 96, no. 2 (2002): 381–94.

Kaid, Lynda Lee (ed.) *Handbook of Political Communication Research.* London: Lawrence Erlbaum Associates Publishers, 2004.

Kariel, Herbert G. and Lynn A. Rosenvall. "Cultural Affinity Displayed in Canadian Daily Newspapers." *Journalism Quarterly* 60, no. 3 (1983): 431–36.

Kavoori, Anandan. "Trends in Global Media Reception," in D. K. Thussu (ed.) *Electronic Empires: Global Media and Resistance.* London: Arnold, 1998.

Kennamer, David J. (ed.) *Public Opinion, the Press, and Public Policy.* London: Praeger, 1992.

Khan, Adnan Sarwar. "Pakistan's Foreign Policy in the Changing International Scenario." *Muslim World* 96, no. 2 (2006): 233–50.

Kim, Kyungmo and George A. Barnett. "The Determinants of International News Flow: A Network Analysis." *Communication Research* 23, no. 3 (1996): 323–52.

Kim, Sung Tae and David H. Weaver. "Reporting on Globalization: A Comparative Analysis of Sourcing Patterns in Five Countries' Newspapers." *Gazette* 65, no. 2 (2003): 121–44.

King, Gary, Robert O. Keohane, and Sidney Verba. *Designing Social Enquiry: Scientific Inference in Qualitative Research.* Princeton, NJ: Princeton University Press, 1994.

Klotz, Audie (ed.) *Qualitative Methods in International Relations.* Syracuse, NY: Maxwell School of Public Affairs, Syracuse University, 2005.

Köcher, Renate. "Bloodhounds or Missionaries: Role Definitions of German and British Journalists." *European Journal of Communication* 1, no. 1 (1986): 43–64.

Kraidy, Marwan M. "From Culture to Hybridity in International Communication," in M. Semati (ed.) *New Frontieres in International Communication Theory.* Oxford: Rowman & Littlefield, 2004.

Krippendorf, Klaus. *Content Analysis: An Introduction to Its Methodology.* 2nd ed. London: Sage, 2004.

Kumar, Martha Joynt. "The Contemporary Presidency: Communications Operations in the White House of President George W. Bush: Making News on His Terms." *Presidential Studies Quarterly* 33, no. 2 (2003): 366–93.

———. "Source Material: The White House and the Press: News Organizations As a Presidential Resource and a Source of Pressure." *Presidential Studies Quarterly* 33, no. 3 (2003): 669–83.

Lash, Scott and John Urry. *Economies of Signs and Space.* London: Sage, 1994.

Leisenheimer, Ilka. "Der italienische Diskurs zum NATO-Beitritt (1947–1949) (The Italian discourse at the time of joining NATO [1947–1949])," in B. Joerissen and B. Stahl (eds.) *Europäische Außenpolitik und nationale Identität: Vergleichende Diskurs- und Verhaltenstudien zu Dänemark, Deutschland, Frankreich, Griechenland, Italien und den Niederlanden.* Münster, Germany: LIT, 2003.

———. "Der italianiesche Diskurs zum zweiten Golfkrieg (1990–1991) (The Italian discourse during the second Gulf War [1990–1991])," in B. Joerissen and B. Stahl (eds.) *Europäische Außenpolitik und nationale Identität: Vergleichende Diskurs- und Verhaltenstudien zu Dänemark, Deutschland, Frankreich, Griechenland, Italien und den Niederlanden.* Münster, Germany: LIT, 2003.

Lendvai, Paul. "What Is Newsworthy—And What Is Not—In the Communist World?" in J. L. Martin and A. G. Chaudhary. *Comparative Mass Media Systems.* New York: Longman, 1983.

Levin, David. "Framing Peace Policies: The Competition for Resonant Themes." *Political Communication* 22, no. 1 (2005): 83–108.

Liebler, Carol M. and Jacob Bendix. "Old-Growth Forests on Network News: News Sources and the Framing of an Environmental Controversy." *Journalism and Mass Communication Quarterly* 73, no. 1 (1996): 53–65.

Livingston, Steven and Todd Eachus. "Humanitarian Crises and U.S. Foreign Policy: Somalia and the CNN Effect Reconsidered." *Political Communication* 12, no. 4 (1995): 413–29.

———. "Indexing News after the Cold War: Reporting U.S. Ties to Latin American Paramilitary Organizations." *Political Communication* 13, no. 4 (1996): 423–36.

Lozano, Jose-Carlos, Edgar Gomez, Alejandra Matiasich, Alfredo Alfonso, Martin Becerra, Ada Cristina Machado Silveira, Magdalena Elizondo, Jorge Marroquin, Luciane Delgado Aquino, and Francisco-Javier Martinez. "International News in Latin American Press," in A. Malek and A. P. Kavoori (eds.) *The Global Dynamics of News: Studies in International News Coverage and News Agendas.* Stamford, CT: Ablex Publishing Corporation, 2000.

Lynch, Marc. "Why Engage? China and the Logic of Communicative Action." *European Journal of International Relations* 8, no. 2 (2002): 187–230.

MacBride, Sean. *Many Voices One World: Towards a New More Just and More Efficient World Information and Communication Order.* London: Kogan Page [for] UNESCO, 1980.

Malek, Abbas and Anandam P. Kavoori (eds.) *The Global Dynamics of News: Studies in International News Coverage and News Agendas.* Stamford, CT: Ablex Publishing, 2000.

Maltese, John Anthony. *Spin Control: The White House Office of Communications and the Management of Presidential News.* 2nd ed. London: University of North Carolina Press, 1994.

Mancini, Paolo. "Old and New Contradictions in Italian Journalism." *Journal of Communication* 42, no. 3 (1992): 42–47.

———. "Political Complexity and Alternative Models of Journalism: The Italian Case," in J. Curran and M. Park (eds.) *De-Westernizing Media Studies.* London: Routledge, 2000.

Martin, John L. and Anju Grover Chaudhary (eds.) *Comparative Mass Media Systems.* New York: Longman, 1983.

Matalin, Mary and James Carville. *All's Fair: Love, War, and Running for President.* London: Hutchinson, 1994.

McAllister, Richard. "Support from a Bicephalous Executive: France," in M. Buckley and R. Fawn (eds.) *Global Responses to Terrorism: 9/11, Afghanistan and Beyond.* London: Routledge, 2003.

McChesney, W. Robert. "Media Convergence and Globalisation," in D. K. Thussu (ed.) *Electronic Empires: Global Media and Resistance.* London: Arnold, 1998.

McCombs, Maxwell, Donald L. Shaw, and David Weaver (eds.) *Communication and Democracy: Exploring the Intellectual Frontiers in Agenda-Setting Theory.* Mahwah, NJ: Lawrence Erlbaum Associates, 1997.

McCombs, Maxwell E., and Donald L. Shaw. "The Evolution of Agenda-Setting Research: Twenty-Five Years in the Marketplace of Ideas." *Journal of Communication* 43, no. 2 (1993): 58–67.

McLuhan, Marshall and Quentin Fiore. *War and Peace in the Global Village.* New York: Bantam Books, 1968.

Mellor, Noha. *The Making of Arab News.* Oxford: Rowman & Littlefield, 2005.

Mermin, Jonathan. *Debating War and Peace: Media Coverage of U.S. Intervention in the Post-Vietnam Era.* Princeton, NJ: Princeton University Press, 1999.

Mohammadi, Ali (ed.) *International Communication and Globalization: A Critical Introduction.* London: Sage, 1997.

Molotch, Harvey and Marilyn Lester. "Accidental News: The Great Oil Spill As Local Occurrence and National Event." *American Journal of Sociology* 81, no. 2 (1975): 235–60.

Musharraf, Pervez. *In the Line of Fire: A Memoir.* London: Simon & Schuster, 2006.

Nacos, Brigitte L., Robert Y. Shapiro, and Pierangelo Isernia (eds.) *Decisionmaking in a Glass House: Mass Media, Public Opinion, and American and European Foreign Policy in the 21st Century.* Oxford: Rowman & Littlefield, 2000.

———. "Old or New Ball Game? Mass Media, Public Opinion, and Foreign Policy in the Post–Cold War World," in B. L. Nacos, R. Y. Shapiro, and P. Isernia (eds.) *Decisionmaking in a Glass House: Mass Media, Public Opinion, and American and European Foreign Policy in the 21st Century.* Oxford: Rowman & Littlefield, 2000.

Nasser, Munir K. "News Values versus Ideology: A Third World Perspective," in J. L. Martin and A. G. Chaudhary (eds.) *Comparative Mass Media Systems.* New York: Longman, 1983.

Nation. "About Us." *Nation on Web.* http://www.nation.com.pk/daily/jan-2007/9/about.php (accessed March 2007).

Ngonyani, Deo. "Tools of Deception: Media Coverage of Student Protests in Tanzania." *Nordic Journal of African Studies* 9, no. 2 (2000): 22–48.

Nordenstreng, Kaarle and Tapio Varis. *Television Traffic—A One-Way Street? A Survey and Analysis of the International Flow of Television Programme Material.* Paris: UNESCO, 1974.

Norris, Pippa, Kern Montague, and Marion Just (eds.) *Framing Terrorism: The News Media, the Government, and the Public.* London: Routledge, 2003.

Nossek, Hillel. "Our News and Their News: The Role of National Identity in the Coverage of Foreign News," in H. Nossek, A. Sreberny, and P. Sonwalkar (eds.) *Media and Political Violence.* Cresskill, NJ: Hampton Press, 2007.

Nossek, Hillel, Annabelle Sreberny, and Prasun Sonwalkar (eds.) *Media and Political Violence.* Cresskill, NJ: Hampton Press, 2007.

Nye, Joseph S. "Redefining the National Interest." *Foreign Affairs* 78, no. 4 (1999): 22–35.

Ostgaard, Einar. "Factors Influencing the Flow of News." *Journal of Peace Research* 2, no. 1 (1965): 39–63.

Page, Benjamin. *Who Deliberates? Mass Media in Modern Democracy.* London: University of Chicago Press, 1996.

Pan, Zhongdang and Gerald M. Kosicki. "Framing Analysis: An Approach to News Discourse." *Political Communication* 10, no. 1 (1993): 55–75.

Paterson, Chris. "Global Television News Services," in A. Sreberny-Mohammadi et al. (eds.) *Media in Global Context: A Reader.* London: Hodder Arnold, 1997.

———. "Global Battlefields," in O. Boyd-Barrett and T. Rantanen (eds.) *The Globalization of News.* London: Sage, 1998.

———. "News Agency Dominance in International News on the Internet." Paper presented at the Centre for International Communications Research, Institute of Communications Studies, Leeds University, Leeds

(UK), 2006. http://ics.leeds.ac.uk/papers/cicr/exhibits/42/cicrpaterson. pdf (accessed October 2006).

Patterson, Thomas E. "Bad News, Bad Governance." *Annals of the American Academy on Political and Social Science* 546, no. 1 (1996): 97–108.

Pfetsch, Barbara. "Government News Management," in D. Graber, D. McQuail, and P. Norris (eds.) *The Politics of News: The News of Politics.* Washington, D.C.: CQ Press, 1998.

Phalen, Patricia F. and Ece Algan. "(Ms)Taking Context for Content: Framing the Fourth World Conference on Women." *Political Communication* 18, no. 3 (2001): 301–19.

Pietiläinen, Jukka. "Foreign News and Foreign Trade." *Gazette* 68, no. 3 (2006): 217–28.

Popkin, Samuel L. "Voter Learning in the 1992 Presidential Campaign," in S. Iyengar and R. Reeves (eds.) *Do the Media Govern? Politicians, Voters, and Reporters in America.* London: Sage, 1997.

Potter, Jonathan and Margaret Wetherell. *Discourse and Social Psychology: Beyond Attitudes and Behaviour.* London: Sage, 1987.

Pye, Lucien W. and Sidney Verba. *Political Culture and Political Development.* Princeton, NJ: Princeton University Press, 1965.

Rapin, Anne. "An Interview with Serge July, Director of Libération: An 'Actively Contemporary' Newspaper." *Label France* 32, July 1998. http://www.diplomatie.gouv.fr/label_france/ENGLISH/COM/july/july. html (accessed March 2006).

Rhee, June Woong. "Strategy and Issue Frames in Election Campaign Coverage: A Social Cognitive Account of Framing Effects." *Journal of Communication* 47, no. 3 (1997): 26–48.

Reese, Stephen D. "Theorizing a Globalized Journalism," in M. Loeffelholz and D. Weaver (eds.) *Global Journalism Research: Theories, Methods, Findings, Future.* London: Blackwell, 2008. Available from http://communication.utexas.edu/journalism/faculty/reese/publish/theorizing%20global%20journalism.pdf (accessed November 2006).

———. "Understanding the Global Journalist: A Hierarchy-of-Influences Approach." *Journalism Studies* 2, no. 2 (2001): 173–87.

Reisinger, William M. "The Renaissance of a Rubric: Political Culture As a Concept and Theory." *International Journal of Public Opinion Research* 7, no.4 (1995): 328–52.

Risse, Thomas. "Let's Argue! Communicative Action in World Politics." *International Organization* 54, no. 1 (2000): 1–39.

Robertson, Roland. *Globalization: Social Theory and Global Culture.* London: Sage, 1992.

Robinson, Cherylon and Lawrence Alfred Powell. "The Postmodern Politics of Context Definition: Competing Reality Frames in the Hill-Thomas Spectacle." *Sociological Quarterly* 37, no. 2 (1996): 279–305.

Robinson, Piers. *The CNN Effect: The Myth of News Foreign Policy and Intervention.* London: Routledge, 2002.

Rogers, Everett M. "Theoretical Diversity in Political Communication," in Lynda Lee Kaid (ed.) *Handbook of Political Communication Research.* London: Lawrence Erlbaum Associates Publishers, 2004.

Roosevelt, Franklin D. "Address to Congress." January 6, 1941. *American Rhetoric.com*, The Four Freedoms. http://www.americanrhetoric.com/speeches/fdrthefourfreedoms.htm (accessed May 2007).

Rusciano, Frank Louis. "Framing World Opinion in the Elite Press," in P. Norris, K. Montague, and M. Just (eds.) *Framing Terrorism: The News Media, the Government, and the Public.* London: Routledge, 2003.

Schaefer, Todd M. "Persuading the Persuaders: Presidential Speeches and Editorial Opinion." *Political Communication* 14, no. 1 (1997): 97–111.

———. "Framing the US Embassy Bombings and September 11 Attacks in African and US Newspapers," in P. Norris, K. Montague, and M. Just (eds.) *Framing Terrorism: The News Media, the Government, and the Public.* London: Routledge, 2003.

Schiller, Herbert I. *Communication and Cultural Domination.* New York: International Arts and Sciences Press, 1976.

Schimmelfenig, Frank. "The Community Trap: Liberal Norms, Rhetorical Action and the Eastern Enlargement of the European Union." *International Organization* 55, no. 1 (2001): 47–80.

Schlesinger, Philip. *Putting "Reality" Together: BBC News.* London: Constable, 1978.

———. "Media, the Political Order, and National Identity." *Media, Culture & Society* 13, no. 3 (1991): 297–98.

Schmidt, Vivien and Claudio M. Radaelli. "Policy Change and Discourse in Europe: Conceptual and Methodological Issues." *West European Politics* 27, no. 2 (2004): 183–210.

Schönback, Klaus. "News in the Western World," in J. L. Martin and A. G. Chaudhary (eds.) *Comparative Mass Media Systems.* New York: Longman, 1983.

Schudson, Michael. "The Sociology of News Production" (1989), reprint in D. Berkowitz (ed.) *Social Meaning of News: A Text-Reader.* London: Sage, 1989.

———. "The Objectivity Norm in American Journalism." *Journalism* 2, no. 2 (2001): 149–70.

———. *The Sociology of News.* London: Norton, 2003.

Schultz, Kenneth A. "Domestic Opposition and Signaling in International Crises." *American Political Science Review* 92, no. 4 (1998): 829–44.

Seib, Philip. *The Global Journalist: News and Conscience in a World of Conflict.* Oxford: Rowman & Littlefield, 2002.

———. "Hegemonic No More: Western Media, the Rise of Al-Jazeera, and the Influence of Diverse Voices." *International Studies Review* 7, no. 4 (2005): 601–15.

Semati, Mehdi (ed.) *New Frontiers in International Communication Theory.* Oxford: Rowman & Littlefield, 2004.

Semetko, Holli A. and Patti M. Valkenburg. "Framing European Politics: A Content Analysis of Press Television News." *Journal of Communication* 50, no. 2 (2000): 93–109.

Shearman, Peter and Matthew Sussex (eds.) *European Security after 9/11.* Aldershot: Ashgate, 2004.

Shoemaker, Pamela J. "A New Gatekeeping Model" (1991), reprint in D. Berkowitz (ed.) *Social Meanings of News: A Text-Reader.* London: Sage, 1997.

Shoemaker, Pamela J. and Stephen D. Reese. *Mediating the Message: Theories of Influences on Mass Media Content.* 2nd ed. London: Longman, 1996.

Sigal, Leon V. *Reporters and Officials: The Organization and Politics of Newsmaking.* London: D. C. Heath, 1973.

Singh, Robert. "Superpower Response: The United States of America," in M. Buckley and R. Fawn (eds.) *Global Responses to Terrorism: 9/11, Afghanistan and Beyond.* London: Routledge, 2003.

Snow, David A., E. Burke Jr. Rochford, Steven K. Worden, and Robert D. Benford. "Frame Alignment Processes, Micromobilization, and Movement Participation." *American Sociological Review* 51, no. 4 (1986): 464–81.

Soley, Lawrence C. *The News Shapers: The Sources Who Explain the News.* London: Praeger, 1992.

Soloski, John. "News Reporting and Professionalism: Some Constraints on the Reporting of the News" (1989), reprint in D. Berkowitz (ed.) *Social Meanings of News: A Text-Reader.* London: Sage, 1997.

Sorrentino, Carlo. *I percorsi della notizia: La stampa quotidiana italiana tra politica e mercato* (The news paths: The Italian daily press between politics and the market). Bologna, Italy: Baskerville, 1995.

Sparks, Colin. "Is There a Global Public Sphere?" in D. K. Thussu (ed.) *Electronic Empires: Global Media and Resistance.* London: Arnold, 1998.

Sparrow, Bartholomew H. "A Research Agenda for an Institutional Media." *Political Communication* 23, no. 2 (2006): 145–57.

Sreberny-Mohammadi, Annabelle. "The 'World of News' Study: Results of International Cooperation." *Journal of Communication* 34, no. 1 (1984): 121–35.

Sreberny-Mohammadi, Annabelle, Kaarle Nordenstreng, Robert Stevenson, and Frank Ugboajah (eds.) *Foreign News in the Media: International Reporting in 29 Countries.* Paris: UNESCO, 1985.

Sreberny-Mohammadi, Annabelle, Dwayne Winseck, Jim McKenna, and Oliver Boyd-Barrett (eds.) *Media in Global Context: A Reader.* London: Hodder Arnold, 1997.

Stahl, Bernhard. "Der französische Diskurs zum Maastricht-Referendum (The French discourse about the Maastricht Referendum) (1992)," in B. Joerrissen and B. Stahl (eds.) *Europäische Außenpolitik und nationale Identität: Vergleichende Diskurs- und Verhaltenstudien zu Dänemark, Deutschland, Frankreich, Griechenland, Italien und den Niederlanden.* Münster, Germany: LIT, 2003.

————. "Der französische Diskurs zur Europäischen Verteidigungsgemeischaft (The French discourse about the European Defence Community) (1952–1954)," in B. Joerrissen and B. Stahl (eds.) *Europäische Außenpolitik und nationale Identität: Vergleichende Diskurs- und Verhaltenstudien zu Dänemark, Deutschland, Frankreich, Griechenland, Italien und den Niederlanden.* Münster: LIT, 2003.

Steele, Janet E. "Don't Ask, Don't Tell, Don't Explain: Unofficial Sources and Television Coverage of the Dispute over Gays in the Military." *Political Communication* 14, no. 1 (1997): 83–96.

Stevenson, Robert L. *Communication, Development and the Third World: The Global Politics of Information.* London: Longman, 1988.

Swain, Kristen Alley. "Proximity and Power Factors in Western Coverage of the Sub-Saharan Aids Crisis." *Journalism and Mass Communication Quarterly* 80, no. 1 (2003): 145–65.

Tahir, Malik. "Report on the State of the Journalists in Pakistan." Journalists Resource Centre, 2000. http://www.syberwurx.com/jrc/ (accessed June 2006).

Talbot, Ian. *Pakistan: A Modern History.* London: C. Hurst, 2005.

Thogmartin, Clyde. *The National Daily Press of France.* Birmingham, AL: Summa Publications, 1998.

Thussu, Daya Kishan (ed.) *Electronic Empires: Global Media and Resistance.* London: Arnold, 1998.

————. "Localising the Global: Zee TV in India," in D. K. Thussu (ed.) *Electronic Empires: Global Media and Resistance.* London: Arnold, 1998.

————. *International Communication: Continuity and Change.* London: Arnold, 2000.

————. "Selling Neo-Imperial Conflicts: Television and US Public Diplomacy," in J. Curran and M. Gurevitch (eds.) *Mass Media and Society.* London: Hodder Arnold, 2005.

Tomlinson, John. "Cultural Globalization and Cultural Imperialism," in A. Mohammadi (ed.) *International Communication and Globalization: A Critical Introduction.* London: Sage, 1997.

————. *Globalization and Culture.* Oxford: Polity, 1999.

Tuchman, Gaye. "Objectivity As Strategic Ritual: An Examination of Newsmen's Notions of Objectivity." *American Journal of Sociology* 77, no. 4 (1972): 660–79.

————. "Making News by Doing Work: Routinizing the Unexpected." *American Journal of Sociology* 79, no. 1 (1973): 110–31.

————. *Making News: A Study in the Construction of Reality.* London: Collier Macmillan, 1978.

Tunstall, Jeremy. *The Media Are American: Anglo-American Media in the World.* London: Constable, 1977.

Van Belle, Douglas A. "New York Times and Network TV News Coverage of Foreign Disasters: The Significance of the Insignificant Variables." *Journalism and Mass Communication Quarterly* 77, no. 1 (2000): 50–70.

Varis, Tapio. *International Flow of Television Programmes*. Paris: UNESCO, 1985.

Verba, Sidney. "Comparative Political Culture," in L. W. Pye and S. Verba (eds.) *Political Culture and Political Development*. Princeton, NJ: Princeton University Press, 1965.

Vlahos, Michael. "Entering the Infosphere." *Journal of International Affairs* 51, no. 2 (1998): 497–525.

Weaver, David, Maxwell McCombs, and Donald L. Shaw. "Agenda-Setting Research: Issues, Attributes, and Influences," in L. L. Kaid (ed.) *Handbook of Political Communication Research*. London: Lawrence Erlbaum Associates Publishers, 2004.

White, David Manning. "The 'Gate Keeper': A Case in the Selection of News" (1950), reprint in D. Berkowitz (ed.) *Social Meanings of News: A Text-Reader*. London: Sage, 1997.

White, James. "Limits to the Indexing Hypothesis: A Case Study of the Reykjavik Arms Control Summit." Paper presented at the Association for Education in Journalism and Mass Communication annual conference, Atlanta, Georgia, 1994. http://list.msu.edu/cgi-bin/wa?A2=ind9603a &L=aejmc&T=0&P=1203 (accessed June 2005).

Wilson, Richard W. "The Many Voices of Political Culture: Assessing Different Approaches." *World Politics* 52, no. 2 (2000): 246–73.

Wu, H. Dennis. "Systemic Determinants of International News Coverage: A Comparison of 38 Countries." *Journal of Communication* 50, no. 2 (2000): 110–30.

———. "Homogeneity around the World? Comparing the Systemic Determinants of International News Flow between Developed and Developing Countries." *Gazette* 65, no. 1 (2003): 9–24.

Wu, Wei, David Weaver, and Owen V. Johnson. "Professional Roles of Russian and U.S. Journalists: A Comparative Study." *Journalism and Mass Communication Quarterly* 73, no. 3 (1996): 543–48.

Yasmeen, Samina. "Unexpectedly at Center Stage: Pakistan," in M. Buckley and R. Fawn (eds.) *Global Responses to Terrorism: 9/11, Afghanistan and Beyond*. London: Routledge, 2003.

Yin, Robert K. *Case Study Research: Design and Methods*. 3rd ed. London: Sage, 2003.

Zaller, John and Dennis Chiu. "Government's Little Helper: U.S. Press Coverage of Foreign Policy Crises, 1946–1999," in B. L. Nacos, R. Y. Shapiro, and P. Isernia (eds.) *Decisionmaking in a Glass House: Mass Media, Public Opinion, and American and European Foreign Policy in the 21st Century*. Oxford: Rowman & Littlefield, 2000.

Zincone, Giuliano. "Ipocrita lettore, simile a me... (Hypocritical reader, just like me...)," in BUR Fondazione Corriere della Sera (ed.) *Come si scrive Il Corriere della Sera: Dentro il quotidiano tra storia e attualità*. Milano, Italy: BUR Fondazione Corriere della Sera 2003.

INDEX

Note: Figures in bold.